Ashley S. Tyler
124 SE 11th St
Oak Island, NC 28465

 **W9-BBA-130**

Making More Plants
The Science, Art and Joy of Propagation

Ken Druse

Designed by
Alexander Isley Inc.

Clarkson Potter/Publishers
New York

TO LB

Published by Clarkson Potter/Publishers,
New York, New York.
Member of the Crown Publishing Group.
Random House, Inc.
New York, Toronto, London, Sydney, Auckland
www.randomhouse.com
CLARKSON N. POTTER is a trademark and POTTER and
colophon are registered trademarks of Random House, Inc.
Printed in USA
Library of Congress Cataloging-in-Publication Data
Druse, Ken.
    Making more plants: the science, art, and joy of
propagation / by Ken Druse.—1st ed.
    1. Natural landscaping. 2. Plant propagation. I. Title.
    SB439.D658 2000
    635.9'153—dc21   00-026277
ISBN 0-517-70787-X
10 9 8 7 6 5 4 3 2 1
First Edition

Note: *Many of the procedures described in this book involve sharp instruments. Please follow all instructions carefully and take all necessary precautions when using these instruments. Also, wear gloves when handling plant parts that are not well known to you and always wash hands thoroughly before eating or drinking. Contact with some plants may cause irritation, and many have toxic components, if consumed. Some plants may cause allergic reactions in some people.*

Note on the photography: *The majority of the photographs in this book were taken with a Mamiya 6/4.5 camera. Fujichrome Velvia (RVS) was the film stock used for most of the pictures. Additional film stocks included Kodak Ektachrome EPP, VSW and Fujichrome RAS. Several of the photographs are double exposures. None of the pictures were manipulated by computer or digitally altered after processing. Most of the hands in the book are the author's taken with a nonmechanical cable shutter-release.*

All of the photographs in this book are available as fine-art prints by custom order. Visit www.thenaturalgarden.com for custom printing information.

Page 1: A tall, sunset-colored dahlia finds its way back to the garden each year from divisions of stored tubers. The unnamed selection was plucked from a batch of mixed seedlings. **Page 2:** Louis holds two boxwood plants that were taken as semi-ripewood cuttings and rooted over winter. **Above:** The dry fruits of the American sycamore *(Plantanus occidentalis)*. The sycamore was one parent of the ubiquitous urban tree, the London Plane *(P. x acerifolia)*, an aged example of which grows in New York City **(opposite). Pages 6 and 7:** A black walnut seedling from a nut that sprouted while being conditioned in the refrigerator. A gift was received of an *Arisaema taiwanense* grown from seed harvested by Dan Hinkley on a plant in the garden of Heronswood Nursery that originated as a tuber raised by Bleddyn and Sue Wynn-Jones of Wales by means of seed collected on a 1993 trip to Taiwan. And so, propagation perpetuates the lives of plants.

HELPING HANDS

For Ken Druse Studio:
George Waffle, Business Manager; Ann Kearney-Dutton,
Photo Editor; John Beirne, Plant ID; Louis Bauer,
Horticultural Consultant; Jill Hagler, Webmaster.
Helen Pratt, Literary Agent.
At Clarkson Potter/Publishers:
Chip Gibson, President and Publisher; Lauren Shakely,
Editorial Director; Olivia Silver, Editorial Assistant;
Marysarah Quinn, Art Director; Jane Treuhaft, Associate
Art Director; Amy Boorstein, Managing Editor; Mark
McCauslin, Associate Managing Editor; Nancy J. Stabile,
Copy Editor; Teresa Nicholas, Director of Production; Joan
Denman, Senior Production Manager; Tina Constable,
Senior Publicist; Merri Ann Morrell, Compositor.
Special thanks to *House Beautiful* magazine:
Oliver Louis Gropp, Editor in Chief; Peggy Kennedy, Editor;
and Betsy Hunter, Senior Editor.
The author also wishes to thank: Suzy Bales; Edmund Cyvas;
Norman C. Deno; Marcia Donahue; Helen Druse; Bill Fidelo; Bobbi
Fischer; Kelly Grummons; Eric Hammond; Dan Hinkley;
Vicki Johnson; Tom Koster; Jody Lathwell; Jean Lundberg; Seamus
Malarkey; John Mapel; Craig Masching; Bill Mills; Robin Parer; Bob and
Brigitta Stewart; John Trexler; Rosemary Verey; Nigel and Lisa Wright;
Robert Zeleniak; Wave Hill and the staff and gardeners headed by
Marco Stufano; The Garden Club of America.

CONTENTS

I was born in the spring, and I never got over it. I am obsessed by seasonal changes; am far too susceptible to the blahs as daylight hours shorten in autumn, get a little too high for my own good when the evening light lingers. I love plants—the way they look and smell, leaves crisp in fall and flower buds bursting into bloom in spring.

Above left: The fast branch of the river that runs around the island site of the new garden. **Above right:** New gardens need plants—lots of them. Wonderful ones come from friends, such as this fawn-colored iris. A piece of a rhizome for *Iris* 'Aztec Gold' came from the Wenbergs, who garden at the top of the hill.

Passersby may call any landscape a garden, but a well-trimmed lawn and tidy flower bed are not evidence of a guiding hand. The soul of a garden is an expression of its guardian, the person who orchestrates arrangements of plants; plans as they grow, thrive, or die; and constantly refines the picture. If you never moan about how much time it takes to garden but wish you had more time to spend in the garden, you probably are this person. If you've come to a point in your gardening life when your dreams outpace your means, if you would just as happily grow dozens of the plants you need as purchase a few from the garden center, you are ready to grow your own.

Long ago, I learned the necessity to know each plant as an individual in order to help it grow; and when I needed many plants, I had to discover more about them. I had to become aware of the way plants work, and their place in the world. Then, I thought, I could practice the magic of propagation.

In 1996, I started a new garden beyond the confines of the narrow yard behind my Brooklyn townhouse. I had been searching for a place in the country, where I could garden by the acre. Months of hunting in the area passed, and on a cold rainy day in December, I took what was to be my last exploration into the countryside. Friends Louis Bauer and Petie Buck came along, and after hours of driving and walking, we were hungry and tired and our clothes were damp. My companions moaned when I said there was just one more place to see.

As we drove down a steep hill and around a sharp turn in the road, Petie sat up and said, "This is it." We were coming to a one-lane bridge over white water to the site of the new garden: 2.6 acres with a house on an island in a river.

I dreamed. I shopped for plants. I negotiated. And five

Above: The canal garden (shown in its third spring) was planted with perennials and shrubs from seeds, cuttings, layers, and divisions. Every spring, around seven weeks prior to blooming, many of the candelabra primroses are dug and divided.

months later, the first moving truck arrived, completely filled with plants. These first arrivals were barely enough to start the new garden, for as I planned and plotted my designs, I realized I needed many, many more. Because of cost and rarity, and just for the reason that some plants beg to be propagated, I began producing my own. And, like every gardener discovers, making more plants is one of the most rewarding, exhilarating, and addictive aspects of our passion.

An early planting was called "the buff border" for its flowers in tawny tones—cream to chamois to toast. I hoped a restricted palette might curb my shopping frenzy, but I didn't stop to think exactly how few flowers are available in these colors. My desire intensified. Reference books and horticultural journals yielded names of promising genera such as the more esoteric foxgloves—*Digitalis lamarckii* and *D. ferruginea*. And I surprised myself when I turned to vintage bearded irises, plants I'd long overlooked. I hunted through old catalogs for mentions of forgotten varieties and out-of-fashion oldies, and I lingered over descriptions of blossoms with butterscotch or copper tones, such as 'Tanbark', which bears flowers in the colors of crème brûlée. Finding the plants themselves, however, was much harder. But if I am at the right place at the right time, when gardener friends need to divide their iris plants, they generously give divisions away.

I know that I am not the only person who has been turned on by propagation. I walked into the kitchen of Saida Malarney's house in a suburb of Detroit and noticed, instead of houseplants on her windowsill, five plastic saucers. A friend had gotten her hooked on starting ferns from spores. In a town nearby, Betty Sturley, a painter who specializes in flower portraits, was propagating annuals and perennials for the church bazaar. In an adjoining town, the annual home gardeners' perennial swap was slated for that weekend. There was a picture in the newspaper from the previous year's event in which a thirteen-year-old boy was wearing a sandwich board that read: "Got Heuchera. Want Hellebore."

If like that young man, you receive a piece or pot of something wonderful to nurture when you get home, you will have a lasting reminder of a place, a time, or a friend— as sentimental as a postcard—a living memento.

Ever since I saw the candelabra primroses at North Hill, the Vermont garden of Wayne Winterrowd and Joe Eck, I wanted to grow them on the banks of the canal that cuts across the island garden. I started with a few plants in a few colors. To have more shades, I would have to grow plants from harvested seeds. I wondered if the seeds would germinate on their own if scattered around the parent plants, so I asked Wayne about his experiences with the same Asian *Primula* species and hybrids. His first comment was a general one about propagation: "It's so different for everyone," he said. As for the primroses, his do not seem to appear from seed on their own. In March, he prepares a flat of medium for a mass sowing of the seeds. The resulting seedlings spend their first Vermont winter in a cold frame. Then they are planted among the other primroses.

Above: June's glowing display features scores of these *Primula* × *bulleesiana* that began as a half-dozen mail-ordered plants. However, in order to expand the color range, the genetic diversity, seeds from harvested fruits had to be sown.

It was encouraging to hear Wayne talk of diverse experiences and varying practices in propagation, because such things are encountered time and again. That was also proved by something else Wayne said about our primroses: "The one thing I know for sure about propagating the *Primula* is that they cannot be divided." He'd tried without success. "They melt, they rot, they disappear," he explained. Oddly enough, I'd been successfully dividing my primroses since my first half-dozen plants were in their second spring. When the growth is about 1½ inches tall, I dig the plants, rinse them off in the canal, pry the little side shoots away from their parents, and transplant them all. The plants bloom about seven weeks later. By the second spring, there were too many to count.

Wayne applauded what he reasoned to be a special technical proficiency. But that is not necessarily the case. My success is due more to one thing we certainly agreed upon—the timing is crucial. I'd recognized the precise moment to operate, when the plants were beginning their surge of growth and were most eager to generate new tissue.

With an open mind and eyes wide, I have tuned in to the biorhythms of the plants in my garden and, without much deliberation, drawn the right conclusions—what might be called "learned intuition." Through propagation, I've learned to appreciate the life within a seed, the promise of a stem cutting or a piece of a bulb; it's the thrill of life beginning, and irresistible to anyone who loves to watch plants grow.

I want other gardeners to know how it feels to sow a seed or root a cutting and watch the results grow to maturity, to experience the freedom and convenience of being able to produce plants in numbers. Enough of the craft and science of propagation can be learned in this book so that anyone with curiosity, practice, and a little luck can master some of nature's skill. You will read about each step and witness them in photographs, taken over three years of performing the magic of making more plants for the garden.

INTRODUCTION

You probably have propagated plants more often than you realize—when you sowed sunflower seeds, for instance, or divided a large perennial. If you've tried your hand at a more complex act of propagation and failed, take heart. Trial and error are great teachers.

A gardener's excitement to do everything at once—or, put another way, nervous anticipation—might seem a problem for a

Above: The young "Buff Border" was carved from brush and tree stumps and planted with dozens of propagated plants. Gardeners propagate more often than we realize: when we nurture a slip of something special from a friend; discover a branch that has bent to the ground, rooted, and can be removed as an independent plant; scatter seeds of poppies on the snow; or tend seedlings of giant sunflowers. Dividing perennials, alone, is a propagation rite of spring.

practicing propagator. After all, some of these experiments take a year to deliver results. But it doesn't feel slow because there is always something going on—the first step of one process, the last of another, a few cuttings to take, rooted ones to pot up.

Over time, gardeners develop a feel for when things have to be done, and with propagation even more so. At the very moment plants are beginning their most active growing period, the gardener seizes the opportunity to divide some perennials or to strike herbaceous cuttings. The announcements of these activities can't be found on a calendar. To use the example of the *Primula* again, in 1997, I divided them on April 19. In 1998, following a particularly mild win-

ter, the task was performed on March 21. Some garden books might just call this spring.

On the first day of spring, according to the published calendar, many gardens are still asleep. By March 21 in northwestern New Jersey, the witch hazel has been blooming for a month and the crocuses are on their way. But across the country, in northern California, the saucer magnolia's flower show is at its peak and the buds on the roses are swelling.

Producing a daily garden guide for one county would be hard; for the country, it's impossible. So in this book, you will not see dates but rather references to moments in the year, such as "early spring" or "midautumn." You need to know a bit about your climate and your garden to apply these expressions. Think of the seasons and the conditions of your plants not as days or dates but as events in the life cycle of plants.

A PROPAGATOR'S YEAR

If there is a beginning to the year of making more plants then, perhaps it starts as daylight hours lengthen, just after the winter solstice. The houseplants in the window garden begin to sprout new stems, and a few of them set flower buds. At a moment counted backward from when it's safe to plant out after all danger of frost has passed, it is time for sowing seeds indoors.

Later, when underground buds of herbaceous perennials such as phlox are beginning to swell, crowns can be divided. Crown division of perennials carries on until the growth is too tall and soft to continue, or if flower buds are forming on early-blooming ones.

When the weather warms, tender tubers and rhizomes are brought up from the dark spot in the cellar where they were kept around 50 degrees F (10 degrees C) for the winter. Some dahlias have already sprouted, and cuttings of their blanched top growth can be taken before their tubers are divided.

In midspring, as the lilac flowers peak, the seedlings from under lights can move to the cold frame. The rooted cuttings of indoor tender perennials and some of the dahlia shoots can be potted up and placed in the cold frame as well. The new growth on some of the herbaceous perennials outside is sufficiently hardened for stem cuttings to be taken, which will root quickly. The very first softwood cuttings of shrubs can also be taken now; beg slips from neighbors with

will blacken the foliage of the cannas and dahlias, and their rhizomes and tubers will be lifted for winter storage. For the next three to four months, cuttings of needle conifers can be taken. Deciduous woody plants, completely dormant in late autumn, will yield twigs for hardwood cuttings and, later, for grafting.

From the time the tree leaves fall to the arrival of the new seed catalogs, there are a few quiet days to rest and reflect on the excitement to come. For the plant propagator, the year is full of opportunities to make more plants.

shrubs that bloom in a color you don't have.

The first week of summer will be the last chance for taking softwood cuttings, but some of the ones taken earlier may already be rooted and ready to be planted in containers, which can be placed in a protected spot away from bright sunlight and wind.

In midsummer, as seed stalks begin to ripen, certain plants receive paper-bag hoods to capture their precious harvest. The seeds of annuals are ripening, too, and in late summer they will need to be collected, cleaned, and stored. The houseplants grown from last winter's cuttings have spent the summer outdoors under the trees and in the shade beneath the porch. They will need to come inside now. Soon a killing frost

A NATURAL PRESENTATION

There are many books on the subject of propagation (as you can see from the Bibliography). I found a textbook from the 1930s with good ideas that are still included in most modern guides. Other practices, however dubious, are also found in modern publications, such as fungicide drenches and chemical sprays. No book seemed to capture the beauty of plants and their propagation, or to impart the sense of wonder that comes from participating in nature's schemes.

Real gardeners helped to write this book by sharing wisdom gleaned from experience.

Sowing of seeds, dividing perennials, and taking cuttings are not difficult operations left exclusively to those schooled in the disciplines of horticulture—they're just everyday parts of gardening. For example, several of the temporary residents beneath an aged magnolia—tall hollyhocks, blue larkspur, double poppies, golden feverfew **(left)**—were simply sown in place to be stand-ins while young perennials and flowering woody plants became established. In the back of the same bed, a rare *Franklinia* **(right),** from a softwood cutting, begins its seasonal foliage display in late summer when the leaves turn scarlet and the camellia-like flowers appear. In autumn, the tropical-looking bronze canna leaves in the foreground will be blackened by the first killing frost. Their harvested rhizomes will be stored in the basement until spring, when each one can be divided into a dozen plants.

Although the propagator's calendar has no specific dates, there are daily accomplishments and milestones along the way. When it is cold outside and most of the garden is fast asleep **(below left)** the appearance of the ribbonlike flowers of the witch hazel **(below right)** is a sign that the outdoor gardening season is on its way. Indoors, in the sunny south-facing window and under fluorescent lights in the basement, seedlings are emerging above the surface of their medium **(above right)**. By summer, seedlings in pots **(above left)** will be hardened off and some will be ready to go into their permanent homes.

Experiments compared accepted recommendations with alternative techniques. For example, cuttings rooted faster and more successfully when the medium was tamped down so hard that a hole had to nearly be drilled in to insert a cutting.

The chapters that follow begin with an overview of how plants naturally reproduce and then the practices for gardeners are presented, arranged not from the ground up but from the top of plants themselves—flowers and the seeds they make for us to sow—to the bottom, with beneath-the-soil methods for propagating even more plants from tiny bits of their roots.

A guide to propagating over 700 genera begins on page 225.

forming, whether you are performing a simple yearly ritual of starting plants from seeds, or grafting fruit trees in your own backyard. If some of the tasks presented in this book seem beyond your expertise or ability, start small. Try

Opposite: Rooted cuttings of woody plants and herbaceous perennials from this summer will spend their first winter in the cold frame.

When you need to know how to reproduce a particular plant, consult the guide to find out the possible methods, which are described in the following chapters.

The magic of propagation can become habit

one technique, then another. Your skills will grow through the year, and so will your garden. This book may be your guide throughout your gardening career. And, wonderfully, gardening is something you can do for the rest of your life.

1

The Botany of Propagation

It is not essential to learn about

botany to garden well: it's inevitable.

Why is the science of plants relevant

to the propagator? For the same reason

that the physician needs to know

about human physiology.

By observing the extraordinary truths and beauty of the plant kingdom, we can recognize where to go, how to get there, what to do, and when to do it. Gardeners can discover how to capitalize on plants' primal goal: to perpetuate themselves, by either passing on genes through seeds or by regenerating tissue, sometimes creating an entire new plant from a single leaf.

The fact that many ancient organisms still exist today is proof that the reproductive strategies that evolved over time are extremely reliable. Well before the first flowers appeared for sexual procreation, fungi reproduced asexually via fruiting bodies—mushrooms—which release billions of spores into the air. A few of these spores would settle in comfortable spots, divide as cells do, and create new beings. The spores grew into exact copies of their single parents.

Evolution and natural selection favor chance: sexual propagation, with its exchange of genetic material, increases the odds for accidental improvements. Mosses and ferns, among the earliest plants, produce spores, but unlike fungi, these plants have sex. A fern spore grows both male and female organs, and a reproductive structure called a *prothallus* has an aqueous film in which a male gamete (fertile reproductive cell) travels to the female. On rare occasions, however, one of the sexual partners might arrive from a neighboring plant, carried perhaps in the splash of a raindrop. The resulting hybrid—containing genes from both parents—is evolution's dividend. The new fern may prove better able to survive environmental changes and in time dominate the species.

Gardeners need to understand fern reproduction when sowing spores to grow more plants, but recognizing the impact of hybridization reveals the achievements of natural selection. The sexual plants that evolved after ferns—the *gymnosperms,* such as conifers, cycads, and the ginkgo—came up with a way to exchange genetic material through the dry medium of air. The gymnosperms encased their male gametes in pollen; and even more revolutionary, they introduced the seed.

Preceding pages: Flowers of *Stipa gigantea* are the largest of all grasses.

Above: Fungi were once thought to be part of the botanical kingdom, because they have spores like mosses and ferns. A mushroom produces many millions of spores that are set adrift on the wind in an effective, if not economical, method of asexual reproduction: only a few find the perfect spot to grow. If all of the spores of a single fungus grew, the progeny would soon cover the earth.

Below: Thousands of fern spores are stored in *sori,* seen as golden dots beneath a frond. Ferns introduced sexual reproduction, while still relying on huge numbers of spores.

Opposite: Gymnosperms, the sexual plants that evolved after ferns, such as this fir with immature purple cones, use air as a vehicle to transport reproductive material. But the trees do not produce spores; they flood the air with male pollen in search of receptive female cones.

The Botany of Propagation   19

Flowers fine-tuned the delivery system, but at a great cost. Intricate and elaborate blossoms enlist the help of animals in swapping chromosomes with like flowers in distant neighborhoods. But it takes a great deal of energy to produce a fancy flower. Adaptations to environmental circumstances must be made, as well as adjustments to the independent evolution of the specific animal partner.

Some of the most recent plants that have evolved returned to the strategy utilized by earlier plants. These plants have found that the energy conserved in producing modest flowers can be directed into building large colonies of individuals in close proximity.

It is probably no coincidence that the world's most important food crops—rice, wheat, and corn—come from the grass family, whose barely visible flowers grow in vast numbers.

The next time you husk an ear of corn look at the withered silk. Each thread is actually a pistil leading to a single kernel.

Left: The great food plants of the world—rice, corn, and wheat (shown)—are members of the grass family. Grasses, the most recent flowering plants to evolve, found it efficient to produce unassuming flowers in huge colonies. Airborne pollen is transmitted and received over a relatively short distance.

Above: In order for an ear of corn to be filled with kernels, the tips of each of its pistils—the silk—must come in contact with a grain of pollen and be fertilized.

Above left: Exchanging genetic material is the goal, and although the *Codonopsis* flower is perfect, self-pollination is unlikely. The female pistil (upper flower) ripens a day before the male anthers (lower flower), by which time fertilization is under way.

Above right: The receptive stigma is at the top of the female pistil, and ovaries—containing immature ovules that will become seeds—are at the base. Pollen-bearing anthers are to the left and right.

Below: A squash plant produces a separate male flower (at left) and female flowers (right, above an immature ovary) that open at different times. Other plants, such as holly, bear flowers of one gender on one plant and the other gender on another. At least one male must be included among female shrubs for pollination and berries.

The innovation of flowers sped up plant evolution and adaptation, and as animals proliferated, plants began to change in ways that could exploit the creatures' mobility. In order to attract animals such as insects, plants developed incentives, such as rewards of nectar, and advertised them with flowers. Refining this symbiotic relationship led to more intricate floral lures, guaranteeing that specific animals would visit specific flowers, easily pick up pollen, and make a special delivery to another flower of the same species. Our love of flowers —their colors, forms, fragrance— is purely coincidental. When we wish to participate in pollination —either to produce fruit or perhaps to create our own hybrid— we need to know what to look for.

The parts of a flower are arranged in concentric rings, or whorls. The innermost whorls comprise the male *stamens* (usually in multiples) and a singular female *pistil*. When one flower has both male and female organs, it is considered "perfect," and if it has all parts—petals, sepals, stamens, pistils—it is "complete." These flowers grow on plants that are *monœcious* (from the Greek for "one household"), which may be capable of self-pollination. Since mixing genes is the goal, many flowers stagger the ripening of their organs so that self-pollination does not occur. Some plants can even recognize their own pollen grains and reject them, while accepting pollen from another individual member of the same species.

To improve the odds for innovation, many other plants are *diœcious* ("two households"). These plants evolved male and female flowers on separate plants. Independent male plants bear only male flowers, and female plants with only female flowers bear the fruit that results from pollination. That is why at least one male holly bush, such as *Ilex verticillata* 'Rhett Butler', must be included in the garden to play stud to the female holly plants, for example, of the variety 'Scarlett O'Hara'.

Birds generally see colors the way humans do, and a red flower is as conspicuous to a hummingbird as a stop sign. Hummingbirds love to visit the red rose-of-Sharon (*Hibiscus syriacus*) common to many backyards. Other pollinators drawn to this flower may not see the same colors, but are drawn by the "target pattern" of light and dark directing them to the spot where nectar is to be found. Thousands of other flowers produce landing patterns in wavelengths of light invisible to the human eye.

Certain orchids seem more deceptive, seducing male insects by presenting what appears to be a female insect at the center of the blossom. A male flies to the female look-alike, attempts to copulate, and picks up pollen before flying off to the next encounter.

Few gardeners can pass by a fragrant flower without leaning over for a sniff. Perfume is a way flowers invite pollinators to make contact, though the fruity and spicy fragrance of the rose, the cool and sweet scent of freesia, and the

Plants have devised ingenious methods to ensure that pollination takes place. Some of these lures are beautiful, some invisible, and some rather devious. Bright color seems obvious. Bees see the color blue best, and many plants have evolved to produce flowers in this hue. To make sure bees are attracted at just the right moment, some of these flowers, such as Virginia bluebells, emerge pink and then turn powder blue when the pollen is ripe and the nectar is flowing.

cherry-baby-powder smell of the heliotrope please people, too. The cloying, honeylike fragrances of linden, autumn clematis, and privet may or may not attract us, but they are potent advertisements for bees that there is nectar to be found. The common petunia produces an intense aroma of clove, but only after dusk, when its pollinator, a nocturnal moth, is about.

Opposite: A bumble bee slides below the tight foxglove flower's anthers and is covered with pollen. **Above, clockwise from bottom left:** Insects often see more than we do, and the deep color at the center of the rose-of-Sharon flower may just be part of a guidance system visible as infrared or ultraviolet light. Virginia bluebells announce their ripe flowers and gift of nectar by changing from pink to blue, the color bees see best. Birds and people are attracted to red—*Lobelia cardinalis* acts like a stop sign to a hummer. The skunk cabbage's attracting strategy is to provide shelter and warmth in winter when the temperature within the hooded spathe can reach 70 degrees F (21 degrees C).

FRUIT

The next step for plants was to disseminate their seeds. Many of the conifers produced winged seeds to use the wind just as the plants' pollen did. There are seeds produced with tempting rewards; those with elaisomes—yew shrubs, for

with a barbed capsule to hitch onto a hiker's pant leg. Other dry fruits may have seeds attached to fluff that can become airborne (like a dandelion's parachute).

Buoyant pods float on streams and rivers, but the coconut is probably the champion long-distance traveler—Caribbean coconuts are

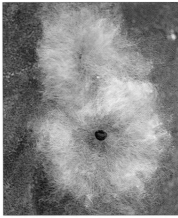

Above, left to right: If the product of a pollinated flower has seeds, it's a fruit, moist or dry. Fruits may protect seeds, delay germination, or help seeds find a new or hospitable place for germination, which is what burdock fruits do, using hooks to hitch a ride on unsuspecting passersby. Kapok seeds are encased in airborne fluff. Water arum plunges its ripening fruits into the surrounding muck.

Below: Behind the familiar star-shaped sepal of a rose **(left),** berrylike hips form around seeds called "achenes." A single strawberry flower **(right)** has many pistils and each swells and fuses into a pulpy fruit. But strawberries are not classified as moist fruits; they are aggregates of achenes with dry seeds on the outside.

example—attract insects, which carry these seeds off to their burrows, where the tasty parts are consumed—leaving the seeds unharmed and in a perfect haven for germination.

The seed vessels that result from floral pollination and the swelling of ovaries or ovary-like structures are fruits—regardless of which side of the produce aisle fruits are found on—whether they are sweet and juicy, hard and dry, pea pods or luscious peaches—anything that contains seeds is a fruit. The containers have been thoughtfully designed by nature to protect the precious contents and, in many cases, to help disseminate the cargo. Moist fruits encase seeds in sweet flesh to entice, and colorful skins are used to publicize delicacies to animals that might eat them and help distribute the seeds.

Prickly dry fruits may enlist animals as well,

occasionally seen sprouting on the coast of Scotland, delivered there by the waters of the Gulf Stream. Violets produce two kinds of fruit: ones at the base of the plant drop seeds on the soil; others face skyward and, when ripe, explode. Harvesting even a few seeds presents a challenge when violets shoot their seeds 6 to 7 feet away to test uncharted territory.

Fruits and seeds take many forms, and it is important for the gardener to know about their guises—for harvesting, cleaning, storing, or sowing at just the right time.

THE RIGHT PLACE AT THE RIGHT TIME

One defense against a seed's premature sprouting is its coat. This outer layer, often covered by water-resistant wax or shellaclike resins, protects the seed while it lies in wait. In nature,

microorganisms may eat through the seed coat. An animal may snag a fruit, and the seed might emerge having passed through the animal's gut with the coat scarred by digestive acids. For the propagator, drying, chilling, nicking and filing, hot-water baths, or a simple overnight soak may be needed to compromise the coat's integrity. Once there's a breach in the coat, moisture can be imbibed. But moisture is not the only agent effecting germination.

Seeds don't sprout at the wrong time in the wrong place. If moisture and warmth were all that was needed for a seed to sprout, nicotiana seeds would germinate when their goblet-fruits filled with water from late-summer rains; the seeds would die as soon as they dried again. If pumpkin seeds sprouted inside their vine-ripened fruits, the seedlings would die without light. Given the complexity of nature, mechanisms more elaborate than the seed's

coat can be suspected of delaying germination.

Scientists conducting research on the elements that affect plant growth have discovered that the hormonal compound abscisic acid (ABA)—the same chemical that is responsible for winter dormancy of mature plants—accumulates in seeds as they ripen. But it isn't accu-

rate to think of seeds as experiencing a dormant cycle. Seeds can remain in suspended animation for months or years. ABA stops the clock, and in order for seeds to move to the next phase in their development, this chemical inhibitor must be removed or destroyed.

The key to this process lies in the origin of the individual seed: the type of plant that produced it and the environment of its homeland. One can speculate that when a bird consumes a fruit and expels its seed, the flesh may have contained the inhibitor. For a plant indigenous to an alpine meadow, exposure to frigid winds and snow could be necessary to prepare its seed. The seeds of annuals grown in our gardens must be harvested when ripe and stored in a frost-free place until it is time to sow the seeds indoors or out. This dry storage may be just what these seeds need—perhaps sitting in a packet on the garden-center shelf provides a coincidental

Left: A chestnut seed's nearly impenetrable coat helps it stay fresh and viable until the right time and place for germination—perhaps where it was buried and forgotten by a squirrel.

Right: Although depicted with a bird in an eighteenth-century illustration by naturalist Mark Catesby, the North American native sweet bay magnolia (*Magnolia virginiana*) is not an aggressive spreader. But keep in mind that birds eat fruits, clean away the pulp, sometimes etching a seed's hard coat with digestive acids, and deposit seeds away from their sources with a nutritional bonus. This method of preparation and dissemination should be a warning against planting potentially invasive bird-attracting plants, such as barberry and autumn olive.

advantage. The seeds of hardy plants are subjected to fluctuations in temperature, and it is likely that this contributes to the gradual destruction of inhibitors.

Gardeners often have to discover how to turn off the inhibitors to "condition" seeds in preparation for germination. The seeds of hardy plants can be sown outdoors, but there are many reasons why pretreating them indoors—perhaps by subjecting the seeds to periods of warmth, cold, and warmth again in the home nursery—may be advantageous. Conditioning could be called for to get a head start on the growing season, to make up for lost time when seeds arrive in winter—months after natural conditioning would have begun outdoors—or to achieve a higher success rate with precious seeds under the gardener's watchful eye and controlled surroundings.

GERMINATION

Once the inhibitor is destroyed, moisture and warmth will initiate germination. Seeing the inside of a seed is like viewing a human embryo

with ultrasound. To glimpse the next steps, consider a large seed such as the fast-sprouting lima bean (*Phaseolus lunatus*). Soaking the bean in warm water will begin the process.

When the seed coat (*testa*) of the bean is wet, it will loosen and slip off to reveal the *cotyledon (seed leaf)*. The bean has two cotyledons, and they can be pried apart to reveal the embryo attached to one part. The miracle of nature is breathtakingly apparent, displayed as a plant in miniature with tiny leaves and an appendage called a *radicle*. After imbibing water, the radicle elongates, emerges from the seed, and becomes the plant's first root. The emergence of the radicle is an indication that growth and life are under way, but the sprouting of the cotyledons is considered the sign of germination. These cotyledons grow to become the seed leaves—predecessors of the

plant's first true leaves. This version of the process is *epigeal* germination.

Some plants, however, do not act so simply, or swiftly. In *hypogeal* germination, the cotyledons remain underground and nourish the seedling without emerging. Sometimes, as with "two-step germinators" (see page 74), several

seasons pass before the process is completed.

Plants such as the epigeal lima bean that produce two seed leaves are classified as *dicotyledons*. Plants whose seeds send up a single seed leaf, like a blade of grass, are *monocotyledons*. When sowing seeds, it is helpful to note the distinction: some seedlings will emerge with two semicircular sections joined at the stem, and others with a solitary shoot. The second set of leaves to appear are the *true leaves,* which resemble the leaves of the plant-to-be.

The dicots again produce a pair of leaves, and the monocots bear a second single leaf. The true leaves of the dicots have veins that branch; monocots have parallel veins. When the plants are mature, the distinctions persist—consider the dicotyledonous maple tree and the monocotyledonous palm. Recognizing the differences between these types of plants affects options for vegetative propagation.

Below left: Inside a bean seed are the embryonic makings of an entire new plant. Visible on the right half is the immature root called the "radicle" with tiny "true leaves" above it. The remainder of the bean, the nutritional endo-carp, becomes the cotyledons, or seed leaves. When germination begins, the radicle elongates. The process is complete when the cotyledons emerge.

Above right: Plants that produce seeds are either dicotyledons with two seed leaves, like the bean, or monocotyledons with one. As they grow, leaves of dicots develop a network of branching veins that can be seen in the skeletal remains of a linden leaf. Leaves of monocots, such as *Canna* 'Tropicana Phaison' **(opposite)** and other members of the lily family, have parallel veins.

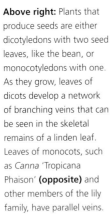

ALL POWERFUL

Plants reproduce sexually via seeds, but the mechanisms that allow them to repair themselves after injuries also enable us to reproduce them asexually, or vegetatively. Buds, which are nestled in the nodes where leaves and lateral shoots emerge from stems, produce hormones that prompt cells to grow and make necessary repairs. Latent buds, or "eyes," are signaled in the event of an emergency, such as defoliation by insects. A gardener can pinch terminal growth, causing the plant to develop new branches or leaves. A young tree damaged in a snow storm may grow a straight and tall new leader. The newest cells of the bud's growing point, or *meristem*, can transform into fresh growth because of an ability called *totipotency*, a term that derives from the Latin for "all powerful."

Totipotency makes reproduction from cuttings possible as well. The *cambium layer* of meristem tissue, which contains cells in a formative stage, lies beneath the corky bark of woody plants and the epidermis of soft-tissue ones. The cells of the cambium can differentiate to become any part of a plant, from leafy growth to protective calluses to new roots. When a large branch breaks off a tree, the cells around the wound divide wildly to form a callus that seals off the exposed tissue. When a woody stem cutting is made, a callus forms through which tiny roots will emerge.

OLD GROWTH

A cutting taken from a mature plant, one that is making flowers and fruit, is using its energy for sexual reproduction, not vegetative propagation. For example, a stem taken from an herbaceous perennial in spring will root easily. If taken later, when flowering, the cutting will be difficult, if not impossible, to root. Likewise, cuttings from young woody plants root more easily than ones from mature, aged plants. Trees, being the longest-lived plants, are often the most difficult to root, although they readily grow from seed. If there is a special cultivated variety of tree that cannot be replicated from sown seed, however, it has to be reproduced asexually through vegetative propagation. Stem sections taken from older trees (known as *scions*) can be grafted onto young plants (called *understocks*), grown from seeds of similar species. The cells of the cambium layer divide to knit one plant to the other. The sapling imparts its youth and vigor to the scion.

Top: It is possible for plants to reproduce without sex through various mechanisms. One explanation can be found beneath the bark of a dicot. A thin layer of cambium cells has an undetermined destiny. Under particular circumstances, these cells can grow to become stems, leaves, or even roots.

Opposite: The water lily multiplies by producing new plants from eyes on rhizomes that creep freely through the earth bottom of a shallow pond.

Clockwise from right: Mature plants, such as trees, and ones that are in flower or fruit are not eager to return to a juvenile state when they were actively adding leafy tissue and easier to propagate. Transformations may begin when the cambium produces a gnarled mass of cells through which roots will grow. Adventitious buds, seen as pale bumps on a *Dieffenbachia* cane, may grow into new stems and leaves or roots. Dormant buds on hardy plants can be "switched on" by hormones when there is trauma to the terminal growth and sprout stems and leaves. The eyes of a potato can grow roots and shoots.

THE MAGNOLIA
MASTER

Dick Figlar wanted to possess every interesting magnolia he ever saw or heard about, but buying hundreds of trees would cost a fortune, even if the magnolia varieties were all available. To satisfy his craving, he learned how to graft. Dick capitalizes on the fact that cells of the cambium layer of a tree can differentiate to grow into a kind of scar tissue that closes a wound. When two plant parts are cut and held closely and firmly together, either through a natural phenomenon or on a nursery bench, the cells in contact fuse, and the plant parts become one. By grafting, Dick has been able to amass an impressive collection of magnolias from the half-dozen or so twigs he receives from fellow enthusiasts each winter.

Sometimes Dick can harvest three or more buds from one of these sticks of scion wood. Each bud will be grafted onto a seedling grown to become the "under stock" or "root stock" that will eventually support the top growth of the chosen magnolia species or variety.

To perform the operation, Dick cuts a small piece of the wood that includes a dormant eye, or "chip bud," of the scion and grafts it onto his magnolia understock, which provides the trunk and roots. In short order, cells of the understock and the graft begin to grow together, and the swollen leaf bud transforms to become a branch. When the graft is well established the following spring, he cuts off the top of the understock seedling and the scion

shoot straightens to become the new leader—the primary vertical shoot of the tree.

The "arboretum" at Dick's vacation property in North Carolina houses over a hundred different specimen magnolia trees. In fact, his grafting has been so successful that he has gone into the scion business, selling to fellow magnolia lovers all over

the country. His is a rather efficient mail-order nursery—there are no rows of plants in pots to be watered or heavy shrubs to ship. When Dick receives an order, he just seals some wrapped twigs in a padded envelope and sends them off.

Opposite: Grafts occur in nature when limbs of a tree grow to touch firmly and the cells of the cambium layer fuse, as they have in these Japanese maple branches. **Clockwise from above left:** Dick Figlar's magnolia collection includes a fifteen-million-year-old leaf fossil from Idaho that closely resembles today's *Magnolia grandiflora*. Dick acquires varieties from twigs sent by other collectors—a chip with one dormant bud is used (page 180). Dick finds *M. grandiflora* 'Bracken's Brown Beauty' to be the hardiest and most floriferous evergreen variety for his New York State garden. Among his one hundred deciduous varieties is the fragrant *M.* x *wiesneri*.

ADVENTITIOUS OUTGROWTHS

Some plants are so eager to reproduce vegetatively that they don't wait for gardeners to propagate them. They produce adventitious growths, known as *propagules* or baby plants. Many *Kalanchoe* species, collectively known as "mother of thousands," produce plantlets along the edges of their leaves. When large enough, the offspring drop to the ground and grow. Tropical water lilies may produce new plants that grow in a bit of captured water in the mature plant's leaf, and new flowers may even bloom there. *Aloe vera* produces brood after brood of offsets around a mature plant. Some orchids do the same; their progeny are called "keikis." One of the most familiar plants to bear live young is the spider plant *(Chlorophytum comosum)*. Its babies grow from the ends

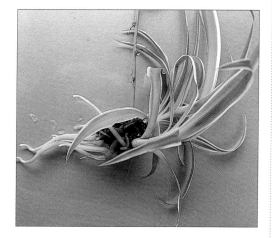

of the flower stalks, and they are easily rooted for new plants.

A few plants that are *monocarpic* (they fruit only once), such as bromeliads, die after they flower and set seed, but they may prepare for their demise by producing compact plantlets around the central parent. Hardy succulent hen-and-chicks *(Sempervivum)* follow this pattern.

Suckers are sometimes produced from adventitious buds on shallow roots, leading to sprouts around shrub clumps of plants such as lilac or sumac. The same action causes straight shoots, called water sprouts, from the trunk and branches of trees or shrubs if they are damaged, severely pruned, or attacked by disease.

Grass plants, such as those in a traditional lawn, also reproduce vegetatively, from rhizomes—underground stems just below the surface of the soil. New roots, stems, and leaves push out from nodes along the subterranean stem. While that's good for a lawn, consider the grasses' cousin, the bamboo, on the rampage across your garden, having escaped from the property next door.

Latent buds, or eyes, on roots are virtually invisible, but in many cases, roots are capable of reproducing entire new plants from cut tissue. These buds are not unlike the eyes of tubers.

Opposite: Many plants exhibit adventitious growths in nature. The mother of thousands *(Kalanchoe pinnata)* produces baby plants along the margins of its leaves.

Top: The familiar spider plant *(Chlorophytum comosum)* grows offspring at the ends of its flower stalks.

Above: The viviparous piggyback plant *(Tolmiea menziesii)* **(left)** sprouts a new plant from an old leaf. The mother fern *(Asplenium bulbiferum)* **(right)** bears its bright green young from the veins of a frond.

Below: Bromeliads, such as *Aechmea chantinii* 'Samurai', produce offsets called "pups" from the base of the plant that can be removed and grown into independent plants.

MODIFIED STEMS

Some plants produce stems and leaves that swell with stored carbohydrates and sugars. We know these organs as bulbs, tubers, corms, and fleshy rhizomes—collectively, the plants are called *geophytes*.

The scales of flowering bulbs may either be

arranged in concentric layers, as those of an onion, or be separate, as in lily bulbs. The lily's scales are arrayed like the bracts of an artichoke. Tulips and daffodils—tunicate bulbs with papery coverings—split to form new bulbs. Tunicate bulbs can be cut into sections for propagation. Lilies—nontunicate bulbs—can be propagated from individual scales.

A few lilies—the tiger lily, for instance—pro-

duce miniature black "bulbils" at their leaf axils. These bulbils roll off the plant, fall onto the ground, sprout roots, and push up stems and leaves. In about two years, the new plants flower and form bulbils of their own.

Other geophytes arise from tubers. As is easily seen with a potato, tubers have dormant buds—eyes—-with cells that have the ability to transmogrify into roots, shoots, and all other plant organs. (Similar buds can be found at ground level at the crown of dormant herbaceous perennials in winter.) Some tuberous plants form tubercles similar to lily bulbils. A few

tuberous vines produce their tubercles in midair, such as the true yam and the aptly named rosary vine.

Gladioli grow from corms, which resemble bulbs but do not have scales, and reproduce by growing whole new corms beneath the shriveled ones of the season before or by making tiny cormels around the base of old ones.

There is one other geophyte: a subterranean rhizome with a growing point and the ability to store nutrients and moisture during times of drought or cold. During the summer, a tiny chunk of a canna rhizome with a single eye will produce leafy growth above ground that is reflected below the soil by an elongating, thickening structure, which by season's end, might sport a dozen dormant buds. Some canna rhizomes also produce appendages—2-inch spherical nodules nicknamed "toes." The rhizome buds bear the "meristem" or newest cells addressed in the anomaly of the *Sansevieria* clone that follows and on page 194.

CLONES

New plants that are produced vegetatively are called *clones*—identical in every way to their parents. A flowering maple (*Abutilon*) cultivar, for instance, may exhibit variegation caused by a virus, and it will pass on this characteristic through cuttings. However, certain traits, harbored only in the new cells of the most terminal growth, will not be passed on. In the case of certain variegated plants, for example, the genetic instructions for producing the colorful trait are carried only in these "meristem" cells and will not appear on new plants produced from stem or root cuttings. Immature meristem cells have not fully differentiated into the tissues of organs they are to become.

Early in the twentieth century, scientists began to experiment with these undetermined cells, growing entire new plants from the emerging new growth of leaf buds or slices from a nugget or callus. This micropropagation, like all forms of vegetative propagation, is a testament to a plant's determination to survive. Glimpses into the science of plant reproduction —the botany of propagation—may or may not be proof of evolution's divinity, but they are evidence of nature's mastery.

Opposite, clockwise from far left: Geophytes can be propagated asexually in several ways. The prolific tiger lily (*Lilium lancifolium*) produces black bulbils at its leaf axils that roll to the ground, root, and grow. A narcissus bulb not only contains everything necessary for next year's flower show (including incipient blossoms with immature anthers), it can also be propagation material propagated from sections of the bulb and basal plate below. Potatoes can be cut into pieces that include at least one growing "eye."

Above: Plants propagated vegetatively produce clones—genetically identical replicas of their parents. Variegation is reproduced asexually; however, in the case of the flowering maple (*Abutilon pictum* 'Thompsonii'), the mottling is caused by a virus that is transmitted to cuttings. But in a variegated snake plant (*Sansevieria trifasciata* 'Bantel's Sensation') **(below)**, the characteristic is developed by mutating meristem cells at the tip of the new growth. Cuttings grow roots and a new rhizome from their bases, so the result reverts to the species form.

2

Why Sow?

Sexual propagation comes down to the seed. Shake a few seeds into the palm of your hand and behold the essence of creation. This dazzling feat of packaging compresses all the genetic information necessary to reproduce an entire plant, plus opportunities for travel and, often, some sustenance for the journey.

A seed is one of nature's most ingenious gifts. The spirited cosmos starts from seed, as does the giant redwood.

The acquisition of a startling new plant for the garden is one of the most compelling reasons to sow seeds. Producing a great number of plants is another. Scores of seeds can be sown, frequently at low cost (and sometimes for free).

Seeds can be shipped around the world with minimal packaging and handling. (*Begonia*

seeds come about a million to the ounce.)

The next phase of the seed sower's career might be to discover and select a distinctive variety from a mass sowing. There is also the potential to "invent" a new plant by interbreeding two plants or a succession of plants, although such manipulation may be controversial. Agribusinesspeople, native-plant enthusiasts, plant purists, and explorers have strong opinions on the subject. A good case is made by the seed savers, who promote the old-fashioned heirloom varieties. The gardener's plea for "new" varieties should be balanced by efforts to perpetuate the old varieties of vegetables and flowers. The possible loss of an entire crop grown in a monoculture, for instance, might be staved off by promoting horticultural and agricultural diversity.

Nature doesn't necessarily need new plants, either, just safe places for indigenous ones to grow. Conservation is another reason to propagate plants from seeds. Stealing plants from the wild is just plain wrong; the theft may contribute to a mini-ecosystem's demise. The best

way to stop people from digging plants in the wild is to make those plants available from nursery-propagated stock; the home gardener can obtain seeds of a wildflower from a native-plant society and grow them to help a species persist, even if its homeland does not survive.

There is one more incentive for sowing seed: it is so much fun. There is the challenge of the hunt for seeds of the species or variety, the thrill of watching them sprout, and the satisfaction of nurturing the seedlings. Ultimately, the joy of propagation is seeing the results in first flowers, or basking in the shade of a tree that will live on beyond the length of our own lives.

Preceding pages: A strain of deep mahogany sunflowers was encouraged by collecting and sowing seeds from the darkest blossoms of the season.

Opposite: For the highest volume at the lowest cost, bedding plants are grown commercially from seeds.

Left: The last wild *Franklinia alatamaha* was seen in 1790, but it exists today because seeds were grown by John Bartram, who named this shrub for his friend Benjamin Franklin.

Right: Hybridizing for desired characteristics is another reason to sow.

SOWING FOR SELECTION

It is said that good luck is simply taking advantage of opportunity. Cultivars, varieties of plants that can be cultivated and introduced to the nursery trade, are found in intentional mass

command hefty prices: $200 or more. Gardeners can search for their own. Instead of deadheading all your hostas after flowers fade, let one stalk form plump fruits. When the fruits are still green but the stalk turns brown, cut the stem and bring it to a safe place indoors. It could be

Above left: A sampling of autumn oak leaves represents some of the fifty varieties grown by Nigel and Lisa Wright in Pennsylvania. The oaks begin as acorns received through the mail from commercial seed suppliers, botanical gardens, and fellow members of the International Oak Society.

Above right: Unusual varieties can be selected from mass sowings of "open pollinated" seeds as John Beirne found with pumpkin-colored coleus— dubbed 'Beirned Orange' by a fellow gardener.

Below: Sean Conway plucked a distinctive coleus seedling from his nursery row—shown with its namesake, son Emmett. Cuttings have to be taken each year to have new plants of coleus 'Emmett' and 'Beirned Orange'.

sowings all the time. More frequently, however, they are simply discovered by someone who spends a moment taking a second look. Careful scrutiny of flats of seedlings on the benches at the nursery in spring, or of seedlings sown at home, often reveals something special. The more seeds sown, the greater the chances of discovering a unique plant.

Hostas are among the most popular herbaceous perennials, with new introductions appearing each year and vying for the top spot on the annual list of favorites chosen by the American Hosta Society. A hosta with the brightest golden leaves, sweetly perfumed flowers, or a shapely leaf with a wave or a wiggle can

stood in an empty vase set in a box where the warm air can dry the pods so any seeds that drop when the pods split open will be collected. Hosta seed can be sown fresh and will come up quickly (see chapter 5, "Sowing," page 76).

The signs of something different will show quickly. Seedlings with promise can be potted up to be grown on in the garden, and the rest can be discarded. Thankfully, the seedlings that don't measure up do not have to go to the compost heap. There's a gardener born every minute, so the surplus should easily find homes.

The popularity of hostas demonstrates the growing interest in plants for foliage. Coleus, for instance, have never been grown for flowers. These plants—formerly familiar in dish gardens made to brighten the sickroom—offer an incredible range of leaf colors, and that has led to the plants' dramatic comeback. Today's coleus barely resemble their forebears. They

have even gotten an up-market name change, to *Solenostemon scutellarioides*. The current crop includes individuals with striking leaf shapes, intricate color patterns, or vivid solid shades in every hue but blue. The vegetatively propagated cultivars have also been given evocative monikers such as 'Inky Fingers', 'India Frills', 'Purple Duckfoot', 'Ella Cinders', and 'Evil'.

John Beirne, a young horticulturist and self-described "foliage freak," discovered a distinctive variety in a batch of mixed seedlings. A gardener at Wave Hill, the public garden in the Bronx, New York, where John worked one summer during college, named the incredible coppery-pumpkin discovery 'Beirned Orange'.

"×" MARKS THE CROSS

A plant name with the designation "×," such as *Abelia × grandiflora*, denotes that it is more than a selection among the progeny of a species.

The plant is the product of either an accidental mingling of independent species or an intentional one. The "×" notes that this plant is a "cross," or hybrid. While a hybrid is commonly thought to be made from two different but closely related species, it is actually the result of interbreeding any two distinct individuals, either within one species (an intraspecific hybrid), between two species of one genus (an interspecific hybrid), or, in the rarest cases, between genera (an intergeneric hybrid). In the latter case, the plant's name usually begins with the symbol ×—as in × *Mahoberberis* (a hybrid of the genera *Mahonia times Berberis*).

With all this crossing going on, seedlings often exhibit characteristics that might make them attractive additions to the ornamental garden. Blossoms with extra rows of petals (double flowers) may appear, as they do in roses. A seedling may be stockier than its brethren, what we call compact. Plant breeders frequently predict the results by choosing parents for particular characteristics.

The process begins when the pollen from one plant is brought to the female stigma of another. The fertilized flower is then sheathed

Top: A maroon *Helleborus orientalis* flower chosen to be "father" was cut and floated in water in the refrigerator for a few days to keep its pollen fresh for "mother".

Left: Betty Sturley made a dense sowing of fresh hosta seeds in a flat, hoping to find something wonderful. Distinctive traits, such as variegation, appeared early.

Below: A hybrid is the product of any cross-pollination, but when many gardeners hear the word, they picture something like this mix of annual impatiens. The latest offerings from commercial houses are usually "F_1" hybrids, or first-generation seeds produced in highly controlled conditions. A debate rages on as to whether there is a need for ever more "new and improved" plants. There's a worry, too, that flashy introductions might supplant species, replace favorite heirloom varieties, or threaten to dominate agriculture. However, producing your own hybrid should be guilt-free when the subject is not invasive and just for your own garden.

in gauze or a paper covering to ensure that the cross will not be contaminated by undesired pollen. From generation to generation, selections are made and interbred. The final cross produces a seed that will result in a plant with predictable attributes.

The familiar seed packets of "F_1" hybrid annuals indicate a first-generation crossing of two inbred lines. These "improved" versions have hybrid vigor (as opposed to inbred depression). However, if a gardener likes the hybrid and wants to grow it again, more seeds will have to be purchased, if possible. A newer introduction may already have taken its place. Although overblown double-petaled marigolds might seem better than the comely single types to some gardeners, others find something missing in these manufactured, and sterile, products (figuratively, and sometimes literally).

GROW YOUR OWN

While the thought of big-business breeding seems unnerving, keep in mind that hybrids occur in nature all the time. It may be prudent to remain wary of some manipulative agriculture—especially in the production of food crops—but on the small scale of the home garden, the interest in creating a "new" plant can be benign—just for fun. Consider the daylily.

One wonders whether with 50,000 named varieties of *Hemerocallis*, there is any point to making another one. But daylilies are popular candidates for amateur hybridizers because the male and female floral organs are large and accessible. The seeds that form are easy to handle, and in just three years (fast for hardy perennials), the characteristics of the new creations will be revealed in the first flowers. And every now and again an introduction appears with honestly original traits.

All of the *Hemerocallis* in our gardens today originated from only a handful of species. Crosses between the resulting hybrids and species or hybrids and hybrids led to the proliferation. For instance, a cross between the lavender-flowered *Hemerocallis* cultivar 'Prairie Blue Eyes' and the fragrant old favorite cultivar 'Hyperion' yielded a variety of offspring. A few plants had spidery, lavender-pink petals.

Most *Hemerocallis* species have yellow or orange flowers, but a pink variety, *H.* 'Rosea'—discovered in Kiangsi Province, China, and imported to the New York Botanical Garden in 1939—presented the opportunity to breed hybrids in shades from pink to red; for example, *H.* 'Prairie Blue-eyes' **(top)**. In a recent cross for fragrance, shape, and color, this broad-flowered lavender hybrid contributed pollen to the sweetly scented yellow introduction from 1925, *H.* 'Hyperion' **(center)**. The half-dozen progeny included a rose-pink flower with spidery petals, one with mauve petals and contrasting ivory midribs, and one **(bottom)** with broad recurved petals, thin sepals that curl at the ends, a dark "eye," and a yellow throat that deepens to lime green at the center. None of the flowers were as "blue" as their father or as fragrant as their mother, but the one shown stays open late into the evening, when the sparkling colors turn tan.

Another bore blooms that stayed open late into the evening, and its mauve-pink and yellow flowers faded to tan and taupe. The nameless hybrid offspring may not have "improved" upon their father by having bluer flower color, but they all were fragrant and unique.

To create your own daylily hybrid, select parents with characteristics you think would produce something special. For example, choose a plant with very fragrant flowers to match with one that blossoms in an unusual color; or, perhaps, join a plant with low foliage with another that produces a funnel-form bloom on slender, tall scapes.

Visit the chosen mother-to-be early in the morning, when the dew still glistens on the leaves and the flowers are just opening. The anthers will be evident but will not have split open to reveal their pollen. Self-pollination is unlikely, but for safety's sake, snip the anthers off with scissors. In half an hour or so, the anthers on the father plant will ripen and they should be used at once. A small artist's paintbrush is an efficient tool for collecting the pollen. Just as the brush picks up pigment and then deposits it on the canvas, so too will it collect and release pollen. The drawback with a brush, however, is that unless you are pollinating several flowers by one male, you will need to scrupulously clean the brush between procedures. Alternatively, you can pinch a bit of pollen between your fingertips or simply pluck the entire anther to bring to the stigma of the mother-to-be.

Daylily blossoms last only a single day, and the pollen begins to "grow" at once. It is unlikely that unwanted pollen from another flower will ruin the cross, since the race is over as soon as the first batch is delivered and pollination has begun. So coverings of gauze or paper will not be necessary. Tie a tag labeled with names of the father and mother and the date of the cross. The petals will soon fall and the ovary containing the developing seeds will swell. A paper bag should be lowered over the fruits and tied shut. (For information on harvesting, see page 55.)

(1)

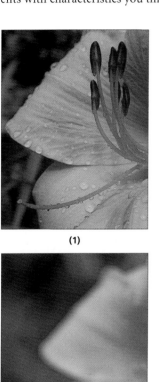

(2)

(3)

(4)

(5)

(6)

There are 50,000 named varieties of daylily, and no wonder: the sexual components are accessible and results can be seen in as little as two years—quick for a long-lived perennial. The process includes these steps: When the mother-to-be opens early in the morning but its anthers have not yet split to reveal the pollen (1), snip off the stamens (2). Shortly thereafter, pollen is collected from the father, and if several crosses are to be made with contributions from this single parent, a clean artist's paintbrush may be used to gather and deliver the golden grains (3). Or simply pick one ripe anther and touch it to the stigma (4). Label the cross with the parents' names and the date of the merger (5). Very soon, fruits will appear. Cover the swollen fruits with a paper bag before they begin to shrivel and turn brown, so when the capsule splits open, the seeds can be retrieved (6).

HEIRLOOM PURITY

Where are the hollyhocks that grew in the farm-house yard? Who can recall the redolent fragrance of violets or remember pears you could eat with a spoon? These were plants once grown in quantity, but for whatever reason—perhaps because they fell out of favor, or there were

difficulties in large-scale production and shipping—are uncommon today.

Advocates of "heirloom" varieties generally oppose modern genetic fusion. The fear is that old-fashioned "strains" will be ignored and ultimately lost in the ongoing quest for "new and improved" ones. If you harvest and sow seeds from a modern F1 hybrid flower, the result will revert to something that resembles one or both original parents—not the hybrid you began

with. On the other hand, when a propagator perpetuates individual plants with desirable characteristics by cultivating them in relative isolation and collecting their seeds to sow again each year, a strain may emerge. Although a plant from a strain is not a species, it will "come true" from saved seed.

Producers of heirloom seeds often work on a somewhat small scale. They enclose their crops with frames covered with screening on the top and sides to keep insects from introducing the genes from other varieties in the species. If

gardeners continue to segregate these strains, usually annuals or biennials, they will retain their traits. For example, seeds harvested from the antique 'Brandywine' tomato will grow to produce that fruit again.

Although it is too late for the lost varieties, other plants are making a comeback because of the growing number of "seed savers," gardeners dedicated to preserving heirlooms as essential resources. More than nostalgia is driving this movement. Heirlooms, grown from seeds that have been handed down through generations or rescued and resurrected from an abandoned plot of ground, help maintain diversity within our natural world.

3 Hunting
and
Gathering

When human beings started to collect, save,

and sow seeds of the plants that their animals ate,

their nomadic life was over and civilization

began. Plants put down roots and so did people.

Stationary communities formed, and over the

next few thousand years, pastures turned into

farms, and, sometimes, farms became

gardens created simply for pleasure.

The notion of hunting and gathering for sustenance is far from our minds today. But most of us hunt through plant-catalog pages, and we might gather some interesting propagation possibilities inside fruits bought at the farmer's market. More often than not, however, the seed we harvest will come from our own plants and those of friends. Picking seeds from private property, parks, or (perish the thought) a public garden is out of the question; however, it may be acceptable to collect a few seeds of plants in the "wild" when their habitat is threatened.

It is customary to cut wildflowers from the roadside, even de rigueur, but if everyone did it, there wouldn't be any flowers left. The same goes for picking seeds. As a general rule, take no more than one in ten seeds that you come upon, and if there are only nine, do not take any.

There are organizations dedicated to native plants, such as the New England Wildflower Society, which offers a yearly seed list of native plants. These groups do the collecting for you and also carry the responsibility of harvesting only from their nursery-propagated stock. If you are interested in specific types of plants, look to associations such as the North American Rock Garden Society or the Hardy Plant Society (see Resources, page 244). Often there is a yearly seed exchange featuring seeds that may not be available from any other source. Members who collect and donate seeds to the plant society's exchange have first pick from the season's offering.

There's always something "new and improved" offered on the colorful pages of the commercial seed catalogs. To find seeds of plants that are less refined, not quite so well bred, subtler, and in keeping with a low-key, sophisticated aesthetic, look to the less flashy catalogs. Mom-and-pop

seed companies that have catalogs without color pictures, or even just lists of species or old-fashioned varieties, can become enticing sources for rare, unusual, or curious plants.

THE SOURCE

Although you will rarely be collecting from the wild, you will want to collect seeds from plants that are "originals"—species, that is—not commercial hybrids or cloned selections. Exceptions would be heirloom varieties, cultivars that "come true," and the seeds of your own cross-pollination experiments. Seeds sown from most

hybrids will not reproduce their parent; they will "revert to type" and resemble one or more of their previous ancestors. Some hybrids may even be sterile, as are many daffodils whose swollen fruits are barren. You should also avoid harvesting fruits from weak or diseased plants. Those plants that are deformed or weakened by viruses may pass on this condition to their progeny.

When collecting seeds, consider the general environment. Was the seed from a tree that lives in a cold climate or from an indoor vine native to the tropics? What was the vessel like that held the precious cargo—in other words, the fruit? Was it a dry fruit with a papery shell or a moist fruit with seeds encased in juicy flesh? The physiological characteristics of a fruit offer valuable hints to its source's culture.

Preceding pages: After the opium poppies' petals fall, ornamental blue-orb fruits are revealed—filled with next season's seeds.

Opposite: The shapes, sizes, and colors of fruits are nearly as varied as those of flowers—a fact wonderfully illustrated by capsules of species in the single genus *Eucalyptus*.

Above left: Seeds of rare plants, such as *Meconopsis grandis,* can be "harvested" through the mail from plant-society seed exchanges, which is often the only way to procure the rarest plants.

Above right: In order to collect the seeds of many plants, a gardener has to be in the right place at the right time. Milkweed seeds take flight the moment their ripe dehiscent fruits split open.

ALL IN GOOD TIME

It isn't always easy to know the best moment to collect fruits and seeds from a plant. The generalization is to get them when they are ripe. If the fruit is ripe, then it can be assumed that the seeds inside are fully matured. But when is that perfect moment?

You can check the fruits of a certain plant each day, only to discover that the moment you thought they would be ready, some animal had a similar notion and collected the seeds before you were able to. Then there are plants with explosive fruits; when you want to harvest these, a minute late is too late. Witch hazel, impatiens, and rhododendron capsules all "shoot" seeds, and once scattered, they are impossible to find. These fruits have to be removed before they open and release their seeds.

When you come across a fascinating but uncommon plant that you're eager to sow from seed, carefully observe the plant and its fruits. A moist fruit is most likely ripe when it turns color and yields when pressed. As a dry pod begins to shrivel and also changes color from green to brown, it will probably be ripe enough to harvest. When the pinecones are heavy and the conifer's branches seem to weep with their weight, it is time for the harvest. After harvesting, the next step is cleaning the seeds before either storing them, sowing them, or beginning the treatments that will lead to germination.

EASIER BEING GREEN

Fresh is usually best. The seeds of jack-in-the-pulpits germinate quickly when they are harvested and immediately processed (see page 60),

Following fertilization in flowering plants *(angiosperms),* structures containing developing ovules swell. These vessels with seeds are fruits—whether moist and succulent like a melon or dry like a vanilla bean. The *gymnosperms* (with naked seed) have no fruit. The conifers, for instance, have ovules within the overlapping spiral layers of their dry cones. Examples of seed sources include: the moist berry of star fruit *(Averrhoa bilimbi),* which when sliced makes the origin of its common name clear **(left);** the dry capsules of *Papaver atlanticum* **(center)** are reminiscent of minarets with "portals" at the top from which seeds spill as the papery fruits lean in the breeze; little winged seeds slip out from the scales of the hemlock's tiny cones **(right).**

Elm and other seeds with papery wings are ripe for harvest and ready for specific sowing treatments as soon as they turn papery brown. Maple seeds are ready to harvest when their winged helicopter-like fruits spin to the ground.

Food crops, forestry trees, and ornamental annuals have been studied extensively, and information on harvest dates can be found in agricultural journals and books. But far less documentation exists for ornamental trees, shrubs, and perennials. Nonetheless, help is available. A public garden's library, or one at an arboretum, may have the information needed.

but those I receive from society seed exchanges, which have been dried for shipping, do not. Even after a 24-hour soak, some take six to eighteen months to germinate. It is possible that chemicals known as "germination inhibitors" (discussed in chapter 4) are formed at the end of a fruit's developmental cycle. Perhaps some seeds will have better germination if they are harvested and sown just before the fruits are completely ripe.

Seeds harvested from the ripe, red fruits of trillium species can take one to two years to germinate. But some trillium enthusiasts have experimented with seeds taken *before* the fruits are ripe, when they were full-size but still green. These seeds germinated almost at once.

How does one know to "suspect" a plant's seeds should be harvested green? A few gardeners have been led to try plants by their own intuition, by trial and error, or perhaps by guessing that similar plants may do well when harvested and sown the same way.

COLLECTING DRY FRUITS

Dry brown pods should not be thought of as the detritus of fall, but as gems in intricate parcels. When you are looking for seeds, a walk through the autumn garden becomes a treasure hunt. Suddenly, a faded flower doesn't represent the end of the season but signifies the beginning of next year's garden.

Pods and capsules, sheaths and spiny orbs—papery, brittle coverings containing seeds—are all *dry fruits*. There are two general types: *dehiscent* and *indehiscent*. Dehiscent fruits burst open when the walls of their ovaries dry, and their contents, the seeds, pour out. When a pea pod dries, for example, one side splits along its seam and the halves open. With dehiscent fruits, you have to be diligent to garner a respectable crop before things pop, slip, or spill. Some indehiscent fruits can also get away. Just consider the dandelion's parachute or the maple's double-winged schizocarp. Those seeds have to be

chased. On the other hand, an indehiscent fruit, such as a pecan, which stays shut, still must be watched. Although there may be a bounty of nuts, some furry creature may beat you to the harvest on collection day.

Harvesting dry fruits requires diligence. Fruits won't split until they are dry, and animals rarely take seeds until they are completely ripe. The early signs that ripening is occurring in herbaceous plants may show in the stems. For example, the stem of a plant such as a sunflower will visibly toughen—the ridges becoming pronounced as the fleshy tissues shrink. Fruits begin to desiccate, showing a few wrinkles, but the most obvious sign is when pods or capsules lose their vivid green color. They may become pale or start to turn tan, brown, or gray.

Even experienced gardeners sometimes miss the moment. Annuals started from seed indoors under lights mature and present ripe seeds earlier than the same species sown later outdoors. An individual plant might ripen earlier because it occupies a warmer spot in the garden, perhaps in brighter sunlight or near a wall that radiates heat. Obviously, you cannot be everywhere at the perfect moment, so you will need to adjust your tactics to reap in order to sow.

The maple samaras can be cut off the trees in a cluster, if you can reach them with a ladder. Sometimes a stick or pole might be necessary to knock a few fruits free (without damaging the tree, of course). Cones may also have to be collected this way. Spread a sheet of plastic or a tarp on the ground beneath the tree or tall shrub to catch and gather a few cones.

If you've had a go at creating your own daylily hybrid as described on page 44, you'll be anxious to collect its seeds. When the flower fades, the ovary at the base of the pistil begins to swell.

Above: Some seeds must be harvested before their fruits "explode." Impatiens fruits **(far left)** are filled with water to the breaking point; any contact can split their seams violently **(left)**, shooting seeds up to 15 feet—suggesting one common name: "touch-me-not." A magnolia's scarlet seeds should be harvested before their fruits **(above)** reveal them; but these slow-to-sprout seeds could be sown "green," not completely ripe, a strategy that works in a few cases.

Shortly thereafter, the pod will stop enlarging and will turn pale green. That's the moment to slip an inverted paper bag over the fruit, close the open end, and secure it around the flower scape with wire or string. Daylily fruits are dehiscent, and without the bag, the seeds would be lost. When the flower stalk below the bag turns brown, the fruit is ready for harvest. Cut the stem and bring the bag to a protected spot before carefully tearing it open to retrieve the split pod and the half-dozen or so seeds of the new hybrid daylily.

Columbine seeds are even easier to miss. The ripe fruits spill their contents without warning. To ensure a harvest, these seeds can be contained, just like the daylily's. The bag containing the columbine fruits should not be opened outdoors, however. When the stem turns tan, cut it with the bag attached and hang the package, fruit side down, in an airy spot indoors. When the fruits are ripe, you can hear hundreds of loose seeds rattling in the bag. Fruits of other plants harvested this way may not open up inside the bag, but you can tell they're ready when the stalk sticking up out of the bag dries. Carefully open the paper sack to check if the seed heads and their contents are dry.

As for the sunflower, its succulent head could rot if it were covered with a bag. But if it were left to dry outdoors, birds might harvest the seeds first. When the ribs along the stem of the sunflower become pronounced and the nearly ripe seeds are beginning to dry, cut the stems about a foot below the heads, tie a string around the severed ends, and hang the stems upside down in an airy spot indoors. You could also lay them across a slatted rack, such as the kind used for drying cloths. When the dry seeds are ready to harvest, you can easily rub them off the head with your thumb. Save what you'll need, and toss what is left out for the birds.

CLEANING UP

Most dry fruits collected before they are completely dry must finish the process before their seeds are extracted, stored, or sown. But if you cut a ripe milkweed pod, for example, and brought it into the house, the warm and dry conditions indoors would cause the pod's cells to desiccate, the tissues would shrink, and the fruit would split apart at its seams. One morning you would wake up to a house full of tumbling, silky fluff.

Above right: When green dehiscent fruits of *Nicotiana alata* turn brown, the cover dries and opens, making ½-inch-long chalices ready to cast their seeds to the ground. **Above left:** Louis Bauer uses a coffee filter to harvest seeds because he can hold the cone open with one hand and bend the fruits over to safely pour the contents into the paper funnel.

If a seed head is of the explosive kind, put it in a box to dry or in a paper bag. As for the columbine and other flower stems bagged outside and cut, simply lift the stalks out of the bag one by one, tapping the stems as you go. Tip the bag to gather the seeds, make a crease in the side of the bag, and pour them into a labeled envelope for storage. Fading flower stalks of primroses can be cut and placed upside down in a bag. If any debris and bits of dried fruits are present, the contents may be poured through a coarse sieve that lets the seeds pass through and captures the refuse.

Other plants do not, however, always give up their seeds as graciously. Strawflower seeds, for instance, must be hand-separated. Winnow the dried flowers from the seeds by rubbing them between your fingers repeatedly and gently blowing away the chaff, or grate them on a coarse screen sieve to separate the seeds from their scaly petals. (Be sure to wash your hands before eating or drinking, since ingesting parts of some plants can be harmful.)

STORING DRY SEED

Many seeds—especially dry seeds—can remain viable for years, decades, or perhaps centuries. There are many tales of archaeologists finding two-thousand-year-old seeds in a Pharaoh's tomb that still germinated and grew. But the point is clear—seeds retain their optimal physical condition with consistent low temperatures and in a dry environment. Luckily, there are alternatives to stone tombs in the Egyptian desert. Cleaned dry seeds can be stored in 2½- by 4-inch translucent, oil- and moisture-resistant, glassine envelopes, sold through camera shops or stationery supply stores; regular paper envelopes; or polyethylene bags.

Record the species name and harvest or storage date on the sealed packets, then slip them into a glass jar with a tight-fitting lid. Place the jar on the top shelf of the refrigerator, where it will be kept at an even temperature of about 40 to 45 degrees F (4.5 to 7 degrees C). The relative humidity should be below 40 percent. The small

Top row: Some seeds do not part with their contents so easily. When the time comes, remove the dried flower stems of plants such as pearly everlasting from their bags **(left)**. Rub the flowers between your fingers **(center)**. The flowers may have to be held over a sieve to catch the seed or scraped across the screen to shred the fibers, which can then be winnowed by sprinkling seeds and chaff over a bowl and gently blowing across the falling debris **(right)**.

Bottom row: Columbine flowers are beautiful in the garden, and frequent sowings guarantee a yearly show from this short-lived perennial **(left)**. As soon as the fruits turn brown, seeds shake free. In order to have seeds for other places in the garden, they must be captured, which is easily accomplished by covering one plant with a paper bag **(center)**. As the stems (and nearby columbine fruits) begin to brown, cut the stalks, invert the bag, and hang it in an airy spot indoors **(right)**.

packets of silica gel that are found in vitamin bottles or new camera equipment can be dropped into the jar to absorb moisture. Some gardeners sprinkle powdered milk or cornstarch into the bottom of the jar for this purpose.

TOO MUCH OF A GOOD THING

Envelopes from rare-plant societies may contain as few as five or six seeds. On the other hand, commercial packets may be sold by weight, and when the contents are tiny seeds from a prodigious producer, the bounty may be passed along to the consumer. Ask yourself if you really need 200 or 300 common foxglove plants. If you buy too many seeds (and you will), you can store the extra seeds by folding the packet closed, taping it shut, and placing it in the closed jar.

Seed-gluttony—overordering and overplanting—is a problem when your eyes for the future garden are bigger than the space in which you can grow the seedlings. Seeds are tiny, and so are seedlings, but not for long. Picture the results of sowing nicotiana, for example: after six weeks, one hundred seeds in one 3-inch pot will become one hundred 6-inch-tall plants needing attention.

Rather than thinning seedlings as most books recommend or saving too many seeds, go in on your seed order with a few friends. Consider sharing seedlings rather than seeds. You might assign yourself all the plants that should germinate at a similar time, grow to a consistent size, or require the same temperature. Ultimately, you will be able to have more different plants than sowing space and conditions could allow.

COLD MOIST STORAGE

The seeds of several kinds of deciduous trees—especially those with a high moisture content—should not be stored as described above. This may seem odd, since the casings of these seeds

seem quite dry. The seeds of chestnut, beech, maple, ash, and some other trees must be stored with moisture. For example, if a maple's seed dries, germination will be delayed at best; at worst, prevented altogether. Put the seeds in a wad of damp whole sphagnum moss slipped into a plastic bag, and place that in the refrigerator. Label the bag with the date and the source.

Some seeds, such as acorns and chestnuts,

may sprout inside the refrigerator and will need to be watched. In early spring, or sooner if you have a cool greenhouse, pot up the seeds, with the usual regard to gravity— root pointing earthward.

COLLECTION DAY

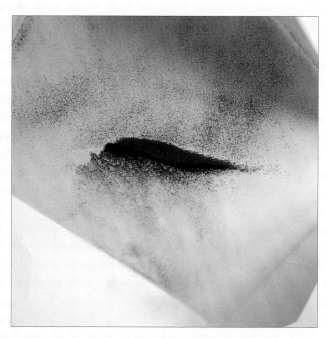

tures for their spores. The cinnamon fern *(Osmunda cinnamomea)* is named for the fertile, leafless fronds that turn brown as the spores are shed in spring. The sensitive fern *(Onoclea sensibilis)* produces sturdy wands covered with shiny, espresso-brown beads from which the spores are shed from winter to spring. Cut one of these conspicuous erect fertile fronds and bring it inside. Hold the wand over a sheet of white paper and tap it. The spores will fall.

The first step in growing ferns from spores, making a fern "print," is nearly as beautiful as the end result. A fern frond with ripe spores has to be found. Most ferns have sori (page 19). If the sori have dulled from gold to tan, and the spores drift into the air when the frond is tapped, they are ripe.

Pick a single frond and lay it spore side down on a piece of white paper overnight in a draft-free place. In the morning, carefully lift the frond to behold its portrait rendered in spores and chaff *(left)*. Carefully fold the paper in half so that the spores and chaff roll to the center crease.

Gently rock the paper back and forth to see the dark brown spores separate from the paler brown chaff *(above)*. You can sow spores immediately or store them by folding the paper and placing it in a jar in the refrigerator. Varying by species, spores can remain viable for several years.

Not all ferns present their sori as precise dots. The hardy maidenhair *(Adiantum pedatum),* for instance, produces sori on the edges of the leaflets. A few ferns grow separate struc-

THE CONIFER'S SEED

Gathering all seeds is an act of trust, an investment in the future. Never is this more obvious than when standing in the center of a forest of towering firs, gazing at a small blue circle of sky far above. It is nearly unfathomable that conifers such as 300-foot-tall sequoias or ten-thousand-year-old bristlecone pines started from tiny seeds, but they did. Few people ever see conifer seeds in nature, but everyone knows their carrier—the cone.

Neither dry nor moist fruits' cones are scaly bracts with seeds inside. The seed-collection process, however, begins as it does for most plants, by harvesting the receptacles in which the seeds are held. You'll find some cones lying on the ground in autumn. If they're on the trees, be sure that the cones are plump and that their color has changed from green or silvery blue to shades of tan and brown—the more familiar dry-cone colors. Most important, the cones should still be tightly closed.

Cones are usually covered with a sticky tar, so disposable gloves will be useful. If you're collecting more than one kind of cone, bring a separate paper bag for each species, and write the plant's name on the bag.

If the collected cones are dry, keep them in the paper bag. When you get back home, place the bag in a warm spot and in a few days, shake it to free the seeds and gather them for sowing or storage. If the plump cones were not completely dry or open, roll a band of paper or cut a section of an empty paper-towel roll, to act like an eggcup to support the cone while it is drying. Try to set the cones in the same orientation in which they grew on the tree—pointing downward, for example. Place the paper collar and cone on a screen in a warm, sunny place with good air circulation, perhaps by a radiator or in an oven with a pilot light. As the cones dry, the scales will begin to open, at which point you can put the cones back into a paper bag to shake and collect the seeds, or leave them on the screen, where you can watch the winged seeds slip from between the layers of open scales.

Gather up the seeds with an index card or brush them onto a piece of paper. Hold the seeds over a bowl and rub them between your fingers to separate them from their wings. The cleaned seeds can be stored in a labeled envelope with other dry-fruit seeds in the refrigerator—a potential forest housed in the space of a thank-you note.

Below: To extract seeds, place a fresh, moist cone in a warm spot with good air circulation and at the same orientation that it grew on the tree. A paper collar makes a helpful stand. As the cone dries, scales rise and winged seeds fall.

Opposite: Cones come in all sizes, from the hemlock's tiny ones to the Coulter pine's—nearly a foot long. Animals, including humans, eat pine "nuts," *piñole*, such as the pinion pine seeds on the tile.

MOIST FRUITS

Partridgeberry, doll's eyes, fuchsia, lowbush blueberry, false Solomon's seal, holly, magnolia, sand cherry, and shadblow are all ornamental plants, but they have another characteristic in common: succulent fruits. These plants have evolved fruits attractive to animals that will help in seed dispersal. When a bird plucks a wild cherry, for example, the fruit (drupe) travels through its digestive system. The nutritious pulp is dissolved by the bird's stomach acids, and the seeds are excreted by the bird in its travels. Microorganisms may also be attracted to the moist fruit when it falls to the ground and perform a similar service. Indoors, these

and stepping on them to crush the fruits' soft outer coating.

If you are processing small batches, place the fruits in a container of water and let them soak for one or two days. (Seeds with oily fruits, such as holly, often benefit from a few drops of dishwashing detergent in the water.) The jack-in-the-pulpit fruits, and those of most other ornamentals, become soft and plump overnight and sink to the bottom. Fruits found floating after a day or so often do not have viable seeds and can be discarded. After this treatment, place a sieve in the sink and rinse the bloated flesh away. (Note that some plants have toxic parts, so make sure to wash your hands thoroughly after all seed washing. If you need to

Opposite: *Arisaema triphyllum*—the stately North American jack-in-the-pulpit—is typified by its T-shaped, three-lobed leaves, hooded spathe, and spadix of tiny flowers within, which if pollinated, will become a club-shaped aggregate fruit.

This page: Seeds harvested from plants with moist fruit, such as jack-in-the-pulpit **(left)**, must be cleaned before they can be conditioned, sowed, or stored dry in envelopes. Most moist fruits should be soaked in water for 24 hours **(center)**, after which time a few empty or spoiled ones will float, the viable seeds will sink, and the flesh will be soft. Press the fruits between paper towels and then wash them in a sieve under running water **(right)**. When cleaning many seeds, use sheets of newspaper, step on them or crush them with a block of wood, and wear protective rubber or vinyl gloves if washing a large quantity.

same agents would not be welcome; they might destroy the seed or emerging seedling as well.

Most of the fruits from plants we grow for their aesthetic value and not for food do not have a great deal of succulent flesh—jack-in-the-pulpit seeds versus a watermelon's, for instance. The jack-in-the-pulpit presents an excellent example to illustrate how the seeds of hardy ornamental plants with moist fruits can be processed. *Arisaema triphyllum* and its relatives produce club-shaped aggregate fruits covered like a corncob with bright red individual growths (which might be called berries) containing one or two seeds. Horticulturists who have a great number of seeds to clean may start the process by placing the small fruits between a few sheets of newspaper

wash large quantities of seeds, wear rubber or vinyl gloves.)

When the seeds of these hardy plants have been cleaned of all flesh, blot them dry on a paper towel. They will then be ready for the next step, which may be storing, sowing, or conditioning (as you will find out in subsequent chapters). If you are drying the seeds of moist fruits because you need to store them or intend to contribute them to plant-society exchanges, spread the cleaned seeds on a fresh paper towel so that they are not touching, and place them in an open airy spot—on a wire rack or screen. When the seeds are thoroughly dry, seal them in labeled and dated envelopes, and store them in a lidded jar on the top shelf of the refrigerator.

4

Conditioning

"I have great faith in a seed," wrote Henry David Thoreau.

"Convince me that you have a seed there, and I am

prepared to expect wonders." Faith in a seed—is there

any truer embodiment of nature's brilliance?

Within this miraculous package is a

miniature leaf and root, an embryo

of a plant   that we may never

have seen before.

The seed is a perfect time capsule: it can remain viable for days, years, or even centuries, snug in a water-resistant coat. Common wisdom has long held that when the light, temperature, and moisture are just right for germination, dormancy ends and the embryo stirs. But *dormancy* is not really the right word for this state. Unlike established perennial plants that have elaborate mechanisms to allow them to cope with seasonal extremes such as leaf loss and underground hibernation as a root or tuber, seeds are not taking a siesta from active growth; their lives as green plants have not yet begun.

A seed may seem to be "sleeping" while it waits to germinate. But unlike dormant hardy plants, the seed's rest does not end when the daylight hours increase in length or the snow melts. Water plays a large role in germination —quick-sprouting zinnias, marigolds, and foxglove all germinate soon after they have absorbed moisture in the indoor propagation area or in warm weather outdoors. However, these same seeds don't germinate while they are still held in seed heads—even if they are drenched by the hose or summer rains. Nature has built into each seed germination inhibitors that prevent premature sprouting—encrypted codes that only specific conditions can decipher.

Pepper seeds rarely sprout inside their moist and sun-warmed vessels, although you may have cut a fruit open to find a dislodged seed sprouting as it free-floats inside the fleshy chamber. Dr. Norman C. Deno, professor emeritus of chemistry at Pennsylvania State University, has devoted years to studying methods of counteracting the chemical devices that suppress germination. He hypothesizes that the seeds inside of a pepper may receive chemical inhibitors through the fine thread that holds them in place, because pepper seeds often germinate as soon as they detach. His studies have also shown that a lack of oxygen may be an inhibitor, perhaps explaining why seeds enclosed in other fruits do not germinate until after dispersal.

In nature, chemical and physical inhibitors are automatically destroyed as part of the life cycle. Natural "conditioners" can range from simple changes in moisture to complex chemical shifts relating to weather, or even symbiotic relationships with animals, fungi, or plants. Dr. Deno suggests that instead of thinking in terms of trying to break seed dormancy, we consider "conditioning" seeds instead. The propagator's task becomes more than just adding water or heat; she or he must eradicate these ingenious mechanisms just as nature does. Giving thoughtful consideration to a particular plant's native habit and environment, we can deduce the necessary procedure for conditioning its seeds and sowing: indoors or out.

For example, many seeds from cold climates have germination inhibitors to ensure that the seeds don't sprout until spring, when the weather settles and mild temperatures are guaranteed. However, storing dried seeds in envelopes in the refrigerator should not be confused with an artificial winter. Often cold-climate seeds need a period of damp cold followed by a prolonged period of warm and moist conditions before they will germinate. Other seeds have nearly impenetrable seed coats and may not germinate for years until their outer defenses have broken and water can reach the embryo. To initiate germination for growing these seeds indoors, the propagator must damage or scar the seed coats so the endocarp and embryo can absorb moisture.

Seeds that are easily cultivated from plants that grow well year-round in your area might best be sown outdoors so that they can be conditioned naturally. However, precious seeds and those that pose specific challenges for germination might benefit from the intervention of the gardener-cum-alchemist.

Preceding pages: Dry sweet pea seeds are soaked for 24 hours to condition them prior to sowing.

Opposite: Ripe crabapple seeds must not germinate inside their fruits in winter, and the ice that covers these is part of the conditioning process. Freezing breaks the cells of the fruit, beginning its disintegration. Cold also destroys the inhibitors, so when the seeds find warm soil, moisture, and sunlight, they will germinate and grow.

Above: Seeds have chemical and physical inhibitors that prevent them from sprouting prematurely. Chemicals may be supplied to seeds, such as the pepper's, through the filament that attaches them to the fruit wall. When the seeds are liberated, germination will be possible.

PRE-GERMINATION

Although seeds may appear to be inert, they, like every other organism, have a life span. Commercially packaged seeds of vegetables or flowering annuals are labeled with their packing date and should be used in the year packed. Most vegetable seeds can remain viable for from two to fifteen years, depending on the type and conditions of storage.

the center of a paper towel and fold over the sides so that the seeds are completely covered. Dampen the towel with a spray bottle, and slip it into a plastic sandwich bag with a zipper lock. Place the package in a warm spot—about 75 degrees F (24 degrees C). The flat top of a water heater, away from the vent, maintains this temperature quite well.

The seeds of most annuals will sprout in three to ten days, but other plants can take longer. Check the package to determine the standard germination time. Halfway through the number of days supposedly required, hold the bag up to a light. If the

If you have annual and vegetable seeds left over from just last year and have stored them in their packets, folded shut and taped closed, in the jar in the refrigerator, you can risk sowing them at the appropriate time. But if they were not stored in optimal conditions or have been stored for two years or more, a viability test could be worthwhile.

Convention suggests that you use ten of each kind of seed to determine the viability percentage. Space the seeds evenly in

seeds have life, there will be a recognizable change in their shape. Remove the towel from the bag and carefully unwrap and examine its contents.

If eight out of ten seeds have swollen and distorted, owing to the expanding radicles, 80 percent germination can be expected from this batch of seeds. If only one or two seeds react, consider replacing the entire lot with the closest variety you can find.

I perform the paper-towel test close enough to the normal

sowing date so that I will not have to discard the test batch if the seeds are good. I pot the seeds in medium and grow them along with my other late-winter sown plants. If any roots have grown through the paper towel, I cut them out with the surrounding moist paper to minimize root disturbance.

If you are testing annual flowers and fruits with large seeds, you can pot these into biodegradable containers, such as peat pots or recycled-newspaper ones, so they can be planted directly into the garden with the least disturbance. If you use peat pots, be sure to tear as much of the pot away as possible. Peat shrinks, breaking roots, and if the top edge of the pot becomes exposed to dry soil or air, moisture will be wicked away from the developing seedlings.

The paper-towel germination scheme can have other applications, such as for pre-germinating certain species and for two-step germinators—described on page 74.

The result of a viability test of last year's pumpkin seeds is seen after about a week (**opposite, left**). If fewer than half of the seeds react, consider replacing the entire lot with the same or a similar variety (**above**). The sprouted test seeds do not have to be discarded; large ones destined for a vegetable or annuals garden can be planted in peat pots that will disintegrate (**opposite, below**). Newspaper can be recycled to make degradable pots with a special form (**opposite, above**).

DRY CONDITIONING

Commercial seed sellers happen to provide one method of conditioning, simply by cleaning and drying certain seeds. Drying may be nature's principal means of destroying chemical inhibitors. Ripe seeds on a sunflower, for instance, do not germinate while they are attached to the seed head because the inhibitors are active. These and other warm-season annuals may require a certain amount of desiccation before exposure to moisture can initiate germination. Generalization is nearly impossible, but it may be that seeds that are exposed to the air and sun while ripening, such as those in the daisy, mustard, and grass families, need a period of drying, or curing, as a precursor to sprouting.

There may be some seeds that need only a short period to dry sufficiently, which occurs in their capsules while they are still attached to the plant. Bob Stewart of Arrowhead Alpines Nursery in Michigan has extensive experience sowing seeds and notes that many ornamental species, however, require an extended time in dry storage. *Campanula* and *Penstemon* are two examples where "old seed germinates much better than fresh seed." This aging could be useful in the case of store-bought perennial seeds or ones received from plant-society exchanges. But as a general practice prior to conditioning or sowing, the dried seeds from perennials with moist fruit should be soaked for at least 24 hours—with the water changed once or twice or the seeds rinsed in a sieve—for a bit of refreshing.

In the last chapter, bending the rules in some cases produced excellent results, such as the fresh sowing of certain deciduous woody plant seeds and others collected just before their fruits were fully ripe. The seeds of warm-season annuals such as marigolds, nasturtiums, and zinnias you harvest from the garden, as well as

Above: The inhibitors in many seeds are destroyed during drying and aging. Ripening seeds of cosmos, black-eyed Susan, and purple coneflower (shown), for example, do not sprout in their flower heads, even if they are drenched by rain. The drying process delays the ability to germinate—the approaching winter postpones the opportunity. The seeds will sprout outdoors when spring rains and warm days arrive, or if harvested when those conditions are simulated earlier indoors.

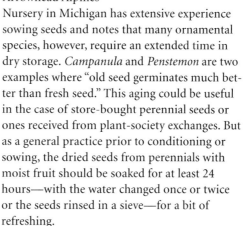

those of fruits such as tomatoes, cucumbers, and zucchini, or courgettes, need to be first cleaned and air-dried before they are placed in envelopes and stored until the proper day for sowing. Then, these annuals often sprout within days. Chances are good that by the time you are ready to sow store-bought seeds of easy-to-grow annuals, they will be "old" enough.

NICK OF TIME

Hard seed coats protect the tender embryos within, but they also prevent germination by excluding moisture. Without intervention, seeds such as those of the perennial pea vine (*Lathyrus latifolius*) may not germinate for a year, decades, or ever. The ornamental castor bean plant (*Ricinus communis* and varieties) has a beautiful seed—exquisitely mottled and patterned like snakeskin in tan and maroon. (It should be noted that all parts of this plant, the source of castor oil, are poisonous.) When thoroughly dry, the seeds have a glass-smooth coat as hard as armor.

These seeds will sprout when there is a breach in the seed coat. Nicking or filing, a process called scarification, will allow moisture to penetrate to the dormant embryo, triggering germination. To scarify a good-size seed, you can hold it in your fingers and drag it across a sheet of medium sandpaper, or use a metal file to scrape into the coat, creating hundreds of minuscule entryways on the hard surface. Use caution when doing this, filing only a side or a blunt end, so the embryo is not damaged.

Performing this task seed by seed is not practical when one is working with large quantities, so some nurseries tumble the seeds in bins with sand. Horticulturists at public gardens often rub seeds between two blocks of wood covered with sandpaper to penetrate the coats. At home, you can put small seeds in a jar with about an inch or two of sand, cover, and shake vigorously. Although it is preferable to separate the seeds from the sand, if the seeds are too small to sift or pick out, you can sow pinches of seeds and sand together.

Getting moisture into the seed is the goal of scarification, but water itself can be used to effect this process in some cases. Morning glory seeds are notoriously hard; you can nick or file

Opposite: The mechanism for delaying germination is often a moisture-resistant, rock-hard seed coat. The castor bean is an 8-foot-tall ornamental annual (mature leaf shown in framed photo) with mottled seeds (in dish) that have a lacquerlike surface. The coat will have to be breached before seeds can imbibe moisture—the first step toward germination and seedling production. Many kinds of seed might be peeled by hand, such as a lemon's, but take care with the castor bean: all of its parts are poisonous.

Top to bottom: Morning glory seeds are used for a demonstration of nicking using a single-edged razor blade to cut a chip off the seed's pointed end. The seeds can also be filed by dragging the point across sandpaper or, when there are many seeds, by mixing them with sand in a jar and shaking vigorously. Morning glory seeds can also be soaked in warm water for 24 hours, which will soften their coats and plump them for immediate sowing.

them by cutting their points off with a single-edged razor blade or dragging them across sandpaper, but they will also soften with a soaking in warm water overnight (mimicking the warm spring rains of tropical climes perhaps). The coats will tear and the seeds will be swollen by the next morning. Sow the morning glory seeds as soon as you remove them from the bath, for, just as with every seed, they must not be allowed to dry out after the germination process has begun or they will perish.

Chemical scarification is used to replicate the caustic effects on seeds of an animal's digestive juices. Birds and other animals are attracted to

before beginning any of these procedures (see the Bibliography, page 251).

The hard coats of other seeds, such as legumes (members of the pea family) and pines, can be cracked with nearly boiling water. In one experiment with the seeds of the honey locust tree, water heated to 170 degrees F (76.5 degrees C) was poured over the seeds and let stand overnight. These seeds were planted in one pot, while untreated ones were sowed in another. The pots were given the same culture from that point on. None of the untreated seeds germinated, while all of the seeds immersed in hot water pushed through the medium after a

Right: Most legumes—members of the pea family—have hard coats. Very hot water (160 to 170 degrees F [71 to 76.5 degrees C]) can be poured over some of these seeds, such as those of the honey locust tree *(Gleditsia triacanthos)*. The water may simulate the effects of winter freezing and thawing to crack the seed coat. In an experiment, twenty-four ripe honey locust seeds were harvested from their pods in autumn. Eight were sown outdoors in a bed near the place where the fruits were found. On April 12, eight seeds were sown in pots and placed under fluorescent lights, while the third set were treated in hot water, left to soak for 12 hours, and then sown. Within ten days, the treated seeds began to push through the medium **(center)**, and in ten more days the eager sprouts had become strong seedlings **(far right).** In late June, six of the outdoor seeds sprouted. The untreated indoor seeds never germinated and were discarded three months later.

certain fruits, which they ingest and break down. The seeds are deposited in a new location, their seed coats damaged enough to allow the seeds to absorb moisture. In laboratories, plant scientists experiment with acids. Sulfuric acid, for example, is used to etch the coats of certain species of roses, witch hazel, and linden.

Professional propagators also use hormones such as gibberellin (in the form of gibberellic acid) to stimulate germination in other types of seed. Gibberellic (GB) acid destroys abscisic acid, the primary chemical germination inhibitor. GB is available to the home gardener from specialized sources, but the techniques involved in using it require a great deal of precision, so you should consult references

week—a higher success rate and months sooner than germination in a natural environment, where the repeated freezing and thawing pattern of winter breaks the seed coat.

Extreme heat is used in nature as well to weaken seed coats. When fires swept Yellowstone National Park several years ago, some seeds not only survived, but sprouted and thrived; they needed the exposure to intense heat to break open dried fruits or cones, or to crack hard seed coats. With the fire, the resins that sealed the cones of *Pinus radiata* melted, the cones opened, and seeds fell out onto cleared land where they had the chance to grow.

Seeds of certain plants lie in the duff of the forest floor or the sandy soil of scrubby areas waiting for fire and smoke to destroy their germination inhibitors. A few suppliers of specialty seeds, such as *Rhodocoma capensis* from Australia and *Erica glauca* from South Africa, include bits of paper impregnated with the same compounds found in brushfire smoke. Before the seeds are sown, they should be soaked along with the paper to absorb chemical reminders of their environmental heritage.

LIGHT WORK

Even though the majority of seeds are covered when they are sown, whether indoors or outside, most seeds do not require darkness. Covering the seeds, however, definitely helps to keep them moist, and covering them is a good practice for all but the specific seeds that require "surface-sowing" and light.

Light, however, is another one of nature's ways for destroying inhibitors. Fern spores and many tiny seeds that float lightly to the ground, or the seeds of epiphytic plants, which spend their entire lives above the soil in the crotches

and branches of trees (bromeliads and orchid cacti, for example), need light to germinate. This type of conditioning is accomplished by sowing seeds on a moist medium or sprinkling them over a top-dressing of grit and not applying any additional covering.

STRATIFICATION

Many of the agents that repress germination in hardy plants' seeds are naturally eliminated through the seasonal stages of chilling and warming. These seeds will not germinate until they have experienced the cold of winter and the spring thaw signals that safe temperatures are close at hand.

In horticulture, the term *stratification* is used to indicate that moisture and controlled temperatures are required before germination. Many references use the term when recommending a "pretreatment" with cold. But it is worth noting that warmth with moisture may also be part of the stratification process.

One way to sow and germinate seeds of hardy plants for gardens is to let nature provide the necessary temperature fluctuations outdoors, as described in the following chapter. But in certain cases, providing controlled environments with specific temperatures could have advantages over the vagaries of weather. For example, when there are precious few seeds of a plant, risks are limited by mimicking nature's forces. Artificial temperature controls could also shorten the period needed from sowing, to germination, to having garden-ready plants. When seeds that ripened through the summer are stored and sent from commercial sources, or a society seed exchange, in February or March, six months of what could have been the natural conditioning process are gone.

The first thing to do with seeds that originated in the moist fruits of perennial plants and that arrive dry in envelopes and packets is to

Left: Heat for conditioning commonly calls for moisture and warmth—perhaps simulating a natural state for hardy-plant seeds that ripen in summer. Moist-warm stratification takes place around 70 degrees F (21 degrees C)—far below the temperatures of a desert summer. Certain references say that exposure to light is a prerequisite for cacti germination, but in nature, these seeds need shelter from searing sun in cool, protected spots, for instance, beneath *Opuntia* pads, where juveniles over fifteen years old may be found.

soak them for at least one day, and up to three—changing the water once or twice a day, or rinsing them in a sieve. This reconstitution is one step toward catching up on time lost. More time in the life of a plant may be reclaimed, however, through accelerated indoor treatments. Experiments have shown that the artificial winter can be shortened in the refrigerator. Some seeds will have gained the benefits of cold after as little as three weeks.

Recent research has also demonstrated that freezing—which may occur outdoors and is recommended by several sources—is rarely necessary. Seeds that are subjected to cold may not be damaged by temperatures below the freezing point, but the conditioning process is put on hold at these low temperatures and resumes only when the seeds are not quite so cold. This is one reason that controlled stratification in the refrigerator can be a truncated version of the outdoor process.

By now it's clear that the most important piece of technical equipment for performing the operations of stratification, the refrigerator, is already possessed by amateur gardeners. Moisture and a constant temperature of 40 to 45 degrees F (4.5 to 7 degrees C) works best. Seeds brought out of the refrigerator to a warm environment may sprout right away, offering an opportunity to get a huge head start on the growing season. The outdoor-sown seed might just be appearing by the time the cold-treated seedlings indoors are large enough to transplant in the garden.

Another benefit of using the refrigerator for stratification, followed by germination and development in protective custody, is that the process can be closely monitored and yields will be high. For a plant such as an oak tree, no acorns will be stolen from the refrigerator shelf, as they might be in the garden.

To moist-cold stratify clean seeds indoors, place them in a wad of whole sphagnum moss that has been dipped in warm water and wrung out as much as possible. Small seeds, which would be difficult to pick out from the moss at sowing time, can be mixed into a little clean, barely moistened vermiculite to sow with the seeds at the appropriate time. Or the seeds may be sown (page 88) prior to chilling. The moss, vermiculite, or pots with seeds next go into

Opposite: Cold is one of the most common factors in conditioning. If seeds of hardy herbaceous perennials, shrubs, and trees sprouted as soon as they were ripe in autumn, the seedlings would be killed by frost. However, as noted, there are chemical inhibitors present in the seeds of hardy plants that delay germination. Exposure to cold disables the inhibitors. The process of subjecting seeds to periods of moisture and cold (or moisture and warmth, or both) is called "stratification." As with most conditioning, the payoff is more seedlings—and sooner.

Left: In propagation, we often have to mimic natural circumstances, and in the case of the jack-in-the-pulpit to "trick" seeds into reacting as if they have passed through a winter. The cleaned seeds are placed on moist sphagnum moss **(top)**, which is folded over and slipped into a labeled plastic bag **(center)**, then put in the refrigerator at 40 degrees F (4.5 degrees C) for six weeks to two months. The conditioned seeds sprout soon after they are sown **(bottom)**.

Above: These red-leaved seedlings were the results of a long search for an old peach variety used for grafting—a red sucker would be easy to spot and remove—but a nursery source could not be located. Fourteen peaches were collected from the ground beneath a rare specimen, soaked overnight, and washed of pulp. Seven "stones" were sown and placed in a south-facing window. The rest were cold-stratified for sixty days prior to sowing. The cold-treated seeds germinated quickly; the others did not, except for one—which appeared after two more winters next to the compost pile. By then, one of the original trees, planted behind tree stumps in a shrub border, had reached 7 feet **(opposite),** and fuzzy, maroon peaches were greatly anticipated.

Below: Species peonies take two steps toward germination. During warm-moist stratification, an immature root emerges; then there must be cold followed by warmth to continue germination. In nature, it could be two years before a leaf appears, but with warm and cold stratification, leaves may show in six months.

plastic bags labeled with their name, dates of moist-cold conditioning, and when they should move to the next step of germination. Seal the bags tightly and place them in a prominent section of the refrigerator.

Here's an example: I saw a tree with wine red leaves growing in a private garden on the "Point" in Newport, Rhode Island. I recognized the shape of the leaves as being those of the peach *(Prunus persica)*—and sure enough, the branches bore small, fuzzy, maroon peaches. So began a fruitless search to find a source for this ornamental tree. I discovered a reference to 'Royal Red Leaf' ('Follis Rubus'), an old variety once used as an understock since it would be easy to notice and remove purple suckers that sprouted below the graft.

In 1996, I met the peach again in a Pennsylvania garden, and this time I did not hesitate to ask if I could gather fruits from the ground. After I cleaned the "stones," I sowed half of them in a pot of sowing mix in a sunny window, while the other half went into the refrigerator for

sixty days to then be potted and placed next to the first. All of the treated seeds came up. None of the untreated seeds sprouted.

TWO-STEP GERMINATION

Some plants have what is often called a "double dormancy." Dr. Norman Deno refers to plants that need more than one period of conditioning as "two-step germinators." Seeds that need only one conditioning begin the germination process when the radicle, or immature root, emerges from beneath the seed. Germination is complete after cotyledons, or seed leaves, slip up through the sowing medium, spread open, and turn green as photosynthesis begins. With two-step germinators, there is a resting period between the emergence of the radicle and the cotyledons; in nature, it occurs during the first or second winter.

Species peonies are exquisite plants—but unknown to most gardeners, and rarely available as plants from nurseries or catalogs. The only way to grow these may be from seed. About half of all lilies are considered *epigeal*, and produce leaves from seed quickly, such as *Lilium formosanum* (see page 203). The other half are *hypogeal*—two-step germinators—and produce a leaf only after a period of cold (page 206). The process can be shortened using the refrigerator.

5

Sowing

When autumn brings shorter days and chilly winds, gardeners usually welcome the intermission in the fast-paced gardening year. By January, we've had enough inaction. The seed catalogs arrive just in time to stave off cabin fever for a week or two. Finally, we get to sow seeds indoors, and welcome spring—weeks before the first warm days outside.

A windowsill garden can help bring the cold, dark season to an earlier end. Houseplants perk up in the new year, and their reawakening has a profound effect on us gardeners. The heady perfume of the first citrus flowers fills the house and rouses our need to garden.

Cultivating a batch of seedlings may seem daunting at first. Like new parents, we do not know quite what to expect. Then there is a blessed event, when seedlings appear as a green haze above their pots. Eventually, necessity and desire lead every gardener to master the process of sowing seeds.

GET READY . . .

Timing, as with every aspect of propagation, is crucial. Short-lived perennials and biennials can be sown in situ as they ripen in summer. Seeds of hardy perennials can be sown outdoors in the autumn to take advantage of the natural fluctuations in temperature, light, and moisture. If seeds of hardy perennials from dry fruit are properly stored, they can be sown outdoors up until midwinter. But those of moist fruits and ones purchased from catalogs or received in plant-society exchanges in winter and then sown outdoors may lie in wait an entire year or longer before sprouting. Many of these may benefit from controlled conditioning indoors.

Tender annuals have to be sown indoors at a precise moment—not too early or too late—in order to be healthy seedlings when the time comes to transplant them outdoors. If seedlings are started indoors too early, high temperatures and a lack of sunlight will cause them to etiolate, to become tall and spindly, barely strong enough to hold themselves up. Sowing *hardy* annuals indoors, on the other hand, may produce no results. In temperate climates, the seeds of these annuals should be scattered "au naturel" in winter, as if they had fallen from the stalks of their parents' dried pods and capsules.

Creating a sowing calendar is helpful for tracking propagation activities. To calculate the date to sow a tender annual indoors, for instance, determine the number of days or weeks that the plant needs from the time it's sown until the danger of frost has passed and it can be planted outdoors. (The back of a commercial seed packet usually provides this infor-

mation, along with the estimated days from sowing to germination.) The common lilac's full flush of flowers could be a sign, but the best way to determine the planting date—the *average* last day of possible local frost—is to call the Cooperative Extension Service, listed in the phone book under the state university.

For instance, the marigold *Tagetes tenuifolia* 'Lemon Gem' needs four to six weeks before the seedlings can be placed outdoors. If the last frost date in your area is May 15, subtracting the weeks puts the sowing date around April 1.

Pretreatments, such as scalding, chilling, nicking, and soaking (noted in chapter 4), must also be factored into the sowing dates. (See the Plant Propagation Guide, page 225.) Your sowing calendar could become a permanent journal in which you note the results of your own experiments and experience, and refer to for years to come.

Preceding pages: Square plastic pots of sown seeds in a shallow pan of water.

Opposite: The propagator's year begins in winter with packets sorted by sowing date (under *Oncidium* 'Sweet Sugar Angel').

Above: Information on a commercial seed packet may include a plant's common, Latin, and cultivar names; color; whether annual, biennial, perennial, etc.; hardiness; garden uses; height; indoor sowing requirements; days to germination and sowing before transplanting; depth and spacing in the garden; and ongoing culture.

GET SET: ENVIRONMENTS

Before seed sowing can begin, the proper environment must be prepared—one with light, predictable temperatures, moisture in the air, and a suitable medium. Pretreated and indoor-stratified seeds will go under fluorescent lights or into the greenhouse at the appropriate times. But some of the first seeds to be sown will be the fresh ones of hardy perennial plants that do well locally. These seeds can be sown outdoors to experience the temperature fluctuations for

pots and also breaks the force of heavy rains.

You can easily make a permanent screened box from readily available materials. First determine a manageable box size, perhaps 2 feet by 3 feet and 1 foot tall. The box must be open on the top, but it can be open to the ground below, or set on pavement; if you're using a found box, drill holes in the bottom for drainage. Place the screen in the bottom of the open box to keep worms from entering pots, and add coarse sand to a depth of 1 to 2 inches to stand the pots in, which will keep them

natural conditioning, and where precipitation and light are provided.

In nature, most hardy plants produce an enormous quantity of seeds in the hope that one new plant will survive. Hailstorms, torrential rains, desiccating winds, or foraging animals are obstacles that reduce the percentage of success. The simplest assemblage calls for pots set in a plastic flat with an open grid bottom, and the same kind of flat used for a cover. The best method for sowing the seeds of hardy ornamental plants outdoors is not simply to abandon them in vegetable-garden-type rows but to create special places.

Hardy seeds should be sown in pots and can be placed in a screen-covered box located in a protected spot, perhaps right up against the east side of the house, where they will receive some sunlight, moisture from rain and melting snow, and the temperatures they need, without being subjected to high winds—and be in a convenient spot for monitoring. Screen or an open mesh plastic flat prevents critters from digging in the

upright and help them stay cool and moist.

An old window screen makes a fine cover, and you can size the box you're constructing to match. If you're using a found box but don't have an old screen, you can use artist's wooden canvas stretchers to make a lid with wire or plastic screen stapled over the edges.

If the weather cooperates and you've chosen a good spot, you will not have to water the pots until the seedlings are up and growing in spring. But some seeds sown the previous winter will not appear the first spring, so resist the temptation to unearth them. Seedlings of tiny plants such as dwarf conifers, and long-lived perennials that may develop slowly, such as peonies, are best left undisturbed. They will transplant more successfully with sturdier root systems. These seedlings will do well if sown sparsely and left in their original containers as long as their needs for moisture are met. As hot weather approaches, bury the pots in a special nursery area (see page 113), and bring soil up to the rims to keep the roots and medium cool and moist.

Above: Seeds of hardy plants can be sown outdoors in protected sites, such as a cold frame **(left)** with open sashes glazed with fiberglass panels. This wooden-box frame **(center)** has a screen cover that has been pulled back to show pots of sown seeds. A flat of medium with a mass sowing of primrose seeds is placed in a sheltered spot outdoors and covered with an upside-down grid-bottom nursery flat and weighted in place by rocks **(right)**.

TOUGH LOVE

Some plants are not finicky at all and like a little neglect, or at least independence. The seeds of hardy annuals, biennials, and short-lived perennials can be planted directly outside. Broadcasting the seeds of such plants is a delightful winter project. Ribbons of ruby-red corn poppies will bloom where the January before their scattered seeds made black streaks across the snow (above). California poppy seeds sprinkled along the sunny edge of the flagstone path will germinate in early spring, bloom, and set fruit while the weather is cool. Sweet alyssum and Johnny jump-up (below),

tossed in the cracks between the stones, bloom as the poppies fade. The alyssum quits when the heat's on but returns in autumn and blooms through the first frosts—even in snow.

Of course, not all seeds need to be sown in the dead of winter. In early and midsummer, quick-blooming annuals such as nicotiana can be sown directly in the garden where the same varieties—started earlier indoors under lights—are beginning to flower. The second coming will extend their colorful season. Saved seeds of short-lived perennials such as columbines can be scattered in bare spaces between slower-growing perennials. The fast-growing columbines fill in as more enduring perennials grow to take their place. Ripening biennial foxglove seeds can be shaken out of the dried stalks of this year's plants to grow in the spot that met with their late parents' approval.

THE GREAT "INDOORS"

Nearly all of the tender plants we want to grow in the garden from seed can be started early in a warm and bright environment. Indoor-sown annuals such as begonias, Mexican sunflowers, and other frost-sensitive plants bloom weeks to months earlier than they would if they were planted outdoors in warm weather.

Owning a greenhouse is every gardener's dream. The environment in the glass or plastic-covered structure allows us to alter the growing season. Depending on the temperature range chosen, tropical plants can bloom through the winter, subtropical plants can be kept at the ready to provide yearly additions to the

outdoor garden, and even food crops, such as leaf lettuce, can be grown nearly year-round. Having a greenhouse, however, is demanding on your time and your finances. Maintenance is one issue, space is another. As with just about every garden creation—from lily pond to planting bed—bigger is better, and for a green-house gardener eager to start plants from seed, bigger also means more expensive to heat. Although there are energy-saving designs for greenhouses—double glazing, pit houses set halfway underground, and passive solar systems with barrels of water stacked high up the north wall—building costs are steep. On the other hand, there is no better aid to the gardener's passion for propagation, and in December, money spent to be able to putter about in the greenhouse may seem more attractive than a Caribbean cruise.

If a greenhouse is not an option for you, a greenhouse window is a second choice. These structures are like bow or bay windows, with glass tops as well as sides, and can be attached to a building in place of a regular window. These greenhouse windows, made with energy-efficient glass and insulated floors, are great additions to any home, and with glass shelves provided, they are terrific for growing all sorts of houseplants. Specialty gardening catalogs offer these windows, and most window manu-facturers sell versions of them as well.

A south-facing window of the house could be your next best choice. The windows and green-house windows must face south, and there can be no shadows from buildings or evergreen trees. Even then, several cloudy days in a row could be the death knell for seedlings. But there are other potential problems, such as drafts next to the windowpanes, which may thwart the ger-mination process. A quick fix is to slip a few sheets of newspaper between the glass and pots of seeds each evening, removing the sheets early in the morning. The newspaper task may seem daunting, but an even greater difficulty may be maintaining high relative humidity—at least 40 percent—since the average moisture content of the heated air in winter is around 10 percent (about the same as in the Sahara desert).

Clear plastic domes—supplied with several commercial sowing flats—raise the humidity, but they impede air circulation and facilitate the growth of diseases. A humidifier might help if placed close to the window or inside the green-house window, but that points out another problem: lack of space. There is very little room for flats of pots in the window and greenhouse window, let alone for the burgeoning crop of potted-up seedlings. Fortunately, there is another choice for home gardeners.

Above: High humidity and a way to apply water from below—which is necessary for growing seedlings indoors—can be provided by a commercial flat with a clear plastic cover.

Center: A homemade ver-sion, such as a flat with a wire frame loosely tented with plastic film, may have the benefit of some air movement and exchange.

Below: Elaborate yet inex-pensive "automated" units are available. This one of insulating polystyrene foam has various components stacked to provide the essentials. The bottom is a water reservoir with a red bob moisture indicator. The next tray holds a capil-lary mat that absorbs water from below and makes it available evenly to the cell-like chambers in the flat above for medium and seeds. The top is covered by a clear plastic lid.

Opposite: Besides being the greatest place on a win-ter's day, the greenhouse bench **(left),** with heat source below, offers high humidity and bright light for starting seeds and nur-turing cuttings. A green-house window would be the next-best source of nat-ural light, and a south-facing window **(right)** is another location. But even in the brightest window, hours of light are fewer in winter and skies can be overcast for days.

Top: Let there be light—regardless of the source. The effects of light on plants are cumulative; bright, uniform artificial illumination over a long period may have the same effect as direct sunlight for a short time. But tungsten light-bulbs produce too much heat for seedlings. Fluorescent lights produce the most light with the least heat and energy use; the floral cart **(below right)** has adjustable fixtures and shelves.

Above: Seeds sown indoors do require some heat, usually from below, with appliances such as electric cables or heat mats, and in commercial situations, hot-water or steam pipes set in moist sand to uniformly transmit the warmth.

ARTIFICIAL LIGHT

Although energy-efficient fluorescent lights do not provide the brightest illumination, they run cool, and seedlings can be placed as close to the tubes as 2 inches. "Full-spectrum" tubes approximate the colors of noontime sunlight, but "cool white" and violet "grow lights" work well, too. The light output diminishes in a year or two, so they will need to be replaced for optimal illumination.

Although simple fixtures and tubes are inexpensive, endless tinkering and suffering with homemade lighting rigs of fixtures, shelves, wires, and chains led me to purchase a commercially manufactured unit, often called a "floral cart." The unit has three fixtures, four 40-watt tubes each, that can be raised or lowered over shelves with sturdy removable trays. A vinyl tent keeps humidity contained, and a small fan circulates the air. The unit is plugged into a timer that keeps lights on for 18 hours each day. With this unit, any properly prepared seeds will germinate and thrive.

HEAT FROM BELOW

Most seeds germinate more quickly if warmth is delivered as "bottom heat," simulating the temperature of dark soil absorbing sunlight in spring. For most seeds, the ideal temperature of the medium should range from 70 to 80 degrees F (21 to 26.5 degrees C). Even if the room temperature is comfortable, evaporating water in the medium lowers the temperature in the root zone, so an extra heat source is needed.

In commercial greenhouses, steam pipes are installed under the benches. Some growers adapt modern residential radiant-heat systems, such as hot water in flexible hoses set in moist sand to conduct the heat. The pots or flats of pots are set on top of the sand. For years, home gardeners have used insulated wire heating cables, a spaghetti tangle of wires that resist electrical current and become warm. The cables are placed in a large flat or wooden box and covered with moist sand. Some of these wire devices come with preset, in-line thermostats, but the wires are unwieldy.

Rubber heat mats, similar to old-fashioned electric heating pads, are available, and a modern version is a thin plastic sheet that is about the same dimensions as a plastic flat. The reasonably priced sheet combines a trans-

former with a grid of electrically resistant wire.

With a floral cart, supplying heat is simple. The warm light fixtures, which are under all but the bottom shelf, serve as an excellent source of "free" heat for the seedlings on the shelves above them.

SOWING MEDIA

Soil is the foundation upon which all gardens are built. Plants rely on soil for stability, moisture, oxygen, and nourishment. Good garden soil is alive; it is a mixture of sand, clay, organic  material in various stages of decomposition (humus), and varying amounts of nutrients (elements and dissolved minerals), along with a myriad of organisms—some beneficial, some not—such as fungi, bacteria, diseases, worms, and insects. It may be tempting to use some of this "black gold" for sowing seeds indoors, but leave it in the garden where it belongs. In the warm and still conditions of the indoor nursery, the organisms that break down organic matter in soil may attack the seeds as well. Confined to a pot, indoors or out, where the free forces of nature cannot act on it, the soil may become an impenetrable block. The best approach when sowing seeds is to buy or create a medium suited to the nursery.

Most commercial sowing media in the United States, usually labeled seed-starting mix, are categorized as "soilless" or "peat-lite"—blends of peat moss, perlite, and vermiculite. It is quite easy to make your own medium, but easier still to adjust or amend a purchased one. Peat moss is a renewable resource, but it takes some 250,000 years to renew. If ethical concerns prohibit you from using peat moss, use compost that has been sifted through ¼-inch mesh and sterilized following directions below.

If you buy a premade starting mix, improve it by adding one part drainage material to three parts prepared mix. Use coarse horticultural-grade sand (similar to parakeet gravel) or fine grit. Grit is flaked stone—usually granite—manufactured for the poultry industry as a feed additive.

An easy way to blend the medium is to place the ingredients on a table or in a box and fold them together. You can also put the materials in a tightly closed plastic bag and roll the bag over several times. Then dampen the mix if necessary. The moisture content of the medium has to be "just right." The mix should be light but not dry enough to rise in the air if you blow on it. It should feel cool to the touch, with about as much moisture as a wet sponge that has been thoroughly wrung out. Pour a bit of warm water on the mix in the bag. Roll it over or fold, feel the medium, and add a little more water if necessary. Go slow—the medium must not be sodden either.

DECONTAMINATION

There is almost nothing more frustrating or disheartening than to carefully select, gather, and sow seeds only to watch them wither from disease shortly after sprouting. There are a series of fungal diseases that can plague seed propagators. Collectively termed "damping-off," these dis-

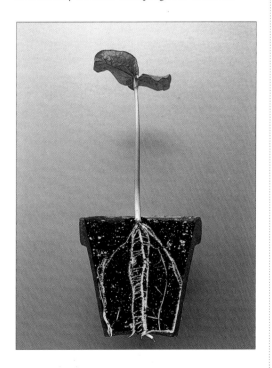

Above: Riddles can be used to sift media. Many kinds are available, including new plastic or antique wood hoops. Wire mesh in various sizes (industrial screen, hardware cloth, chicken wire) can be fitted over a simple square wood frame and stapled in place to make a riddle for sifting material, from fine to coarse.

Below: A perfect sowing medium holds moisture and air and has a fine yet open texture that promotes and supports healthy roots, such as those of a castor bean. A homemade medium using a humus source such as compost must be sifted through ¼-inch mesh.

Below: Horticultural sand has been used to top-dress these square, 3½-inch plastic pots. The square shape provides more surface for sowing, and if set into a flat, the pots are less likely to fall over than round ones.

Opposite: Plastic and clay can both be washed and reused, but durable, nonporous pots offer advantages. Clay pots, however, can be recycled for other garden uses, as Georgia designer Ryan Gainey discovered.

Right: A variety of ingredients can be used in a growing medium. Some of the materials and mixed media that one may encounter include **(shown actual size, left to right, top to bottom):** commercial seed-starting mix; perlite (exploded volcanic rock); commercial humus-based potting mix; number 2 or grower (medium) chicken grit; horticultural sand (coarser than beach or construction-grade sand); number 1 or starter (fine) grit.

eases cause a new seedling's stem to discolor and collapse. Once damping-off strikes, even before the seedlings keel over, the outcome is unstoppable, and an entire flat of seedlings can be leveled in a matter of hours.

The ideal sowing medium must be virtually sterile. Fresh, store-bought soilless mix is usually disease- and pest-free. If the medium has been sitting around in an opened bag, or if any sources from the garden are being used, the

"bad" organisms (and weed seeds, if present) and leave the "good" ones—those that keep the medium active, open, and "alive." Higher temperatures, however, provide greater security and alleviate the need for pesticides and fungicides.

A faster and completely odorless method is to place the medium in a plastic, heat-proof roasting bag in a microwave oven. (The bag also provides a handy way to mix and store the medium.) If the medium is not already moist-

mixture should be heated to kill lurking pathogens. Professionals either process their medium in a steam sterilizer or treat it with toxic fumigants. I have come across a book with a dubious reference to using the kitchen pressure cooker for sterilization, but most references for amateurs suggest baking the medium in a roasting pan in an oven set at 300 degrees F (150 degrees C) for about two hours. This baking—while smelling up the house—heats the medium to about 140 degrees F (60 degrees C), which purports to eliminate the

ened as described above, dampen it evenly, and twist the top of the bag closed, leaving plenty of room for the contents and tumble to mix. Tie the bag closed with string, and heat it in the microwave at full power for about ten minutes. Open the bag, and insert an instant-read thermometer. The temperature in the center of the medium should be at least 180 degrees F (82 degrees C); if it is lower, zap it for a few minutes more. The same temperature can be reached in a conventional oven, of course. In all situations, take precautions to avoid burns.

(1) (2) (3)

(4) (5) (6)

(7) (8) (9)

Traditional sowing steps: Terra cotta is permeable, so gasses flow through a clay pot (1), but moisture is also lost. (If seeds or seedlings dry once they have absorbed moisture they will perish, so nonporous plastic is often chosen for easier care.) Pour moistened medium into a scrupulously clean pot until it overflows (2). Skim off the excess (3) with a stick or striker (this one is a concrete float). Tamp the medium down to remove air pockets (4) (a fence post finial is shown but the bottom of another pot will work). Jack-in-the-pulpit seeds (5) are ready to be distributed evenly (6). Then comes more medium to cover the large seeds, a gentle tamping (7), and a shallow layer of grit (8). Because of the large seeds and pot, the seedlings and tubers that developed were allowed to grow through their second year before transplanting (9).

POTS

Now that plastic stands in for nearly every organic material, even money, it isn't surprising that synthetics are everywhere in the garden too —even the garden of a nature lover. Many horticulturists sow seeds in 12 by 20-inch, easy-to-clean plastic flats that can hold thousands of seeds of one plant type. (Sowing seeds of several kinds of plants in one flat creates problems because the seeds germinate at varying rates and are difficult to handle.) Pots made of nonporous plastic keep moisture in the medium, and are easier to wash than ones made of clay.

flats so they can be moved without toppling.

Everything that comes in contact with the seeds must be impeccably clean. If you are using recycled pots, wash each one thoroughly. Use dish soap, dishwasher detergent, or a 5 percent dilution of bleach in water. Scrub off any crusty salt deposits from fertilizers with a fingernail brush. Rinse the pots thoroughly, and drip-dry them on a rack.

The last step before actually sowing seeds is to fill the pots, and here comes the crocking controversy. Common practice calls for placing extra drainage material such as broken clay pot shards placed concave side down, pebbles, or

Top: A thin layer of fine or medium granite chicken grit is nearly always added and brings the medium up to the pot rim. There may be some settling, but since water is absorbed from below or occasionally misted from above, there is no need to provide extra space for a reservoir as with a potted plant. The grit prevents disease and keeps the medium from being disturbed if sprinkled.

Above: Tiny nicotiana seeds are removed from their envelope **(left)** and, because of their size, are sprinkled on top of a thin layer of grit **(center).** The seeds—about one hundred in a 3½-inch pot—settle in between the spaces of the grit. This one pot produced a brilliant show **(right),** with flowers that opened in the evening and filled the air with their fragrance.

However, there is no question that clay pots are better looking than plastic, and they are also better for plants. If you have the time and patience to tend seedlings in terra-cotta containers, which dry out quickly, by all means do so. The exchange of gases through the walls of the pots is beneficial to plants. On the other hand, plastic is inexpensive, lightweight, and durable. Outdoors, plastic pots hold up to the elements longer than the more attractive terra cotta, which can crack from freezing and thawing. Ultimately, though, ultraviolet light, temperature fluctuations, and even the heat of the indoor nursery will break down plastic—nothing really lasts forever.

While a flat is useful for mass sowings, in most cases, square, 3-inch plastic pots are the most efficient choice for home gardeners. Square pots make the best use of space and hold more medium and seeds than round ones of the same size. Square plastic pots also fit snugly into

gravel in the bottom of containers for drainage and weight. Adequately prepared medium, however, composed of similar particle sizes and aggregate, should provide enough drainage and heft to propel the medium in a single mass out of a pot when it comes time to dump the contents. Another reason not to add crocking is that if a capillary mat (see page 93) is used as the primary watering system or for maintaining moisture when the gardener is away, the medium must touch it. Pots sit directly on the mat, and moisture is transferred by direct contact with the medium in the containers.

SOW!

The preparations are nearly complete, and according to your sowing calendar, it is time to begin. Start by filling each pot to overflowing with the medium. Strike the surface by scraping a tool or flat stick across the rim, then firmly

rap the pot on the table or potting bench to settle the medium and fill all air gaps. If necessary, add more medium and rap the pot again. The surface of the medium should be nearly even with the pot rim for tiny seeds and just below for larger seeds.

The density of the sowing depends on the size of the seeds as well as the size of the seedlings-to-be. Most seeds will range between the size of a poppy seed and those of a pumpkin. Medium-size seed, for example, a lemon's "pip," should be sown one or two per square inch—about a dozen in a 3-inch pot. In contrast, fifty to one hundred columbine seeds fit in the same size container. Helpful hints for achieving an even distribution include sprinkling in plaid grid patterns, but practice is what you'll need.

Most books recommend covering seeds with a depth of medium equal to twice their thickness, often to keep seeds from light. While some seeds *do* need darkness to germinate, as some need light, most will sprout in either condition. Unless noted, cover seeds to assure them of a moist environment.

Large seeds can be evenly set on the medium and pressed into place with a tamper. More medium can be added as needed to cover the seeds. Tap the pot gently to level the surface. Then cover the medium with a fine layer of grit. (If you can't obtain grit or a substitute such as parakeet gravel, use additional medium.) The grit should be flush with the pot rim.

Although bringing the grit or medium to the top of the container counters the tendency to leave a reservoir for watering, it will prevent the obstruction of air movement or the collection of airborne microorganisms, which could attack emerging seedlings.

Medium-size grit, which has particles about

⅛ inch across, is good for most applications. The smallest grade (number 1, or starter) can be used for the smallest seeds. The very tiniest seeds, which often require light for germination, can be sown on top of a very fine layer of grit or sand. Tiny seeds roll into the spaces between the grains, receive light, and are kept moist by the damp flaked rock or coarse sand.

To sprinkle the grit, fill a pint-size plastic tub half full, and then tip and carefully tap it. With practice, you'll be able to make a layer two or three particles thick.

Commercial suppliers often pack the tiniest seeds in little sealed foil or paper envelopes inside normal-size packets. Take out the inner packet, carefully cut it open with scissors, form a crease on one side, and tap it very gently so that the seeds arrange in single file along the

crease and drop one by one onto the grit. Another method is to mix tiny seeds with fine "play" sand, take a pinch, and sprinkle the mixture lightly onto the surface.

Note: To assist gardeners, some companies sell difficult-to-handle, nearly microscopic seeds individually coated in a shell of nutrients and inert material to create larger "pelleted" seed.

For review, see Sowing Summary, page 240.

WATER

The next procedure ensures that the medium will contain just the right amount of moisture for the seeds. Initially, the best way to water is to fill a dishpan or a flat without drainage holes with 1 to 2 inches of room-temperature water, place the pots in it, and allow the medium to soak up the moisture from below. If the water source has been chemically softened or treated, or if the water is known to be naturally very hard, use distilled water. When placing the pots

in the flat, take care not to let water douse the surface of the individual containers and dislodge the seeds.

The absorption process may take a half hour or so, depending on the temperature of the water and the temperature and initial dampness of the sowing mix. The medium has absorbed enough moisture when the grit on the surface turns from near-white to pale gray, or when the light brown medium darkens. If all the water in the tray is absorbed before this color change happens, add more. As soon as the surface has changed color, remove the first pots, add more water, and insert other pots.

Next, place the moistened containers into a

tor faces is to monitor the medium's moisture content religiously. Once seeds have absorbed water, they must never be allowed to dry out. During the weeks between germination and preparing plants for their permanent homes, if you need to be away for more than a few days, plan to have a neighbor come over to check the moisture in the pots, following your written instructions, or consider installing an inexpensive capillary mat. One edge of this sheet of absorbent, feltlike fabric is placed in a trough of water, and the rest is laid beneath the pots. Water is wicked into the mat and transferred to the pots by osmosis. The mat is not a cure-all, nor is it an alternative to attendance.

Opposite: Germination occurs when the seed leaves emerge above the medium, as with these nicotiana seedlings from the sowing demonstrated on page 89.

flat with drainage holes. Note how heavy the pots feel at this time; become accustomed to judging this weight. Lifting the pots is about the best way to tell if the seed mix or seedlings need more water. In many cases, the pots will not have to be watered again until the seedlings are up, possibly even later.

This first watering from below ensures that the medium and seeds are not jostled, which can happen when water is poured from above. However, if the mix in the pots begins to dry, water can be sprinkled from above with a rubber bulb mister or a spray bottle. Later seedlings may be moistened with a watering can fitted with a very fine "rose" attachment.

Perhaps the most demanding task a propaga-

LIGHT

When the seeds are newly planted, the pots are brought to the greenhouse, south window, or should be placed so that the rims are approximately 4 inches beneath the center of the fluorescent tubes (the light in the middle of the tubes is much brighter than at the ends). As the seedlings emerge, the lights have to be raised to maintain a 4-inch distance from the leaves. When all the seedlings do not come up or advance at the same rate, things become complicated. To accommodate the different seedlings, plan to stage the pots using clean, inverted flowerpots to raise individual pots or trays.

Above: Corn is a mono-cotyledon, so its first leaf is a single blade, followed shortly thereafter by another **(left)**. Dicotyledons, such as these impatiens, first produce coupled, semicircular seed leaves **(center)**. The twin cotyledons are followed by sets of true leaves that resemble those of older plants, as seen with these honey locust seedlings **(right)**.

. . . AND THEY'RE UP

At last, the miracle happens, and a green haze appears above the grit in the pots. Most seeds started indoors with warmth from below will germinate in two to six weeks—which can seem like an awfully long time to the eager gardener. But soon, tiny, new sprouts develop with seed leaves, or cotyledons. Monocotyledons resemble a blade of grass; dicotyledons hold two semicircles atop a little stem. These seed leaves are followed by the first true leaves: monocots

overcrowded and their roots would grow into a tangled mass. "Potting up" or "potting on" involves transferring seedlings from the original pots into their own containers. Most seedlings appreciate personal space and will take off, growing larger and sturdier, in just a few days.

Seedlings of hardy herbaceous and woody plants may have to remain in individual pots for up to a year, so they should be moved into sturdy containers. Seedlings that are destined for transplanting to the garden in a month or so can be moved into flats made of flexible plastic.

If you're growing annual bedding plants, 12- by 20-inch flats with drainage holes are handy. If you do not have enough of one species to fill an entire flat, you can mix varieties with similar requirements and rates of growth—perhaps two colors of one kind of marigold. Eventually, the seedlings can be transplanted with a spoon.

Flats with preformed cells or individual compartments that allow each seedling to develop a separate "plug" of roots come in various sizes with as few as 12 cells or as many as 120. At planting time, the seedlings will recover quickly if their roots are disturbed as little as possible, and it's easy to pop the plugs out of their cubicles by pushing up from below.

Below: When seedlings have their first set of true leaves, they will have to be transplanted either to individual pots or flats with room to grow. One

method, to "prick out" each seedling from the medium, is most useful for mass sowings of seeds in communal flats (see page 80); the other calls for easing the entire contents out of the pot at once and pulling off seedlings one by one. To prick out, hold each seedling by its first true leaf and use a sharp stick, plant label point, or a pencil to pry the roots up and out of the medium. These nicotiana seedlings were transferred to a flat with seventy-two cells **(right)** and were ready in three weeks to be hardened off for planting outdoors.

sprout a second blade; dicots, two diminutive replicas of mature ones.

Seed packets give instructions for thinning out the crowd either by pulling some or decapitating half with scissors. Thinning makes sense when hundreds of carrot seeds are sown outside in the kitchen garden, but sacrificing precious seeds of unusual perennials, some of which come fifteen to a packet or less, is not necessary.

Potting up seedlings for more root and elbow room takes the place of thinning outdoors.

Once the seedlings have developed their first set of true leaves, it's time to move them into larger quarters. It is too early to transplant indoor seedlings outdoors, even if the weather is mild; the tender seedlings would perish in the sun, wind, and lower humidity. However, if left in their pots, the young plants would become

DIGS

A good potting medium for seedlings is coarser than the one for sowing. Again, homemade is preferable to store-bought mixes. Commercial "potting soils" vary from poor-draining, loam-based soils to light peat-based mixes. The best choice contains humus—homemade compost or leaf mold—sieved through a $1/4$- to $1/2$-inch mesh. For drainage material, use perlite, coarse sand, grit, or a mixture of these. By volume, use three parts humus to one part drainage material. Plants from shady woodland environments need a moist mix with less drainage material. Species native to prairies or deserts prefer a faster-draining mix with more perlite and grit. The medium should be just damp—cool to the touch—not wet enough to stick in clumps.

(1)

(2)

(3)

(4)

(5)

(6)

(7)

(8)

(9)

Potting up: To transplant seedlings, assemble a flat with or without compartments, potting medium, striker, tamping tool such as a section of dowel or tree branch, labels, pencil, Popsicle stick or similar tool, and watering can or bulb mister. Pour medium into the flat (1), such as this one with twelve six-packs, and smooth to fill every cell (2). Strike the surface even (3) and tamp each receptacle (4). Bring the seedlings to the flat (5), invert the pot, shake it gently until the medium begins to slip free (6), and "dump" the contents on its side. Drill a hole in the medium with a pencil. Peel a seedling from the top of the pile while holding it by one true leaf (7) and lower it into the hole. Push the medium back in place (8). Large seedlings may be set in place while pouring a thin stream of water to settle the mix (9). Transfer the label to the flat.

Aside from the practical benefits of a home-made mix, *feeling* the medium is part of the experience. So much of the pleasure in gardening comes from tactile sensations. A gardener learns to sense if a homemade mix is right by the look and feel of the blended materials. (See page 86 for media ingredients.)

After preparing the potting medium, fill a flat to overflowing, skim the excess off, and gently tamp down the medium. A section of branch or a child's block can make a good tamping tool.

WHAT A DUMP

Some sources suggest pricking out individual seedlings one at a time from the pot. There is an easier way to transplant an entire batch all at once. Dump the pot of seedlings out sideways into your hand and lay the clump on its side. (If you need to leave this task midway, cover the pile with a wet paper towel—the roots must be

Right: John Mapel of the Tower Hill Botanic Garden, Worcester, Massachusetts, makes a cold frame out of seven 8-foot-long and seven 4-foot-long pieces of aged, pressure-treated 2 x 12 lumber. (No food crops will come in contact with the wood.) I chose recycled glass sashes, but John recommends durable acrylic or fiberglass. A 4- by 8-foot rectangle was made by butt-joining the lumber with galvanized deck screws. One 4-foot-long piece was ripped diagonally to create the slanted top, which will face south for the most sunlight. Two more rectangles were built and lengths of 1- by 3-inch lumber were cut. These pieces will be fastened to wrap around the outside of the rectangles, covering the seams and serving as bracing. Two more pieces were cut that will fit inside the box for the sashes to rest upon when closed.

kept moist at all times. Keep the seedlings out of the sun or drafts.)

Make a hole in the center of the cell, new individual pot, or corner of a flat with your pencil. Lift one seedling at a time, holding it by one of its true leaves, not its cotyledons or stem, and peel it from the top of the clump. If the true leaf is damaged, the plant will survive, but

the plant will not survive if the seed leaf or stem is torn. Lower the seedlings one by one into their spaces in the medium.

Roots will not grow in pockets of air, so snug the medium gently but thoroughly with a Popsicle stick or your fingers. If the roots are extra long or wide, "water-in" the seedling by holding it in one hand over the hole and lowering it while pouring a fine stream of water from a small can. Stop as soon as the seedling seems able to stand upright. Try not to overwater.

CARE AND FEEDING

Seedlings need a great deal of light as they grow, but they no longer require bottom heat. In fact, after seedlings have emerged, high temperatures will cause them to become leggy, and they may be useless by the time it is safe for them to go outside. (The bottom shelf of the floral cart has no light below it so it is a cool, bright spot.)

Keep a sharp eye on moisture by judging the weight of the pot or feeling the medium. The mix should feel cool and slightly damp about half an inch down. If the medium becomes too wet, mold and fungus gnats may appear. These tiny, swarming, black insects do little harm, and the problem can be corrected by allowing the medium to dry a bit more between waterings. Apply a water-soluble fertilizer, such as fish emulsion or a liquid organic fertilizer diluted to about one-quarter of the recommended rate for full-grown plants, every other time you water.

If the seedlings seem to be pale, examine the leaves for pests. Red spider mites are microscopic, but you may see what appears to be dust on the undersides of the leaves and, in the worst cases, webs around the foliage.

Whiteflies are tiny mothlike insects barely $1/16$ inch long that take flight if you disturb the leaves. You can vacuum them up as you shake the plants, but don't get too close and suck up seedlings as well. Yellow sticky cards also work.

If caring for the seedlings seems overly demanding, they may have been started too early. Note this on your calendar or journal.

TOUGHENING UP

Eventually, seedlings of outdoor ornamental plants have to leave their pampered life indoors, but the transition must take place gradually. About two weeks before the date the plants are to be set into the garden (the last possible day of frost), they must be "hardened off."

This process acclimates new plants to direct sunlight, wind, changeable relative humidity, and cooler temperatures. Gardeners are often advised to take the seedlings outdoors to a protected spot, for one hour the first day, adding an hour of exposure each day. This regime may work well, but it is not practical for most people.

Cold frames make the necessary process of hardening off much easier. One portable version, of thin, corrugated, white plastic, is available from mail-order suppliers. The bottomless frame is shipped flat and can be stored that way when not in use. Set up the frame on soil or a paved patio, perhaps in a spot that receives just a few hours of direct sun. Place your flats of seedlings into the frame.

If the air temperature during the day is 65 to 70 degrees F (18 to 21 degrees C) or higher, prop the lid open 6 inches. At night, or if a cold snap is predicted, leave the top closed. After a week, open the

frame fully all day but continue to close it at night. In two weeks the seedlings will be ready for transplanting into the garden.

Someday, you'll want a permanent frame (see captions). These are set in full sun and will need a filter of sheer cloth or a temporary coat of whitewash.

Above: Steve Labuda helps by digging a trench 1 foot deep **(left).** The first rectangle is laid in the hole and John lifts the corners as Steve cuts the soil or fills in to level the frame's wooden foundation **(center).** John checks the level one last time **(right).** The next rectangle is set on the first and, finally, the slanted top. The rests and braces are added, and last the sashes are attached to the back of the frame with hinges.

Left: For insulation, dry leaves can be sprinkled over the plants in the frame. One or two layers of bubble wrap can also work. The plastic can be stapled to the inside of the frame. Rigid foam insulation can be placed on top of the sashes and tied or weighted in place when the coldest weather is predicted. But as with all parts of a garden in the North, nature's insulation—snow— is best of all. Under the cover of this airy white blanket, plants stay cozy until spring.

It used to be called pluck, the thing that made amateur gardener Saida Malarney try growing ferns from spores on her kitchen windowsill *(below)*. A love for ferns impelled Jean Lundgren to start a nursery in southwest Michigan. And a need to share the knowledge gleaned from extensive experience inspired John Mickel, curator of ferns at the New York Botanical Garden, to write *Ferns for American Gardens,* the best guide to these plants.

Ferns are most familiar as the plants carpeting the woodland floor, but there are ferns that grow taller than a person and have trunks that look like trees, and there are delicate ferns with wiry stems that aggressively climb trees. A few ferns float on water, and others thrive in the desert. However, the most intriguing feature of these underutilized garden plants might be their manner of reproduction. Ferns produce spores that first grow vegetatively—dividing to grow into male and female organs, which then reproduce sexually. In a way, ferns straddle the line between asexual and sexual propagation.

Despite their global presence, ferns are very particular when it comes to germination, growing only where humidity, light, moisture, and earth are perfect. Competition from other organisms can be fatal, either by crowding or by consuming the devel-

oping spores. Ferns overcome the odds in nature by generating enormous numbers of the microscopic spores. Spores are produced in multiples of 64—up to 512 in each *sporangium,* with the sporangia themselves clustered in groups of up to 100 in basket-like *sori* (singular, sorus). The sori appear as golden dots on the back of fronds. The strategy has proved successful for millions of years.

The challenge of participating in one of botany's more curious marvels might be enough to inspire an attempt at fern propagation, but the promise of an ocean of hardy ferns could be another incentive for a gardener. The time from spore to baby is nearly a year—not instant gratification, to be sure—and it's longer still before the plants are garden-ready. But the process is filled with moments of beauty. This kind of close-up gardening is very personal, and more precious for that reason. Don't be surprised if you lose your heart to the emerald waifs on the windowsill.

Our three enthusiasts—the gardener, the grower, and the author—use slightly different methods, including a variety of containers and locations for sowing fern spores, but all agree that very high humidity and impeccable hygiene are critical. Everything that comes in contact with the spores as they are

FERN SOWING

being sown must be more than clean, it must be sterilized, from the medium to the containers. Saida uses plastic saucers, Jean prefers ones of terra cotta, and John places plastic pots in closed, clear plastic shoeboxes, but all of these are disinfected—either by pouring boiling water over and into the containers or by washing them in a 5 percent dilution of bleach in water. The media— mixtures of humus and perlite—are sterilized (see page 86).

Sowing is simple. Take the paper with collected spores (page 57) to the trash and pour the contents into the can. Enough spores will be stuck among the paper fibers. To sow, just hold the paper face down over the medium and snap the back. In nature, the odds for fern success are banked on numbers. In home propagation, the numbers are smaller, but the odds increase under artificially optimal conditions.

The place for sowing spores must be a warm spot with even, bright light. John will place his shoeboxes about 6 inches below fluorescent light tubes. Saida's saucers go to her kitchen window, and Jean places her clay ones in a greenhouse. A good way to try your hand at propagating ferns is to duplicate Saida's windowsill experiment using readily available materials.

When ready to sow, Saida takes two similar plastic containers bought from the garden center. Both are 5 inches in diameter and clear, but one was molded to be a shallow saucer—about 1 inch deep—and the other was designed as a liner for baskets —at about 2½ inches deep. She sterilizes the containers by holding each one with tongs over the sink and pouring boiling water over it. The medium is sterilized as well. (The mix can be two parts humus to one part each vermiculite and perlite, or packaged, commercial African violet soil.) The deeper container receives some medium, which, after the liner is tapped on the counter, settles to a depth of ¾ inch.

Clay saucer, tray, and glass-pane cover (1). *Prothallus* (center) (2). Jean Lundgren lifts a sporling with a dental spatula (3), and moves it to a flat (4). Sporlings after transplanting (5). Others after several weeks (6).

6

Vegetative Reproduction

It is easy to appreciate the wonder of birth. When we propagate plants from seed, we get to play midwife. Plants can also reproduce in ways that are harder for humans to relate to, generating entire new entities from bits and pieces. Even though we may comprehend the process, asexual propagation seems supernatural—for now.

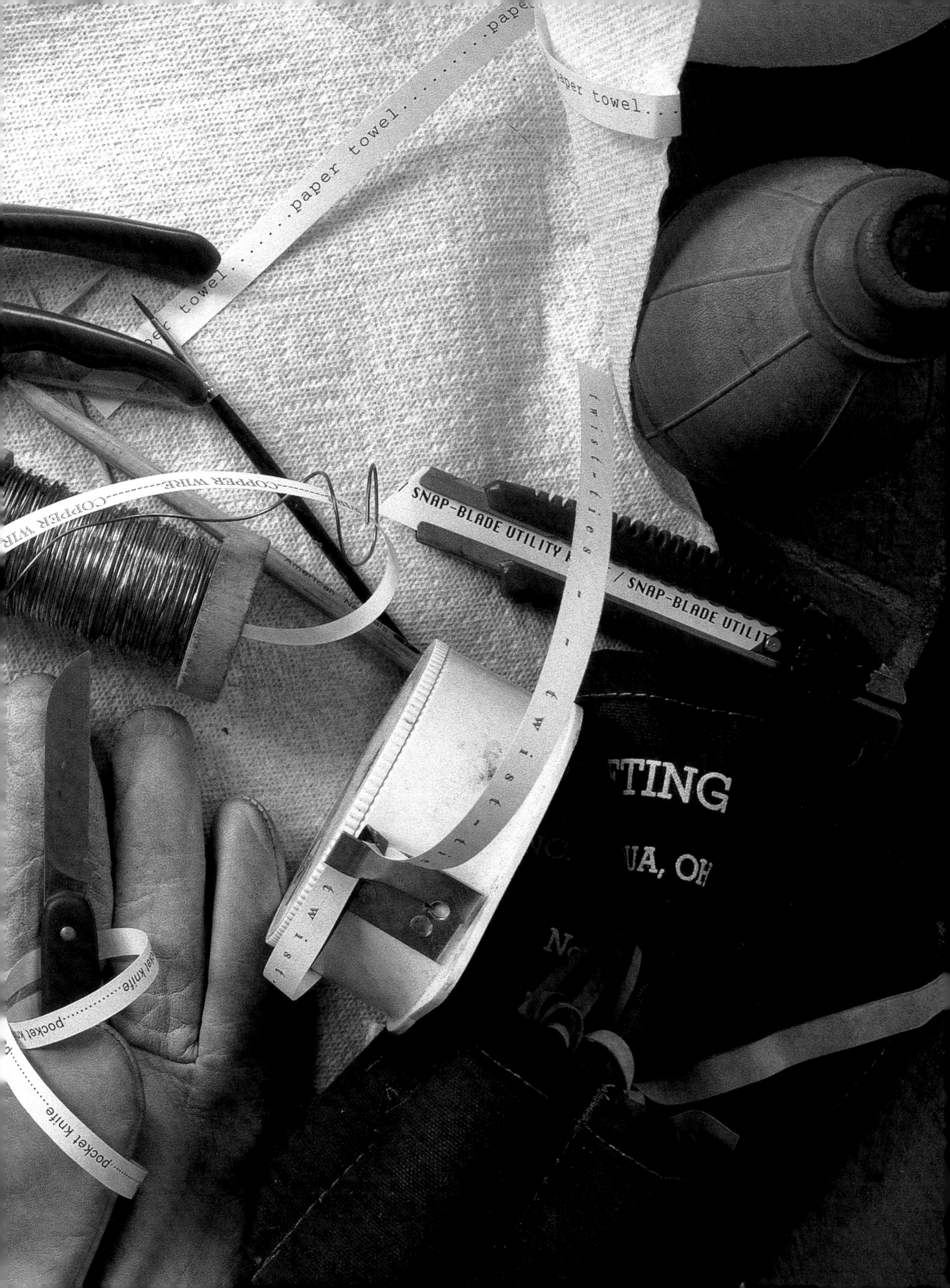

paper towel......paper towel....

paper towel....

COPPER WIRE......COPPER WIRE

SNAP-BLADE UTILITY

SNAP-BLADE UTILIT

twist-ties

twist

FTING

UA, OH

pocket knife

pocket knife

pocket knife

Scientists have recently managed to produce genetically identical animals—clones—without the benefit of a sexual union. Yet plant clones are as old as plants themselves.

Single-celled bacteria produce clones by division. Vines sometimes scamper along the ground and root where their stems touch moist soil. In time, entire plants grow from these spots, pushing out new shoots of their own. A desert succulent might have one of its leaves broken off by a careless lizard. The leaf falls to the sand, the wound heals, and new roots begin to grow through the callus. Soon a tiny plant

produce a fascinating anomaly such as a side shoot with gold leaves on an otherwise all-green plant. The accident may never happen again, but an offspring produced from a golden cutting would carry on the colorful characteristic.

WAYS AND MEANS

Even though taking stem cuttings may be the most frequently used method for reproducing plants asexually, this is only the beginning. There are herbaceous stem cuttings, softwood cuttings, and hardwood ones to harvest from

Preceding pages: The tools are made ready for asexual reproduction.

Opposite: Gracious mirrored borders, surrounded by dignified hedges, barely hint of the craft that goes into producing this scene: the hedges were grown from cuttings, as were many perennials that also have to be divided to rejuvenate clumps or to make more.

emerges, using the moisture in the leaf until it becomes established on its own new roots.

Knowing what we know about the tenacity of plants, we can play a very active role in making more from what we often call "cuttings," in the process known as vegetative propagation.

Why is this form of reproduction so valuable? For one thing, plants made from cuttings will be larger and more mature than their counterparts started from seed. Within a few weeks, a 6-inch-long stem cutting of an elderberry, for example, will have pushed new roots. In a month longer, it may be ready to go into the garden. In a few years, it could be 5 feet tall, flower, and fruit. A seedling grown in this same time frame might be 12 to 18 inches tall, but it would not be mature enough to flower for quite some time.

Vegetative propagation is a way to perpetuate nature's "accidents." A number of factors might

woody plants when they are dormant in winter. Within the stem cuttings, there are variations such as nodal, internodal, leaf-bud, and basal cuttings. Stems can be grafted together, and even bits of one plant can be fused to parts of another; roses, for instance, are passed around the world as twigs with dormant leaf buds to harvest and graft onto established rootstocks.

Modified, fleshy stems that grow underground—tubers, bulbs, and rhizomes—can be cut into sections to make more plants. When scales from a lily bulb are gently removed and placed in an appropriate environment, tiny new bulblets will grow from their bases. Even leaves may be cut to propagate certain plants.

Many herbaceous perennials need to be divided every few years to keep them at peak performance. Division is also the most frequently used method to reproduce perennials,

Above left: New plants can be made from sections of rhizomes, and in the case of bloodroot (*Sanguinaria canadensis*), the rhizome can also be scored in situ— a small incision behind the growing shoot causes multiple buds to develop. In order to perpetuate a sport with a distinctive characteristic, such as this chance variegated branch of a deutzia **(center),** it has to be grown from cuttings. Crown division is the primary means of propagating herbaceous perennials—an annual ritual at the Bellevue Botanical Garden in Washington State **(right).**

and the easiest. When clumps are cut—right through the crown—the divisions grow quickly. A good-size *Hosta lancifolia,* for instance, can be dug up in early spring, cut into three sections, and replanted; by summer, the new plants will be nearly as large as the original.

inside the jars, however, and the cuttings could easily have rotted. This is where my grandmother's intuition came into play. She sensed the moment to take the cuttings—when the tissues were most resistant to disease and would root without rotting.

Growers often make tiny root cuttings when large numbers of herbaceous-perennial clones are needed. A perennial can be lifted in the spring, root-pruned, and replanted. The lush new roots that form—full of sugars and starches and primed to grow—will produce vigorous new plants when cuttings are taken in the autumn.

My grandmother rooted summer rose cuttings under jars. She set the slips in moist, sandy soil in the shelter of shrubs, where the cuttings were protected from the burning rays of the sun but had enough bright light to continue photosynthesis and grow roots. There was no air circulation

What my grandmother may have guessed, I have learned. Gardeners have to observe growing plants and then seize the moment to take and make more.

MAKING UP FOR THE LOSS

Detached parts of a plant have the same basic needs as whole ones do. But they are all missing something: roots, leaves, or stems. The most important job of the propagator is to reduce stress by making up for the losses, so the plants-to-be can focus on growing new cells and use their energy to become self-sufficient.

Without roots to take up water immediately, leafy cuttings, for example, will wilt long before they can grow new roots. The cuttings still need light to carry on photosynthesis, but the searing direct rays of the sun will overheat and dry out the cuttings. In order to help keep the tissues

turgid, there must be moisture coming up from below and in the air all around the cuttings. Air filled with water vapor will draw less moisture from the leaves or stems, and any droplets that settle on the surface of these parts and do evaporate will cool them. The cuttings will need to be placed in "intensive care units" that provide for their special requirements.

What you choose to use for these controlled environments will depend on the needs of your plants and the scale of the project, along with the scope of your ambition and, as always, your budget. Plants grow faster in warm temperatures, but raising the thermostat speeds

up transpiration—the loss of moisture through the pores in the leaves. In most situations, the relative humidity will be maintained at a high level because an artificial closed environment is fabricated. In some cases, though, you'll need to add moisture to the air via pebble trays, mechanical humidifiers, or even a cloud of water vapor from a misting system.

The cuttings will need a temporary substitute for natural earth for the roots they will produce. The medium must provide physical support, close contact, moisture, and air. Once plants have roots and shoots and leaves to carry them on, they must be moved into another medium that will promote further development.

Plants will need assistance adjusting from protective custody to the drier air of the window garden, or a more strenuous transition to a permanent spot in the outdoor garden.

THE ICU

In the best of all possible propagation worlds, there would be bright light all day long, and warm, steamy air—even in the winter. The humid air would swirl around the plants, moving just enough to inhibit disease and to toughen the cuttings' tissues. Electric heating cables or perhaps steam pipes beneath wire mesh counters would warm up sterilized medium in gracious polypropylene flats. The synthetic soil that fills the flats would hold air and moisture, and also firmly grasp stem cuttings—practically tickling them into making new roots. In other words, the utopian ICU is a propagation bench in a warm greenhouse. Well, almost.

A greenhouse has a few problems. One, it is hard to keep cool in late spring and summer when we need it most. Two, when the greenhouse ventilation system is working well, the temperature will drop, but so will the humidity. The fans

Above: The atmosphere under the glass jar was a small-scale version of the best place for making cuttings, a greenhouse. The Enid A. Haupt Conservatory at the New York Botanical Garden is the embodiment of a great glass house, but at any size, the elements of the controlled atmosphere are the same: light, temperature, and, most of all, humidity.

Below: Cuttings must remain turgid. Tissues lose moisture through their surfaces, but they can also absorb it, so a high relative humidity is imperative while the cuttings produce roots to restore water in the conventional way. Providing warmth, especially from below the medium, speeds the formation of roots, but as the temperatures rise the leaves and stems transpire even more quickly. One method to keep the humidity high also keeps the tissues above the medium cooler—frequent misting from devices such as these nozzles above a mist bench in a commercial greenhouse.

PLAY MISTY

Mist is magic. Cuttings of stems and leaves of herbaceous plants and broad-leaved evergreens, conifers, and deciduous shrubs—all but dryland cacti and succulents—root quickly in a cloud of tiny water droplets. The mist is provided by special

systems with nozzles and valves. They create a film of water on the tissues of the cuttings that prevents them from losing their own moisture or overheating, while the medium can be warmed from below to accelerate root formation. Easy cuttings root three times faster under mist, and pieces of hard-to-propagate plants may be coaxed to produce roots.

Mist is created when water is forced through nozzles with pinprick-size openings, or deflection outlets, which push a fine stream of water against an "anvil," breaking it into micro-droplets. The cuttings are allowed nearly to dry off between sprays. Valves turn the water on or off for predetermined periods of time—more frequently during the day, less frequently or not at all at night. Mist systems are expensive.

I produced a lower-cost home misting setup using an inexpensive nozzle made for commercial-greenhouse bench misting, somewhat like the kind that fogs the produce in the supermarket. The nozzle clamps onto readily available 1/2-inch PVC (plastic) plumbing pipe and emits 1.2 gallons per hour. I used the plastic pipe like Tinker Toys to fabricate a frame in a 2-foot cube shape and installed the spray nozzle

in the center of the cross member at the top of the cube.

Two flats of cuttings fit beneath the nozzle. An electric mat under the flats, plugged into a GFI (ground-fault circuit inter-rupter) outlet, supplies bottom heat. I found a battery-operated timer that can be set to turn the mist on for ten seconds every ten minutes during the day. The unit could be placed in a greenhouse or outdoors in the hot summer months. It works!

A homemade misting unit **(left)** was constructed with plastic plumb-ing pipe, an inexpensive nozzle, a heat mat below the flats, and a timer. Easy cuttings become established very quickly under the mist **(above)**, and difficult ones have a better chance of success.

create a great deal of air movement, which can dry out the cuttings. A solution to this problem could be to have indoor rain showers at regular intervals—in other words, a misting system. Someday you may have the perfect greenhouse and misting system. But there are plenty of alternatives right now.

TOO CLOSED FOR COMFORT?

The most important requirement for rooting many cuttings is a controlled environment. Cuttings of tender and hardy herbaceous plants, and of the seasonal growth of woody ones between spring and late summer, demand high relative humidity. The recommendation to make a miniature greenhouse with a plastic bag, placed open end down over cuttings in a pot, didn't work for me. My plants frequently had problems in this confined space, which was more like Biosphere II than a working greenhouse. If mold didn't grow on the cuttings in short order, it ultimately did when the bag collapsed onto the leaves and stems. Then they rotted where condensation collected at the points of contact. The hint to insert wooden sticks into the medium to hold the bag upright didn't fix

the problems, since the sticks got moldy as well. Perhaps it was just too moist and humid.

A modified version of the plastic-bag greenhouse starts with a 4-inch round plastic pot and a gallon-size, heavyweight food-storage bag with a zipper closure. Fold the zipper edge out, like a cuff, and lower a pot with medium and cuttings into it. Then pull the sides back up around the cuttings. These sturdy bags usually stand upright on their own, but if one seems to be folding over, a rubber band placed around the bag and pot just below the pot's rim will pleat the plastic for extra stability.

By opening and closing the zipper, you can adjust the humidity in the bag. Start with the zipper about halfway open, which makes just a slight slit in the top. If there is quite a bit of condensation on the sides of the bag, so much that you can't see the cuttings, increase the size of the "vent." If the cuttings wilt, close the vent some more. Once the cuttings have roots, you can open the bag completely to begin to acclimatize them to lower levels of relative humidity.

An advantage of the single pot is that cuttings of the same size and species or variety can be placed together and monitored closely. They should root at corresponding rates and can be

Below left: The humidity of a flat covered by a clear plastic dome encourages rooting; but pathogens grow, too. Fungicides are available, though cracking the lid for air circulation prevents problems. Plant diseases were just some of the challenges faced by Biosphere II in the Arizona desert **(right),** where microorganisms and macroorganisms (people) shared a giant terrarium.

Above: Opening the top of a zipper-lock bag moderates humidity and discourages mold.

taken out of the bag at the same time. Several of these setups could be placed on a bright windowsill in late winter to mid-spring. But most stem cuttings that need high humidity are taken from the garden in the spring, and there may be hundreds of them. For these cuttings, which can be rooted with controlled humidity and light outdoors, a larger version of the plastic bag-and-pot will be more suitable.

Above, left to right, top to bottom: Making a homemade sweatbox begins by pouring rooting medium into a flat with drainage holes. Moisten the medium with clean water. Tamp the medium very hard with a clean brick or similar tool. Fashion two U-shaped supports from a wire clothes hanger. Insert the points into the corners of the flat and slip it into a dry-cleaning bag or lay a piece of thin plastic-film drop cloth over the supports. The plastic can be closed with a wire tie or a clothespin, or anchored with rocks.

Below right: The sweatbox finds a comfortable spot with very bright light and a breeze, but away from direct sunlight and the full force of the wind.

Below: If needed, a brace can be made from a bamboo stake notched to spread the wire hoops and keep them in place. Customize the sweatbox to meet your needs.

THE "SWEATBOX"

A "propagator" takes the concept of the inverted plastic bag one step further. These units, often imported from England, consist of plastic flats with clear, rigid dome covers. Although they have adjustable vents to control humidity and allow hot air to escape, a lack of air circulation seems to make these propagators better at growing mold than helping stems produce roots. I have had much greater success with a homemade "sweatbox" which keeps humidity high, but allows for an exchange of a bit of air.

By the time the lilacs are in full bloom, mid-May in my region, the "sweatbox" is up and running. Early herbaceous perennial cuttings are already under the plastic tent of the sweatbox. Since softwood cuttings of lilacs are taken from fresh, nonblooming growth, they will soon join the herbaceous ones.

Each spring, I construct a new box. Building

the box is not a weekend project —once the materials are assembled, it takes just an hour or two. The base consists of a plastic flat with drainage holes, filled with rooting medium and fitted with a frame made out of bent coat-hanger wire to support a covering of thin plastic film—such as a dry cleaner's bag. I cut the seam of the bag to produce a single sheet and lay the plastic over the frame. When the sweatbox is placed in its propagation site, I fold the plastic sheet as if making a bed. Small rocks or wood blocks will anchor one side of the sheet to make access quick and easy.

While the plastic cover keeps the relative-humidity levels high, it also is not sealed tightly enough to stop an exchange of some of the air inside and out—it "breathes." The loose tent cover flexes, since I set the box in an area where gentle breezes brush by. The movement of the air inside the box seems to toughen tissues a bit and, since there is some evaporation, cool the cuttings as well. If the surface of the medium is warm or dry to the touch, I add water by misting the cuttings and medium with a spray bot-

tle, perhaps once a week. The spray also helps to wash the cuttings clean.

In the next two or three months, the outdoor temperature will soar. But in the sweatbox—tucked into a cool, shaded spot—the cuttings' tissues should not overheat. The temperature there is generally between 75 and 80 degrees F (23.5 degrees and 26.5 degrees C) during the day, with a drop in the cool evening.

By the end of summer cuttings will be rooted and potted up, and the sweatbox will be retired. The plastic film will be discarded. If the flat is in good condition, it will be cleaned for reuse. The medium—perlite—can be recycled for potting mixes. Starting fresh each spring with new materials and medium provides another deterrent to disease.

NEW MEDIA

The best rooting medium is sterile, makes close contact with the stems, and holds both water and air. And while the white roots that sprout from pussy willow stems in a jar of water are a testimonial to plants' ability to regenerate tissue, water is not a good medium for vegetative propagation. The thick, smooth roots that develop to absorb air in the low-oxygen medium of water are brittle.

To find ideal media, growers in England are using blocks of rock-wool insulation, and in the United States, commercial propagators are trying preformed individual plugs made of Oasis—florist's foam in specially designed flats. A cutting placed into the material makes perfect contact, receives moisture and

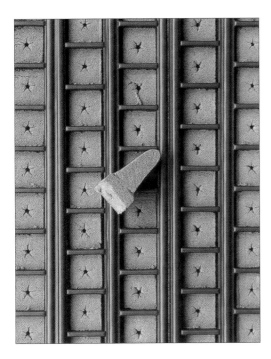

Above left: A rooting medium should hold water and air and be able to come in close contact with the cutting. Coarse white pumice is a superb rooting medium but difficult to come by. For economy's sake, it can be extended with perlite.

Below left: Absorbent foam produced for flower arrangements, such as Oasis brand, has a dense texture (like watermelon flesh when moistened) and is now being made as plugs set into customized flats. The plugs come with or without a hole.

Above right: Plants such as this begonia may be too small for the plug's cube's premade hole, but it can be pushed in the side to root quickly. Other plants, however, find foam cubes too moist, so there must be some experimentation.

air, roots fast, and can be potted plug and all.

Some gardeners recommend two parts perlite to one part pumice; others swear by a fifty-fifty blend of peat moss and perlite, or peat moss and sand. Pure, very coarse sand is a popular choice. Perlite is made of grains of volcanic glass that are heated until they explode—like puffed cereal—with hundreds of spaces to hold air and water. It is slightly alkaline in pH (a consideration when rooting acid-loving plants, such as rhododendrons and heathers).

POTTING UP

Once cuttings have rooted, they are removed to individual pots. Most potting will happen in warm weather and can be done outdoors, but keep the young plants out of direct sunlight. Work in a comfortable spot, on a table or bench.

The recipe for the medium is three parts coarsely sieved moistened humus—peat moss,

Above: After they have rooted, all cuttings will need to be potted in individual containers. The roots must be kept moist during the process. An easy way to do this is to place the roots on a moist paper towel and fold it back and forth between layers.

Clockwise from left: Potting begins by turning over the edge of a plastic bag filled with just-damp growing mix, setting a pot in the center, and holding a cutting in position over the pot. Scoop up medium with your free hand and pour it around the roots, making sure all the spaces are filled. The potting mix can be brought up to the rim and gently but firmly pushed down to make good contact, removing any air pockets and leaving a shallow reservoir at the rim for future watering. Water the newly potted cutting the first time by placing it into a tray with an inch or so of water for a half hour or until the surface feels cool and barely moist.

homemade compost or leaf mold, composted tree bark, or almost any processed vegetable-based material, even coir from the outer husk of the coconut. Add one part drainage material, such as perlite mixed fifty-fifty with coarse grit or horticultural sand (see page 85). Add more humus for plants that like a moist medium or more drainage material for those that would appreciate a drier mix.

If the medium is in a bag, open up the bag and roll the top edges down to make a low-sided container. Place the empty pot in the middle of the medium in the bag. Hold the cutting gently by a few leaves or the stem so that the crown —the place where the new roots emerge from the stem— is even with the pot rim. Scoop up some of the potting medium with your other hand, and pour it into the pot so that it fills in around the new roots; rotate the pot and pour in more medium until it is close to the top.

As the pot fills, tap it on your table or bench. Add more medium if necessary, tap again, add more, and press gently with your fingers to create about a ½-inch water reservoir between the medium and the pot rim. Label the plant by name and include information such as the date that the cutting was made or the source.

As you go, set each newly potted plant into a pan of water about 2 inches deep. Take the pots out of the pan when they feel heavy or moisture begins to darken the surface of the medium.

ELDER CARE

Rooted and potted hardy herbaceous plants, woody deciduous plants, and evergreens will live in pots for weeks to months to a year depending on their size and hardiness and your plans for their use. Indoor tender plants will be potted in small containers—just large enough to accommodate their roots. Place houseplants in bright light but out of direct sun for several days.

If plants wilt when they are removed from the sweatbox and potted, slip them into an open plastic bag or cover them with a cloche—a small portable transparent cover that can be used indoors or out. There are several homemade versions, such as a large, clear glass bowl propped open on a block of wood, or a cloche made out of a plastic soft-drink bottle. Remove the label from a one- or two-liter bottle, cut off the bottom, and place it over the pot or rest it on the medium surface. Removing the cap produces a chimney to help dissipate extra moisture and allow for a bit of air movement.

Cuttings of hardy plants that are potted in late spring can be placed in a protected shady spot for a few weeks. After four to six weeks, herbaceous plants can be planted in the garden. Woody plants may

Top: A burlap tent tempers the sunlight as transplants of tender perennials adjust in their first week in the garden.

Left: Tiny, portable "greenhouses," called "cloches," such as the blown-glass, bell-shaped cover, can be purchased for use indoors or outside, where the glass cloche will have to be propped open on sunny days. Similar equipment can be fashioned from materials at hand; for instance, a zipper-lock storage bag indoors, or a cut plastic carbonated beverage bottle. With caps removed, the bottles have a ready-made chimney for ventilation.

have to spend their first winter in a nursery area and if you plan to grow them there until they reach a good size, transplant them into the soil. Otherwise, sink the pots into the nursery-bed soil all the way up to the rim to keep the medium moist and cool.

Some nurseries, even in extremely cold climates, place young hardy herbaceous perennials in gallon containers close together on the ground and then cover the entire area with a

spun-bonded polyester insulation blanket.

Plants that were rooted late in the season will go to the cold frame (page 97). After all danger of frost has passed, the plants can be removed from the frame and planted in the garden or nursery bed; however, since they might still appreciate some shelter, drape row-cover fabric over hoop supports for the first few weeks.

AND SO, TO BED

Along with a compost area, a nursery bed can be one of the most useful places in any garden. There, small plants can be grown on to good size for later use. You can tuck the bed out of view behind some shrubs perhaps, or it can become a destination on your garden tour, where visitors can see and judge your latest acquisitions.

When you bring home new plants, you won't have to shoehorn them into little crannies in the garden. Instead, they can go into the nursery while you plan and make room in the garden. Some of these plants can be left in their containers for a year, buried to the rim. Other newcomers can be divided to make more plants before they are placed in the nursery.

The nursery bed is like a vegetable garden with paths between rows of carefully labeled plants. Site at least one bed in full sun. Low-growing plants should be set on the sunny side so they are not shaded by the taller ones. If you are planning only one nursery, create a shady area with a row cover or cloth. A burlap screen can be used to shield young broad-leaved evergreens from winter wind. The whole bed should be covered with a thick layer of mulch to retain soil moisture and limit weeds.

Where winters are severe, young plants should be covered with additional loose, lightweight mulch of whole oak leaves or evergreen boughs after the ground is frozen. Pine boughs, without tinsel, from discarded neighborhood Christmas trees are ideal. In early spring, pull back some of the mulch to check the plants. If more cold weather is expected, gently replace the mulch of evergreen branches.

Opposite: A row cover or similar screen or shield is a good temporary device to shelter a rooted cutting from direct sunlight, wind, and low temperatures as it adjusts to transplantation in an open spot. The cover can be made of special spun fiber, burlap, woven plastic, corrugated cardboard, or as in this case, a recycled polyester sheer curtain over wire hoops.

Above left: My first activity in the new garden was to make a nursery bed. Four years later, the sunny bed was empty, but splinter nurseries of baby plants are still tucked throughout the landscape.

7

Cuttings

When you say "cutting" to a gardener,

a piece of stem comes to mind—and

then, perhaps, a person or a place.

One neighbor passed a "slip" over

the fence to another, who rooted

it and gave a piece to a friend

across town.

I gave a rooted slip of a favorite houseplant to my friend Judith Bromley when she gave birth to her son, Daniel. He's out of college now, and I can just imagine how this begonia has proliferated over the years. I know there's a piece of *Begonia coccinea,* or "Dan's begonia," for Judith's new grandchild, Benjamin, born to daughter Emily.

One reason stem cuttings are so satisfying is that once rooted and potted, they instantly look like a plant. In fact, they are miniature versions of their parents in just about every way. The type of stem cutting made is described by the condition of its tissues at the moment it is taken. A cutting can be harvested at any time after its burst of fresh growth slows. Once this new growth becomes firm enough to remain turgid after cutting, the condition of hardness describes the type of cutting taken.

The quality of the growth also foretells the rate at which it will develop roots. The softer the tissue can be without wilting, the faster it will root. Tender herbaceous plants, such as the begonia, are easy to root from cuttings because their tissues never become completely hard. Cuttings of these plants can be taken at any time of year, but roots will form fastest with young material. The next easiest to root is tissue of hardy herbaceous plants taken in midspring, slips of which are quite similar to the tender cuttings.

Slips of the young growth of deciduous woody plants are even called "softwood" cuttings, since that describes the condition of their tissues when the production of new growth slows from mid- to late spring. When the shrub's new growth stops elongating and its bark toughens, and the bright color darkens or changes, it is considered "greenwood." Shortly thereafter, summer dormancy sets in when tissues ripen and harden.

Cuttings of herbaceous perennials taken in midsummer are "semi-ripe," and stems of woody plants taken at that time are called "semi-ripewood" or "semi-hardwood." Broad-leaved evergreens, from boxwood to holly, are rooted from semi-ripewood stems.

Needle-leaved evergreen cuttings remain pliable through their first year or longer. Although many books refer to these cuttings as "hardwood" because they are taken from mature tissue, there could be some confusion with the leafless, dormant twigs of deciduous plants. Since cuttings of evergreens such as the conifers are treated so differently from those taken of dormant deciduous wood, there should be a distinction made here. So we will call cuttings from needled evergreens "evergreen hardwood" and those of dormant deciduous woody plants "hardwood."

Opposite: Many of the plants in Bob Clark's fantastic garden east of San Francisco began as cuttings.

Clockwise from above: The source and condition of cuttings give them their names. The deciduous azalea is grown from softwood cuttings taken when the first flush of growth slows, is turgid but still supple. Perennial salvias are rooted from semi-ripe herbaceous cuttings in late summer. The evergreen hardwood cuttings of *Chamaecyparis lawsoniana* 'Oregon Blue' are best taken in their first autumn. Semi-ripe cuttings of the hardy succulent *Sedum telephium* ssp. *maximum* 'Atropurpureum' are best taken before flower buds appear.

The rhythm of nature again affects the choice of propagation technique, its progress, and ultimate success. With stem cuttings, the time of year and climate are also factors in how fast roots appear. In late spring, warm temperatures

Opposite: Timing is everything for stem cuttings such as the camellia's taken as semi-ripewood. Although a piece of one plant or another can be harvested every day of the year, the source and method change from month to month. Every plant has a moment when cuttings will root best.

Above: Exceptions prove the rule. The sumptuous blue hydrangeas **(left)** can be rooted from "softwood" taken in late spring, "semi-ripewood" harvested in midsummer, or "hardwood" made in winter. Observations of a potted coleus **(right)** suggest a "Goldilocks principle": stems can be too soft, too hard, or just right for rooting.

and increasing hours of daylight hasten root development when high humidity can be maintained around the cutting and there is sufficient moisture in the medium. Besides the condition of the tissues of the plants, the stage in the parent plant's life is also a factor. A plant that is directing energy into making flowers and fruit is considered mature; it will be more focused on sexual propagation than on making new cells for vegetative reproduction. Therefore mature stem cuttings will be more difficult to root. For example, a stem from an herbaceous perennial that is flowering will not be as easy to root as it

would have been earlier in spring, or as it might be if the plant produces a new soft side shoot after flowering.

Sometimes plants can be rejuvenated and encouraged to push lush top growth from which cuttings taken will be eager to root. Older shrubs can be pruned a year in advance to pro-

duce thick stems with soft growth in spring or strong hardwood for autumn harvest. Trees, the longest-lived plants of all, illustrate the maturity clause—they are the most difficult plants to root from cuttings. Trees grow readily from seed, but a unique variety that cannot be reproduced sexually *must* be propagated asexually. Stems taken from some young trees may root from greenwood under mist, but those of older trees usually have to be grafted onto young plants of the same species grown from seeds or cuttings. Understock from the younger plants impart some vigor to the older tree's scion.

HERBACEOUS STEMS

Most cuttings are made from sections of stems, and many of the general techniques apply to taking and making these cuttings from various sources. Herbaceous plants in the following text will serve as examples, and perlite will be the

rooting medium. When most gardeners hear the term *herbaceous* they think of the cold-hardy occupants of a perennial border. The soft growth of these hardy perennials is destroyed by the cold in winter but returns in spring from dormant structures, such as crowns at the soil surface or roots or tubers underground. Hardy

Opposite: Shrubby, tender herbaceous plants, such as coleus cousin *Tetradenia riparia*, are easy to root in spring from pliable stem cuttings.

Above right: Young stems can also be pried free at crown level—basal stem cuttings in spring produce the best results with hardy chrysanthemums, such as the "Korean"-type called 'Single Apricot'.

Below: Keep cuttings fresh during the harvest by plunging them into a bucket of water, or wrapping the cut ends in moist paper towels **(left)** and slipping them into a plastic bag **(right).** Keep the bag out of sunlight, and, if necessary, store the cuttings for up to a week in the refrigerator.

herbaceous perennials return every year and can have a life span of two years or even up to a hundred. A tree is a perennial, as is a shrub, but trees and shrubs have hard, permanent growth that is added to with every growing season. The hard permanent growth distinguishes these plants as *woody. Herbaceous* is a term used to describe any plant with soft tissues.

A tender perennial is also an herbaceous plant. Many houseplants and some garden plants considered annuals are tender perennials; for example, coleus and begonias—which are killed by frost in the autumn in cold climates, but live for years in their warm homelands. A true annual, on the other hand, is a plant that "fulfills its genetic destiny"—from seed to grave —in one growing season. A California poppy, for instance, sprouts, grows, flowers, sets fruit, and dies in a couple of months. Quick-to-mature annuals are not grown from cuttings. Tender perennials, or more precisely, non-cold-hardy herbaceous plants, are among the easiest of all to root. Some can even be rooted from a leaf.

The hardy herbaceous perennial candidates for stem cuttings are mostly dicotyledons characterized by bushy growth, vertical stems, and side shoots. Although young stems need little coaxing to produce roots, the most frequently used method for reproducing hardy herbaceous perennials is by dividing their rootstock as growth begins in early spring. Stem cuttings are useful later in the growing season, and whereas division might yield two or four new plants, dozens can be made from cuttings. When you hope to try a perennial seen in a friend's garden, he or she will be reluctant to dig up and part with half of the plant. Cuttings are easier to acquire, and they also travel well.

If the cuttings you gather cannot be processed immediately, wrap the cut ends in a moist paper towel, put the slips into a closed plastic bag, and store them in the refrigerator for up to a week. Even cuttings of tender plants such as coleus (*Solenostemon scutellarioides*) can be stored in the refrigerator as long as the temperature is above 40 degrees F (4.5 degrees C).

TAKING CUTTINGS

You can practice on a stem of a sacrificial cutting to learn what herbaceous tissue looks and feels like when it is perfect for fastest rooting. If it is just right, it will snap cleanly. Collect cuttings of herbaceous perennials in spring as the new growth is slowing down, and in the morning when the cells are full of water.

Most stem cuttings need to be from three to six nodes long (nodes are the places where leaves emerge from the stem), depending on the

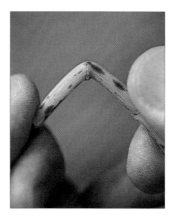

Above: To become accustomed to taking a stem tip cutting that is the right age, condition, and length on tender perennial shrubs such as coleus *(Solenostemon)*, try bending the stem. Too young, the stem rolls **(left)**; too old, it creases **(center)**; just right, the succulent stem makes a clean break with a "snap" **(right).**

Below: Plants such as the easy coleus yield several types and sizes of cuttings that will root at varying rates. One stem has been cut into vertical sections **(left)**; excess pieces of side growth are trimmed away.

source, but when you gather the cuttings, take a little extra length. Severed ends seal quickly, and the final cut will have to be made just before you set the cutting into the prepared medium. Pull off the leaves on the bottom third of the stem; if you meet with resistance or if you cause excessive damage when pulling them off, cut them instead at the base of the leaf petiole with a clean, sharp blade. If there is any sign of a flower bud, pinch it out.

Prepare the cuttings in an area that is near the

other or at alternate spots along the stem. With some plants, internodal cuttings—ones made between the nodes—can be taken. The stems of these plants often have adventitious buds—visible as tiny pale dots between the nodes—which are eager to grow into roots.

Plants that do not have adventitious buds along the stems have similar ones clustered at the leaf nodes. The surest cut for success with these, and with most cuttings, is one made just below the node—toward the earth end of the stem—at a distance equal to the thickness of the stem at that point. These nodal cuttings have good, firm bases and produce strong cuttings with thicker roots.

Because herbaceous plants are so eager to root from fresh material in spring, it may be possible to take a number of cuttings from a single stem that would not be possible at other times of the year. That is when the internodal cuttings might come into play. The cuttings could be as small as a section of stem and one node with a pair of opposite leaves; or, in the case of plants with leaves arranged alternately along the stem, a bit of stem and a single node and leaf. The surgery can be performed on a pane of glass using a sharp blade. To reduce the chance of fungal growth, dip the blade in alcohol and wipe it on a fresh paper towel between cuts. Slice cleanly so there are no ragged edges or bits of hanging tissue. (See page 125.)

These cuttings **(right)** were all taken from the plant pictured on page 118, including the sections cut between the leaf nodes (internodal) and those sliced just below the node (nodal).

sweatbox (see page 108), if possible. Keep the cuttings protected from sun and wind. They must remain moist during the process, especially the cut ends, so cover them with moist paper towels.

Just before sticking, make the final cut. Locate the nodes, which may be in pairs opposite each

STICKING CUTTINGS

When you are ready to place, or stick, the cuttings in the medium, use a dibble or a sharpened pencil to make a hole that is about the

same size as the stem and just deep enough to receive one or two leafless nodes. You may have to twirl the tool in order to drill the hole. In the case of internodal cuttings, make the hole as deep as the length of the stem up to the first node, which should rest on the surface of the medium. Place the stem in the hole. Push the particles of the rooting medium gently at first to fill in the hole and come up to the stem. Then press the medium firmly with your fingers to make it as dense as it was to begin with. Tamp the surface around the cutting's stem using a

chopstick or the blunt end of a ¼-inch wooden dowel so the particles are in close contact with the stem and firmly reset. Sometimes a stream of water from a small watering can could be used to help realign the medium.

Insert a label into the medium with each cutting or group of cuttings of the same kind. Include the date the cutting was made and, for multiples, the number of cuttings in the batch. Don't rely on your memory or experience to identify all the cuttings later. (In the case of deciduous woody plants, the leaves will eventually drop, and then they will be even harder to identify.)

Four-inch-long white plastic labels are the best for cuttings. Although they're not particularly attractive, they are inert—unlike wooden ones, which rot in the medium and can spread pathogens to living tissue. Plastic labels will ultimately break down in ultraviolet light after two to three years, however, and that's a concern, since the labels can follow the cuttings from rooting medium to pots to the garden. A graphite pencil is the best marker, and the writing can be erased or sanded off the labels for reuse. So-called permanent markers are waterproof but not sun-proof, and they fade.

PRY, PRY AGAIN

If the leaves of a cutting begin to wilt in the first days, mist them with water from a hand pump sprayer. If they revive the next day and stay turgid, the cutting is on its way. The amount of time that it takes a cutting to root varies, but most of the spring-stuck herbaceous ones will be

Above left: The idea for the front garden began in an attempt to have a colorful container garden without flowers that might get picked or coniferous evergreen shrubs that would be stolen. The color came from foliage, tiny flowers and sporadic ones on short stems (red *Passiflora coccinea*). The planting shown won an award for neighborhood "stoop" gardens.

Below: A cutting is placed in a hole that has been "drilled" with a pencil into the compressed medium (perlite). Firm the cutting by pushing the perlite back up to the stem for perfect contact **(left).** The medium can also be tamped back into place with the blunt end of a dowel **(center).** When you think a cutting is ready to be removed from the medium and potted up, check for roots. Plunge a flat stick, plant label, or table knife into the medium beside and beneath the cutting and pry it up and out **(right).** If too few roots have grown, lower the cutting and refirm the medium.

ready in two to four weeks. If the cutting starts to produce new growth, you can be fairly sure that roots are growing in the medium. That doesn't mean the cutting should be removed. A common bit of advice to test a cutting—tugging to feel resistance—seems misguided, since that could tear the roots. The only definitive way to tell is to examine the cuttings, or at least one of a group of the same variety, stuck at the same time.

To do this, pry a cutting up out of the medium with a sturdy plant label or a table knife. If the cutting has few roots or none, replace it and refirm the medium. If there is a good cluster of roots about 1 inch long, the cutting is ready to be potted up (see page 110). Do not let roots grow too much longer than an inch. Roots an inch long or just slightly longer easily make the transition to a potting medium and soon begin to push new green growth.

WOODY PLANT STEMS

Plants that do not have soft, herbaceous tissues but instead have ligneose, permanent growth, are known as woody plants. The assorted woody plants—hardy deciduous shrubs and trees, broad-leaved evergreens, conifers—have different characteristics and yield many kinds of cuttings. As usual, the condition of the tissues determines the treatment for the cuttings. For example, cuttings of deciduous shrubs can be taken at nearly any time of year, but every season has its own technique. In spring, a shrub's new growth is as pliable as that of herbaceous plants and stems harvested then are known as softwood cuttings. Later, greenwood and semi-ripewood cuttings are taken, and finally, when the plants are dormant and leafless, hardwood cuttings can be taken.

Softwood cuttings give quick and extremely satisfying results, often producing an independent plant in one season. Although the overseeing of softwood cuttings requires diligence, the demands on time are relatively short. A 6-inch-tall cutting of some wonderful shrub can become a 6-inch-tall shrub in as little as four weeks. These cuttings root quickly because the young tissue is still rapidly producing new cells. Nature does its part, too. In spring, when softwood is available, the air temperature is warm and the hours of daylight are long.

THE KINDEST CUTS

Several types of leafy herbaceous stem cuttings have been described. Some of this information bears repeating, and additional techniques are to be considered for softwood, greenwood, and semi-ripewood cuttings.

Create a space to work near the sweatbox, and assemble an impeccably clean cutting board, sharp knife or blades, and moist paper towels to place over the cut ends during preparation. Pinch out the growing tip of the cutting if there are signs of flower buds. Carefully cut away the leaves from the bottom one or two nodes. You want to prepare enough leafless area to be set into the medium. For cuttings with particularly large leaves, slice the remaining leaves in half with a single-edged razor blade to make more room in the sweatbox and to decrease the surface area of the leaves from which moisture is lost.

Finding the nodes of small plants, such as lavender, heath, or heather, is irrele-

vant. Strip leaves off the bottom third of the stem. (Tiny inch-long heath and heather cuttings could be easier to handle if rooted in sand.)

Single-node or leaf-bud cuttings can be taken of woody vines and ramblers. A piece of Boston ivy, for instance, could be cut to include a single leaf and a dormant leaf bud. Trim the cutting just above the leaf, taking care to not damage the dormant bud. Then make a second cut in the stem at least an inch below the node. A double-node cutting (which includes two leaves) is made the same way from a plant with opposite leaves, such as a clematis, a passionflower, or even an evergreen magnolia. Rooting hormone is a must for these cuttings (see page 128).

Some greenwood and semi-ripewood cuttings include a bit of the older, hardened growth. Picture a new side shoot having grown out from a dormant bud. The cutting can be taken so that a section of last year's growth is included and trimmed later. This is a great technique for rooting difficult candidates, such as Japanese maple cultivars.

Variations on these cuttings include the "heel" cutting. In this situation, a cutting is stripped off its parent and includes a bit of the main stem's hardened growth. The heel is then trimmed so as not to leave any thin or ragged tissue. Another modification, called a "mallet" cutting because of its shape, includes an entire section of the older plant. The new-wood cutting is taken by cutting a section of the older growth completely, about ¼ to ½ inch above and below the new shoot. The mallet not only makes a firm base for the cutting, it also pro-

Opposite: Woody cuttings exhibit various kinds of cuts **(left to right):** nodal, internodal, nodal (trimmed leaf), heel, and mallet. The heal and mallet cuttings take a piece of last year's growth along with the stem of this season's. The mallet makes a solid base and may be cut again if it is large or to make two cuttings of opposite stems. The split mallet opens more area to hormone treatment, water absorption, and callousing while supporting a slender cutting.

Above left: Softwood stems resemble herbaceous perennial cuttings in that their tissue is tender and pliable. The preparation and rooting methods are similar as well. A viburnum cutting stands in. Pinch out any flower buds. Remove the bottom leaves and leaf buds with a sharp, clean blade (hygiene is paramount). Trimming just below the node seals the stem—especially useful for plants with hollow stems. Recut the bottom to a distance below the node equal to the thickness of the stem. Large leaves may be sliced to reduce the area of transpiration.

Below: Judge when to take cuttings by the condition of the tissue, not the date. For example, the common lilac **(left)** will be ready for softwood cuttings two months before those of summer lilac or chaste tree *(Vitex agnus-castus)* **(right)** in the same climate.

 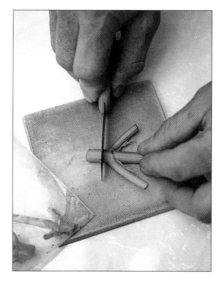 

vides a bit of nutrition, which benefits semi-ripewood cuttings left in a cold frame over winter. Sometimes the mallet is cut further, such as when two alternate cuttings are harvested from the same section of the plant. The segment of the older wood is split down its middle—horizontal to the new growth, which also exposes more tissue to produce a callus.

SOFTWOOD CUTTINGS

Cuttings can't be made by the calendar. Only observation and learning to recognize the condition of the tissues of a woody plant will tell you when it's time to harvest. Softwood is available when the growth of the fresh new stems has slowed. The succulent new tissues are bright in color—the chartreuse of "spring." The right moment to take softwood cuttings is when the leaves are turgid, but not hard or leathery.

On the day of the collection, begin early in the morning, when the plants are filled with moisture not yet lost to the sun and heat. Carry pruning shears and a bucket filled with water for the cuttings; if a bucket is not convenient, bring a plastic bag. Touch some of the stems. The tips should feel very soft, and farther down, the stems should be pliable but the tissue should not yield to a squeeze. At the lowest part of the softwood, where it sprouted from a bud, the growth should be firm and just starting to darken in color.

Make the cut just above this point where the

new growth began. Excess leafy growth can be pruned away, but final trimming is left for later! Plunge the cuttings into the bucket or place them in the bag (kept out of sunlight). They should be processed quickly, so limit the harvest to the quantity that can be made ready for the next steps. If the cuttings are taken from a location away from home, extra care must be given to keep them fresh. When you come to a sheltered spot, lay the cut ends on a moist paper towel, fold it over, and roll the cuttings up. Store the cuttings in closed plastic bags in the refrigerator, if necessary, for up to a week.

Although the use of rooting hormone with softwood is not critical, a quick dip in solution before the cuttings are set in the medium could benefit especially difficult kinds. When you trim the cut ends, experiment. Try a cutting without treatment, and one using a liquid hormone in a low concentration, following the manufacturer's application rates for softwood.

The procedure for sticking and caring for the woody cuttings is the same as for herbaceous stem cuttings (see pages 120–124). To determine if roots have grown, pry up one of the cuttings to check. If a cluster of 1-inch-long roots have formed, the cutting can be potted individually. Young hardy deciduous shrubs spend their first year in individual pots and, for protection in cold climates, their first winter in the cold frame. As winter approaches, check to see that the pots are moist. One thorough watering will probably last the winter with deciduous shrubs

Opposite: Stems should be gathered in the morning, when they are filled with water, such as this cutting of a gold-leaf *Sambucus canadensis.*

Above: A general trimming of side leaves can be done before cuttings are plunged into a plastic bag **(left).** When being prepared for "sticking," the base of the stem is retrimmed below the node **(center)** and the leaf stalks and shoots are cut away **(right).**

and trees. In the spring, potted shrubs can be transplanted to a nursery bed to grow larger for autumn installation in the garden, or if they have developed sufficiently, they can be planted in the garden immediately.

BETTER ROOTING THROUGH CHEMISTRY

Auxin is the natural hormone that triggers growth in plants. Synthetic auxins, introduced to the market in the 1930s, promote root development. A few preparations are available to home gardeners that contain chemicals such as IBA (indolebutyric acid) in alcohol or NAA (a-naphthaleneacetic acid) in talc. The dry hormone preparations of IBA usually contain fungicides and are therefore avoided by organic gardeners. Be sure to read and carefully follow directions on all containers.

The products available for home use may contain between 0.01 and 1 percent IBA. The liquids include directions for preparing diluted formulas with the proportion of active ingredients appropriate to the task. Most eligible cuttings get a quick dip in liquid IBA. The duration of exposure does seem to affect success, and results of recent research suggest that dipping only the tip of the cut tissue may yield a higher ratio of success for some plants than immersion of the bottom $\frac{1}{2}$ to 1 inch.

In situations where there is conflicting information, or when intuition counters an assumption, test both methods with half the cuttings treated one way and half the other way, labeling all the participants. As with all chemical preparations, however, it is best to err on the light side. Natural auxin not only stimulates growth, it signals a bud when *not* to grow.

GREENWOOD CUTTINGS

A greenwood cutting is simply one taken from a woody plant a bit later in the season than the softwood cuttings are harvested. It is a useful method if the softwood-cutting moment has been missed, and some plants root better with

tissue that has toughened weeks after the early-spring flush. Shrubs such as smokebush, tender salvias, and butterfly bush are examples of woody plants that can be propagated this way.

The greenwood stage of a woody plant will be

evident in the appearance of the stems. Stem tips will still be soft, but by now the bright spring color of the new leaves will have given way to the shrub's permanent leaf color. The lower part of the stem that developed in spring will have taken on a color closer to the previous year's growth or the color of the shrub's bark. The stems may appear more slender than the fleshy soft tissue at the tip. Just when in the season the change takes place is variable; the timing depends partially on weather but more on the individual genus, how early in the season the plant's leaves emerged, and how fast the plant develops.

Trim each cutting into the ligneous, or woody, area below a node. Rooting hormone is

Right: When spring stems and leaves harden and the surface begins to take on the color of the previous year's bark (shown on shrub dogwood), the time of softwood has passed. The next cuttings are of greenwood, and though they take longer to root than softwood they are less likely to fail from wilting. The cut ends will benefit from hormone treatment and may callus before roots appear.

important for these more mature cuttings. Treat them with hormone diluted to softwood strength—by dipping the cut ends in liquid—or touch the cut ends to powder. Greenwood cuttings can be set into the sweatbox or grown in a mist propagator (see pages 106 and 108). Although some plants produce roots, others will develop callous tissue first and then push roots through this gnarled mass. These cuttings may not be ready for potting until autumn, or later, and may have to be transferred to the cold frame and grown on in rooting medium.

SEMI-RIPEWOOD CUTTINGS

When the greenwood stage has passed, and no new growth is being made and all the leaves that grew in spring and summer have stopped elongating, the next type of tissue is presented: semi-ripewood, sometimes called semi-hardwood. Some easy-to-root deciduous shrubs such as *Weigela* and mock orange *(Philadelphus)* will root from semi-ripewood. Some conifers can be rooted from semi-ripewood, too, but the plants

most often used for semi-ripewood cuttings are broad-leaved evergreens.

Hardy broad-leaved evergreens—such as boxwood, English ivy, *Leucothoë, Nandina*—can be pruned in winter to force growth for cuttings to be taken the following late summer or autumn, when vigorous stems will be primed to initiate roots. The cuttings root well in a bright environment with high humidity. The temperature

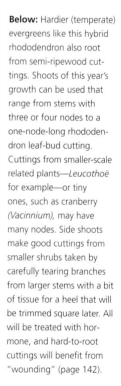

Above: Warm-temperate, broad-leaved evergreen *Aucuba japonica* (varieties 'Picturata' and 'Variegata' shown) is among the easier hardy broad-leaved evergreens to root from semi-ripewood and a good one for a first attempt. Mexican orange, cherry laurel, and evergreen Bullbay magnolia are other examples.

Below: Hardier (temperate) evergreens like this hybrid rhododendron also root from semi-ripewood cuttings. Shoots of this year's growth can be used that range from stems with three or four nodes to a one-node-long rhododendron leaf-bud cutting. Cuttings from smaller-scale related plants—*Leucothoë* for example—or tiny ones, such as cranberry *(Vacinnium),* may have many nodes. Side shoots make good cuttings from smaller shrubs taken by carefully tearing branches from larger stems with a bit of tissue for a heel that will be trimmed square later. All will be treated with hormone, and hard-to-root cuttings will benefit from "wounding" (page 142).

Thousands of cuttings could be taken from a boxwood (*Buxus sempervirens* 'Elegantissima'), but it only took one to produce this plant (1). A cutting is taken in autumn (2). The bottom leaves are stripped away, and the cutting, eight or more nodes long (3), is dipped in liquid or powdered hormone (if that is used). The cuttings are placed in a cool greenhouse, sweatbox, or similar dome-covered flat (4) placed in a cool, very bright window (mist and bottom heat will speed the process but are not necessary). Keeping the cover slightly ajar may help moderate humidity, and allow for some air movement, lessening the likelihood of disease (5). Pry cuttings out of the medium in spring to check for roots or as any of the plants show new top growth (6).

(1)

(2)

(3)

(4)

(5)

(6)

will depend on the method and the location. The procedure for taking these cuttings is similar to that for herbaceous and softwood cuttings, but the treatment is not.

The cuttings are taken when cold weather is on the way, so winter options for locations might have temperature ranges as follows: a cold frame—35 to 40 degrees F (2 to 4.5 degrees C); a cool sunny window in a sweatbox —55 to 60 degrees F (12.5 to 15.5 degrees C); or a greenhouse—60 to 70 degrees F (15.5 to 21 degrees C). Small cuttings of boxwood taken in late autumn rooted well in a domed flat on a chilly windowsill in the 55 to 60 degree F range. In a warm greenhouse, a misting system may be needed to provide moisture for the cuttings and cool their tissues.

For semi-ripewood, choose shoots of this year's growth. The size of the cutting—2 to 6 inches, or so—depends on the plant. For a large plant such as southern or bullbay magnolia (*Magnolia grandiflora*), take cuttings about three to five nodes long; for tiny broad-leaved evergreens such as boxwood *(Buxus)*, six to eight or more nodes long. Prune long cuttings from a stock plant to trim to the appropriate length later. For cuttings taken from side shoots off a larger branch, tear the stems carefully off the main branch with a little bit of tissue or heel. Although a loss of moisture seems unlikely, take along a plastic bag for the slips.

Prune off any tip growth that is still soft (usually paler in color), which may rot. Remove any flower buds, and strip the leaves off the bottom third of the cutting. For plants with large leaves, cut back each remaining leaf by a third to a half. This step reduces the leaf area from which moisture can be lost and allows room for more cuttings to be stuck in a smaller space. (Slicing leaves exposes open tissue, and if you are concerned about disease, which is especially possible in a mist unit, do not cut the individual leaves.)

Square off the heel cuttings by trimming any thin bark remaining from the older plant. Trim the smaller cuttings without heels just below the bottom node before treating them with rooting hormone or sticking them in the medium.

You can encourage difficult-to-root species, such as rhododendrons, by "wounding" the base. Make a few shallow knife cuts straight into

the bark about ½ to 1 inch long, depending on the size of the cutting, and dip the cutting in liquid rooting hormone.

Some of the cuttings in the indoor cool sweatbox will be rooted by mid- to late spring;

these cuttings generally make the most vigorous plants. Cuttings that have not rooted but still appear to be in good condition can be set back into the medium to be checked later. Discard any unrooted cuttings whose stems have turned black. The indoor-rooted cuttings can be potted up individually and hardened off in the cold frame or planted in a nursery bed where they should remain until the following spring. The bed should not be in sun all day, and for the first few weeks, use a row cover (a series of wire hoops stuck into the soil and covered with sheer curtains, or a commercial row-cover system). All of the cuttings should root within a year.

Above: If there are no roots, replace the cutting, but if roots have grown— 1 inch long or longer— prepare to pot up the plant (page 110). The finished product is on its way to becoming a low hedge or potted specimen.

Cuttings of frost-tender herbaceous plants, such as begonias, are easy to root—similar to the soft early-spring growth of hardy herbaceous perennials outdoors. Stems of begonia houseplants can be taken at any time of the year, but like their hardy counterparts, they root fastest from young soft stems. In their homelands, the plants may produce new tissue year-round. But transported to a temperate region and transplanted to a pot indoors, the tropical plant adjusts to the seasons. Even outdoors in a frost-free climate in the Northern Hemisphere—the coast of California, for example, or subtropical Florida—tender plants respond by slowing down in autumn and bounding back with a flush of new growth as daylight hours lengthen in late winter and spring.

Equatorial plants experience periods of dormancy and vigorous growth in their homelands caused by seasonal drought or rains. But without a cold season, different kinds of tissue are produced. A banana tree isn't a woody plant, it's herbaceous. The conventional categories of plants must be reviewed; after all, the spiny *Agave* is a broad-leaved evergreen.

When we think of a broad-leaved evergreen, we picture a woody rhododendron. Succulents and cacti aren't exactly soft like herbaceous plants or hard like woody ones. Their growth resembles that of greenwood cuttings taken from plants in the stage between soft and hard. But familiar Chinese hibiscus (*Hibiscus rosa-sinensis*) and ficus trees are quite like the hardy rhododendron with parts that are woody and parts that are green, and they too can be rooted from semi-ripewood (page 129).

Many tender monocotyledons have obvious adventitious buds, seen as pale dots, which will quickly develop into roots or shoots. In the tropical rain forests the buds develop into roots in the humid air. Tropical monocotyledons, such as *Dieffenbachia*, provide greenwood cuttings from stem-tip cuttings of new growth that is hardening. Sections of mature stem with a single leaf will root like the hardy broad-leaved evergreens. Small sections of mature stem, each with at least one dormant bud, can be set horizontally halfway deep in medium to produce roots and shoots.

Leafless stems of *Cordyline fruticosa*, the Ti plant, are sold as novelties at flower shows and in tourist shops at island resorts. If a 5- to 10-inch-long section is set vertically into a medium, one or two shoots will develop; if set horizontally, several dormant buds will grow new shoots.

The familiar window-box plants of the genus *Pelargonium*—better known as geraniums, the common name retained after the genus was split

from its cousin genus, the true, or hardy, *Geranium*—can grow into large shrubs in mild climates. The stems are succulent and the leaves felted. Cuttings of young growth can be taken after the stems are firm and can be four to six nodes long. Just be sure to pinch out any flower buds. Then *Pelargonium* cuttings should be allowed to sit out in the open air for 24 hours to let the wound "heal." Otherwise, the cut ends will rot when they are placed in moist medium. The seal keeps moisture in the stems and leaves, and disease organisms out.

The leaves of the geranium, however, are soft and will wilt, so place a plastic bag over the top of these cuttings, leaving just the cut end

Opposite: Tender, subtropical shrubs—to propagate for the greenhouse, window garden, annual display in the North, or outdoor garden in mild climates—have similar requirements for rooting as winter-hardy, temperate broad-leaved evergreens. The growth will be of semi-ripewood taken in late summer to early autumn. The stems are ones that began to grow in the spring, have stopped enlarging, but have not hardened completely or gone through a winter.

Right: Sections of the stems of monocots, such as the Ti plant, dracaena, sugarcane, and dumb cane (*Dieffenbachia,* pictured), can be rooted when laid horizontally on moist rooting medium. Not as hard as woody plants or as soft as herbaceous perennials, tropical evergreens do not fit easily into conventional categories, but most of these indoor plants will root if they are treated as greenwood cuttings.

exposed. After a day, the cuttings can be placed in medium in a sweatbox.

Other, more succulent plants, such as *Kalanchoe* and *Crassula* (jade plant), need to heal over at their wounds, but they resent any covering. Cuttings of these plants from dry climates should be allowed to heal for several days before they are placed in a medium. Stem cuttings of these desert plants should be inserted to a shal-

low depth in medium. Leaf cuttings can also be made of succulents. Succulent leaves and leafless cuttings of cacti should be set on the surface of a medium such as perlite. The cacti may have to be propped up to stand vertical. This is a case where coarse sand could be a good choice for the medium. With the possible exception of orchid cacti, these plants will not need the humidity of a covered box.

A cold frame is unnecessary in subtropical climates, of course, but newly rooted and potted plants, indoors and out, should be sheltered from full sun and wind for a week or two before being planted permanently in the subtropical garden or moved in their pots to a sunny window.

EVERGREEN HARDWOOD CUTTINGS

Cuttings of conifers are usually called "hardwood" because they are ideally taken between midautumn and midwinter, when their deciduous counterparts are leafless. However, cuttings can be made from summer up until the buds swell in spring. These cuttings never become completely dormant and have green leaves that may continue to photosynthesize, albeit at a slower rate. The conifer cuttings resemble those of semi-ripewood and must be given light and moisture while they are rooting, unlike deciduous hardwood cuttings, which are stored in cold and darkness. So here, the term *evergreen hardwood* cuttings will be used.

There are a few different types of cuttings that can be taken: short, longer, and heel cuttings. The decision on which type to take depends on the source, the climate in the area where the cutting is taken, and the depth of the rooting medium. Obviously, larger cuttings, ones that include two- to three-year-old growth,

Opposite: Some tender evergreens, such as tropical hibiscus, may be rooted from semi-ripe tissue, but cacti and frost-tender succulents should be propagated as greenwood cuttings.

Above left: Rather than digging up all tender plants or saving every potted geranium *(Pelargonium)* used outdoors in summer, reproduce a few for the following year. Save one potted specimen or take a cutting. Root tender salvias, plectranthus, or coleus, for example, pot up and pinch to become well-branched stock plants. In late winter, make up to a dozen cuttings from each plant. Pelargoniums are succulents, and like cacti and other succulents, they should be allowed to air-dry and callous **(above right)**. But unlike more juicy succulents with impermeable surfaces, like the flat orchid cactus sections **(below right)**, geraniums will wilt and may not recover to become successful cuttings. To handle the potential problem, keep sections out of sun and fit them loosely with a plastic bag that leaves the cuts exposed for 24 hours **(below left)**.

will result in larger plants. But these cuttings are probably too challenging for a first attempt.

The shorter cuttings are taken to include about ½ inch of the ripened growth, often clearly seen on the stems as a color change to brown. The length of the cuttings varies by species, and in moderate climates, such as the Pacific Northwest of the United States, where evergreen growth is fast, the cuttings can be nearly twice as long as those in colder or arid climates, where growth is not as vigorous.

Select tip growth for plants that are to grow vertically, and horizontal side shoots for spreading shrubs and ground covers. If you are rooting the cuttings under mist, remove upper growth that overlaps lower growth. Strip off the lowest growth from the colored stem area on conifers with flat leaf arrangements, or "scales," and just a few from needle-leaved cuttings. The stripping will wound the cutting and aid in rooting. For large cuttings of older wood, wounds must be cut into the stems.

Many species benefit from being taken with a heel. Strip the leaves from the bottom of the cuttings and trim the heel as for broad-leaved evergreens. If stripping would damage the cuttings too much, cut away the bottom growth and wound the cutting by slicing carefully into the stem. Heel cuttings will do better if rooting is to take place outdoors in frames.

The rooting period may be long, and different species within one genus take different lengths of time to root; indeed, individuals of the same species may require varying terms. Lift the cuttings in the following summer to check for roots, and place those that have insufficient ones back in the medium (see below). Conifers such as *Chamaecyparis* and *Thuja* that have scales are among the easier evergreens to root. Yew *(Taxus)* is a bit harder, and the more difficult subjects are the needled evergreen trees such as pines *(Pinus),* firs *(Abies),* hemlocks *(Tsuga),* and spruces *(Picea).*

Because many broad-leaved and needle-leaved evergreens grow in acidic soils in nature, most propagators use a mix of half peat moss (or similar humus material) and half granite grit, coarse sand, perlite, or Turface, instead of the more alkaline pure perlite. (Turface looks as if it were red perlite and is an aerated clay product—like gas barbecue "lava rock.") Use a higher percentage of drainage material for cuttings under mist.

Poke a hole in the medium for each cutting.

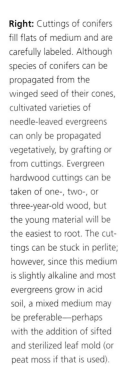

Right: Cuttings of conifers fill flats of medium and are carefully labeled. Although species of conifers can be propagated from the winged seed of their cones, cultivated varieties of needle-leaved evergreens can only be propagated vegetatively, by grafting or from cuttings. Evergreen hardwood cuttings can be taken of one-, two-, or three-year-old wood, but the young material will be the easiest to root. The cuttings can be stuck in perlite; however, since this medium is slightly alkaline and most evergreens grow in acid soil, a mixed medium may be preferable—perhaps with the addition of sifted and sterilized leaf mold (or peat moss if that is used).

Above: Needle-leaved evergreens are crucial to the landscape. Of course, they contribute to the winter garden, but even if they didn't their textures and forms are singular, as often is their color; for example, thread-leaved, yellow-tipped *Chamaecyparis obtusa* 'Crippsii' in front of *C. nootketensis* 'Pendula'.

Below, left to right: In early winter, a young branch of *Chamaecyparis pisifera* is taken that will yield several cuttings. The cuttings should have their lowest side growth stripped away. This action exposes the ripened brown material and wounds the cutting, which will promote the effectiveness of hormone, moisture absorption, and rooting. The cuttings are dipped in hormone (liquid or powder) specially prepared for evergreen hardwood cuttings. In most cases, vertical stems will produce plants that grow up. However, if the plant selected is intended to retain a prostrate habit, such as an evergreen ground cover, horizontal side shoots must be taken.

Insert the stems one or two nodes deep for large species, three or four for small ones. Reset the medium around the stems, but if humus-based, do not tamp it back in place. In cool temperatures, the rate of moisture loss from the medium will be slow. Check the medium occasionally, and sprinkle with some water if necessary. The medium should be just damp to the

high and be covered with a shade material until winter, creating an environment that might not be hospitable to other plants in the frame. Evergreen cuttings taken in autumn need bright light but not direct sun. For spring and autumn shading, a specially prepared greenhouse whitewash can be painted on the glass of the closed sash. The whitewash will become translucent

Left: Most propagators use mixes of peat moss, acidic leaf mold, granite grit, or Turface, a product used in soil for golf courses. The brick-colored product is like the clay version of perlite or micro lava rock.

Right: Rooting evergreen hardwood cuttings under mist with bottom heat is the fastest way to produce plants. Care should be taken to prevent overlapping leaves that can trap moisture and promote disease. Other environments and methods include a flat on a cool greenhouse bench or a sweatbox placed on the floor of a warm greenhouse. A sweatbox in the sun can be draped with an open-weave fabric, such as cheesecloth, before its outer cover of plastic film. The cloth diffuses light and absorbs condensing moisture, allowing it to evaporate into the internal atmosphere. Evergreen and semi-ripewood cuttings can also be rooted outdoors in flats of medium buried to their rims in the earth floor inside a cold frame.

touch on the surface. Remove any fallen leaves, using tongs or even tweezers if necessary. Rooting will be fastest with cuttings taken in late winter and set under mist with bottom heat. A sweatbox inside a greenhouse with bottom heat could come next. Then there are cold frames with a source for bottom heat. But as long as there is bright light and no direct exposure to icy weather, the cuttings will root.

EVERGREEN CUTTINGS OUTDOORS

There are a few options for rooting needle and broad-leaved evergreen cuttings in outdoor frames. Either prepare a medium in a deep flat to be buried up to its rim in the bottom of a cold frame and covered with a clear plastic tent, or excavate the soil in the frame and replace it with medium.

   If you are using a small cold frame or one divided into isolated compartments, try to devote the entire frame or a section to the evergreen cuttings. The outdoor cold frame must be closed tightly in autumn to keep the humidity

when wet, allowing more light in on rainy days. The wash eventually wears away, and if it is applied in spring, it will be gone by autumn. A shade cloth can be used instead; the cloth should be removed when the daylight hours are short and the angle of the sun is low.

   Insulate the cold frame in winter (see page 96), and also keep a minimum/maximum thermometer inside the frame. The interior temperature should not be allowed to rise above 60 degrees F (15.5 degrees C) during the day or dip below 32 degrees F (0 degrees C) at night.

   Cuttings in the frame must stay in place after they have rooted. Open the window sash or other hinged top of the cold frame slowly during the first sunny days in late winter and early spring to prevent warm air from building up. Leave the sash completely open throughout the summer, shading any plants in the open frame with a fabric cover. Water with a can and rose to keep the medium damp. The cuttings can stay in the uncovered frame until autumn, when very hardy ones can be transplanted to pots or a nursery bed. Less hardy types may be kept in the frame for spring planting.

NEARING FRAME

face exact, true north. It is claimed that if the frame veers by even a few degrees, it will not work. The frame is painted white to reflect light, and several should be placed in line, 6 feet apart, to reflect more light and to reduce wind exposure. A medium made of a non-alkaline material such as oak-leaf mold or peat moss (if you use that) and sand from a slightly acidic source (granite grit) or Turface is placed in the frame to a depth of about 12 inches. Five hundred to a thousand evergreen cuttings can fit within a single frame.

The Nearing frame fell out of use and the patent expired, but anyone who

In 1932, Guy G. Nearing, a rhododendron expert, patented a method for cold-propagating rhododendrons that also works for all hardy evergreens. The device is known as a Nearing frame. (The propagation of rhododendrons can be quite specialized; refer to works specifically written on this subject.)

The Nearing frame must be built to precise specifications. Elaborate tests were made to develop the device, which must

is interested in a potentially carefree way to propagate a high volume of evergreens—and especially evergreen rhododendrons—should investigate the frame's design further.

Counterclockwise from top left: Nearing frames in a row at Arrowhead Alpines in Fowlerville, Michigan. Rhododendron cuttings inside one of the frames in winter. The monogeneric shrub *Microbiota decussata*. *Microbiota* cuttings from the frame.

HARDWOOD CUTTINGS

As leaves change color and drift to the ground in midautumn, hardy woody plants cease their growth and become dormant, storing their

energy for the next season in their twigs, branches, trunks, and roots. For the propagator, it will soon be time to begin taking cuttings of dormant hardwood. These are fully mature sections of stems produced during the previous growing season on deciduous woody plants.

You may have taken and rooted hardwood cuttings already, perhaps as pussy willow stems brought indoors to force in late winter. If you set the stems into a vase of water, you probably noticed that roots grew quickly. Most willows will root in water, but they cannot survive in the low-oxygen and nutrient-poor aqueous medium indefinitely. The thick white roots will have to transform into the fine, threadlike ones that grow in soil. If transplanted from water to perlite or a similar medium before the brittle roots grow into a tangle, the plants might survive.

Few hardwood cuttings root

like willows, but the method may still be the easiest for rooting woody plants. The cuttings do not require much attention. The sources and materials are readily available. Cuttings can be transported easily as long as they are kept cold and moist. They can't wilt—they have no leaves. Their stems won't collapse: they are already firm—hard.

Hardwood cuttings are taken anytime after a plant's leaves have all dropped, late autumn through late winter, and prior to bud swelling and the emergence of leaves and new stems. While at rest, the basal, or ground, end of the stems seals and produces prodigious calluses. The callus, a bundle of undifferentiated cells, is necessary for root formation. Unbranched stems are cut into sections about five nodes long. Several pieces may be taken from a single branch or shoot if it is long enough; the terminal tip must be discarded. As with many cuttings, polarity has to be retained—roots will

Opposite: It is fun to see roots growing on willow stems in late winter, and reserved "willow water" may be used to moisten dry medium as a root stimulant. But roots left too long in this low-oxygen medium will rot or, if potted in time, have a hard time adjusting to mixes and garden soil.

Below: Hardwood cuttings are harvested after leaves fall—from autumn to late spring, depending on the source—and most need time in the cold. Willows are just about the last dormant cuttings to take. One such as *Salix integra* 'Hakuro Nishiki' (*S. i.* 'Alba Maculata'), with green, white, and shrimp pink variegated leaves, eagerly roots when cuttings are taken in late winter.

Above: Hardwood cuttings may be the "easiest" of all cuttings to make, as long as the propagator has patience, for some plants, unlike the willows, need to be harvested and chilled for five months. The period of cold is needed for cuttings that have to develop a callus before they will root. These twigs of *Hibiscus syriacus* (rose-of-Sharon) were stored in the refrigerator from November to March. The callus growth can be seen as a circle of whitish cells emanating from the cambium layer of the anterior cuts.

grow only on the earth end of the twig. Draw a small arrow on the wood with a permanent marker to indicate orientation. During harvesting and processing, the cuttings should not be allowed to dry; prepare them immediately after cutting, or store them rolled up in a barely damp

paper towel in a plastic bag in the refrigerator awaiting further preparation, but try to get to the job within a week.

Rooting hormone is essential for hardwood cuttings. Two popular preparations for amateur propagators are 0.5 percent IBA and 0.25 percent NAA dilution in water labeled for hardwood, and 0.08 percent IBA in powder (if used). Other materials needed include pruners, a

blade or knife that can be sterilized between cuts, string or twine, and wooden boxes or similar containers about 8 by 12 by 5 inches tall. The boxes that small fruits are shipped in can be used.

Most hardwood cuttings are trimmed with a straight cut across the bottom, but there are a few alternative configurations that can be made when tissue allows, and these can produce more surface area from which roots will sprout and, in some cases, limit disease. Two of these alternatives are the heel cutting and the mallet cutting. In some methods, the mallet is split horizontally to expose more tissue to hormone or moisture.

Some cuttings that are especially difficult to root can be encouraged to do so if the basal end of the stem is wounded, which exposes more cambium cells to hormone and for callusing. One method calls for whittling off a bit of bark, through the cambium layer, about ½ inch up the stem. In another technique, vertical incisions about ½ inch long are made in two to four places around the base of the stem, directly into it, but no bark is removed. A liquid hormone works best with this wound.

The propagation process for the hardwood cuttings can be illustrated with some easy shrubs that are nearly guaranteed to root and

Above: In early spring, the hibiscus cuttings were planted—callus end down—one-third of their heights in sandy soil **(left).** At the same time the species in the garden developed leaves, the cuttings did as well **(center).** But that is not a definite sign that roots have formed, just that they, too, have begun to grow underground. Leave the plants in place until you need them, perhaps until the following spring. In the future, a handsome rose-of-Sharon, such as 'Diana', will be your reward **(right).**

Below: The deutzia grew fast. These three samples, dug in August of their first year, had prodigious roots and lush top growth **(left).** The cuttings were planted for an informal screen by the road. The shrubs of the variety *Deutzia scabra* 'Codsall Pink' are shown flowering in their third spring **(right).**

produce satisfying early attempts: *Deutzia scabra* and *Hibiscus syriacus* (rose-of-Sharon). Hold a bunch of a dozen or so trimmed stems in your hand and tap gently, earth end down, on a clean surface to even the ends. Tie the bundles in two places. Treat the bottom of the bundle with hormone—the bunch can easily be dipped in one operation into liquid hormone diluted for hardwood cuttings. Don't allow the stems to sit in the liquid any longer than recommended in the product's instructions—usually around five seconds. Too much hormone will inhibit root formation. (Claims that only the cut surface should touch the hormone for efficacy cannot be proved by my anecdotal experiments: results between dipping just the tip and ½ to 1 inch were not evident.)

Pour sand in the bottom of the box or boxes, lay a few bundles on the sand, and pour more sand over them until they are covered. Moisten the sand with water until it is just damp. The ideal temperature for callus formation is around 40 degrees F (4.5 degrees C)—any colder, and the process might not continue; any warmer, and the buds on the cuttings might swell, thwarting callus formation. Although convenient, the refrigerator may not be the best location for boxes of sand (one box might be acceptable). The boxes can be placed in the cold frame, or you can dig a hole in well-drained soil in a cultivated part of the garden, making it deep enough so that the top of the box will be about 1 foot below the surface. Mark the spot with a stake and label for digging up later.

RESURRECTION

Unearth the boxes in early spring and examine the twig bundles. Nearly all the cuttings will have developed robust calluses on their basal ends. In fast-draining soil in a nursery area, insert the twigs upright to a depth equal to one-third to one-half the stems' height.

Roots and shoots will develop quite quickly. Shade the new foliage growth with cloth or rigid translucent plastic for the first few months. A vertical screen to shield the cuttings from the sun is better than a row cover, as the new growth may be prodigious and should not push against the cover. Most cuttings should stay in their rooting place at least until the first

third of their length in potting medium, about four to a quart container, and placed in good light in an unheated room or the window well in the basement. In late winter, bring the cuttings to a windowsill with direct sunlight, where they will begin to produce leaves, and then move them to the cold frame for hardening off close to the last date of expected frost.

Less hardy hardwood cuttings that have callused can also be put in a sweatbox in late winter. At the end of winter, after checking for calluses formed while the twigs were laid in a box of clean, moistened sand in the refrigerator, pot the cuttings in sterilized potting mix. Place the pots in the sweatbox in a very cool spot, perhaps on the floor of the mudroom or an

Left: Edible figs are excellent candidates for rooting from hardwood during their dormant season. Long stems can be harvested and cut into sections, including some one-year-old growth. However, these are not as hardy as some of the woody candidates and they could be destroyed by freezing.

autumn or the following spring. This is often welcome, since the cuttings don't have to be potted, moved to a cold frame, or hardened off. When ready, dig up the plants with a garden fork and the roots should separate easily. The new shrubs and trees can be planted where you need them or passed along to friends.

HARD BUT NOT HARDY

If you are propagating a plant from hardwood that is not hardy outdoors where you live, such as an edible fig perhaps, the cuttings must never be exposed to temperatures below 32 degrees F (0 degrees C). They can be bundled and placed in the refrigerator, or planted to a depth of one-

enclosed porch if the temperature there will not drop below 40 degrees F (4.5 degrees C). The cuttings should have plenty of sun. Gentle bottom heat supplied by an electric mat should cause roots to form quite quickly. Moderate the heat with a sheet of corrugated cardboard.

In a cool greenhouse, pots of calloused non-hardy twigs can be placed on the bench in sun. This method can be tried with some hardy plants as well. Place one of your boxes of bundled twigs in just-damp sand into a plastic bag and then into the refrigerator. Check the cuttings at the end of winter, and then move them into individual pots in the greenhouse. All of these plants will have to be hardened off before going outdoors.

Center: The cuttings are trimmed, wounded, and treated with hormone. Then they are potted in sterilized potting medium and set in a cold room by a window.

Right: In early spring, the buds will swell and break, producing fresh green leaves—the first sign of roots below.

TROUBLE IN PARADISE

Things can go wrong: Here are a few things that might affect the different types of stem cuttings.

- If no—or few—calluses form on hardwood cuttings, the cause may be improper use of hormones; or the cuttings may have been taken too early or too late in the season.
- If broad-leaved cuttings do not break bud in the spring when expected (because parents in the garden have already emerged from dormancy), the problem could be that the plants may not have experienced cool enough temperatures to have sufficiently ripened their buds before they were taken. It is too late for these cuttings. Note the problem and delay harvest of that variety next time.
- If the leaves of cuttings become pale in color, the cuttings, especially those under mist, may be suffering from too much water. Nutrients may be leaching out of the plants and can not be replaced by the nutrient-free medium. The medium may also be waterlogged. Check drainage holes to make sure they have not become clogged. Cut down on the duration of the misting, if not the frequency. (Concurrently, pale color in low humidity could be a sign of a red-spider-mite infestation.)
- Low humidity is more often a problem. Herbaceous and softwood cuttings will wilt. Open the flap on the sweatbox and spray the cuttings with a fine mist. If you are using perlite or a perlite-and-pumice mix, and a flat with adequate drainage holes, it is unlikely that you will overwater. If the temperature of the air in and around the box is too high, make sure that the sweatbox is not in too much sun, and consider shading it with translucent material.
- Mold and other surface fungi may appear. If leaves drop off any cuttings, remove them at once. Mold may be a sign of too much humidity and not enough air circulation. Crack the flap on the plastic cover to dry the atmosphere and medium.
- If there are holes in the leaves, check for pests. Plants love the nice atmosphere inside the sweatbox and cold frame, and insects do too. Signs might also include caterpillar droppings.
- Many plants in pots will enjoy a summer vacation in a sheltered spot outdoors. Rooted houseplants have to be brought back inside at least one month before the heating system goes on so they can adjust gradually to drier air and lower light levels—or else they'll drop up to 50 percent of their leaves. But try to leave critters outside. Earthworms may have entered the pots through the drainage holes. These are great for garden soil but the confined worms will wreck havoc to plant roots. Soak the pots in pails or bowls of water for a few hours about a week before you bring any inside. Worms hate moist soil and will leave the pots.

Right: Cuttings can have some of the same problems as seedlings, such as the mold at the base of this coleus cutting. Insects are rarely a problem. A caterpillar or slug may climb inside the sweatbox and have to be plucked off a cutting. Fungus gnats—tiny black insects that fly loops around cuttings—are usually a sign of too much moisture. Their larvae feed on decayed matter, not live tissue. Just back off on the watering. Fungal diseases pose the greatest threat, so keep everything as clean as possible. Do not reuse medium for rooting; recycle it for the next batch of sterilized potting medium. Avoid chemicals if possible. If cuttings in a flat become infected, cut your losses to keep contaminants at bay.

Opposite: Like seedlings, cuttings have to be coddled in the early days. Some will go to nursery beds; others will be placed under cover. Lucky plants in containers may find a comfortable summering place—probably none more beautiful than this fountain garden designed by Laura Fisher and Hitch Lyman.

8

Leaves

Another miracle of propagation would have to be leaf cuttings. The soft tissues in the leaves of certain herbaceous plants, generally tropical and subtropical species, can grow roots of their own, eventually becoming new plants. The leaves of certain broad-leaved evergreens also have this capacity, as do those of nearly all succulents that have leaves.

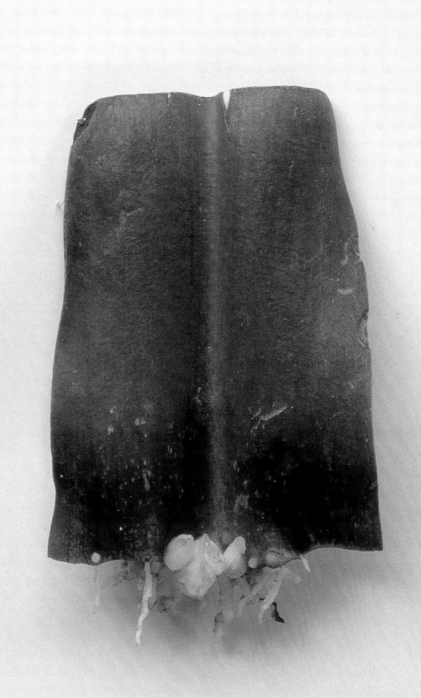

There are three types of these specialized cuttings. In two whole leaves or sections of leaves are used. In another, called a leaf-petiole cutting, a leaf along with a bit of its stem is used. With the first two, roots and tiny new shoots grow at the severed leaf veins, and eventually grow into entire plants. In leaf-petiole cuttings, roots form at the base of the cut end of the leaf stem and, later, so does a new plant.

Leaf cutting from hardy broad-leaved evergreens, such as rhododendron and camellia, is a specialized technique, and care for the cutting is exacting, but professionals needing to produce many plants of a rare variety may resort to this microsurgery. In the process, a section of stem is cut between the nodes to include two leaves and leaf buds (if the plant has opposite leaves) or one leaf and bud (if the leaves are alternately arranged). If the stem is sliced in half lengthwise, the cutting with opposite leaves can be cut into even smaller sections.

Usually the plants we choose to make leaf-petiole cuttings from are the softest, tender herbaceous perennials, such as African violets.

SLICE AND DICE

More unusual cuttings can be made from another member of the African violet, or gesneriad, family. The Cape primrose (*Streptocarpus* hybrids) leaf can be cut into pieces to root. Select a young leaf that is fully enlarged. Place the leaf upside down on a sheet of glass, and slice away the midrib of the leaf with a sharp blade—either a fresh single-edged razor blade or a sharp knife dipped in rubbing alcohol and blotted on a paper towel. (Be sure to sterilize the

blade before working on any plant.) The Cape primrose leaf can also be cut into 2-inch-long, crosscut sections. It is important to note the top or tip end of the leaf because the bottom or stem end must be set in the medium—cuttings set with the tip end in the medium will not root. Set the cut parts shallowly in the medium and lean cross-cut sections to expose their upper surface. The number of new plants that can be produced is staggering. One leaf may yield a hundred or more babies.

Once leaf cuttings have roots, whether visible on the surface of the medium or detected by prying a sample out of the medium, the young plants can be moved to individual pots. The microscopic *Streptocarpus* babies are harder to handle. Unless they are taken off the leaves early, some of the tiny plants may be lost. The small plants can be pulled free with a tweezers and reset in the medium to grow until large enough to transplant to pots. The young Cape primroses in the medium should be watered with a mild water-soluble plant food, perhaps a 10-10-10 at half strength.

Rex begonias (*Begonia rex*) can produce many offspring from one leaf. Turn the leaf upside down on a pane of glass, and make a short slice through each of the thick veins. Then place the leaf right side up on moist medium, and pin it in place with hairpins or U-shaped loops made of bent copper wire; new plants will emerge at the cuts.

Logee's Greenhouses in Danielson, Connecticut—a century-old establishment specializing in begonias and other indoor plants—employs

(1)   (2)   (3)

(4)   (5)   (6)

a method that produces several salable plants from single *Begonia rex* leaves by using leaf-wedge cuttings. The growers remove a leaf, turn it over, and slice it into wedges so that the pointed ends come from the bottom part and include a piece of a large vein. They dip the wedge point in a mild solution of a liquid hormone before placing it about 1 inch deep in their chosen medium—moist, coarse sand. In about six months, four to six new plants can be removed and potted.

An extreme variation on the Rex begonia leaf cutting calls for tiny squares cut out of leaves. The leaves are turned upside down on a pane of glass and cut into 1-inch squares. Edges with a cut vein are inserted into the medium to about a third of their height. Only one or two plants will grow from each square, but dozens of cuttings can be made from each leaf. The rooted cuttings are potted like those of African violets.

Left: There are two ways to make the cuts from the Cape primrose, beginning with a young but full-grown leaf. A pane of glass can be used for a supersmooth cutting surface (1). Place the leaf on the glass (or similar surface) and cut it horizontally into sections with a very sharp blade, remembering to keep track of the orientation (2). The other method begins with a turned-over leaf from which the central vein is removed (3). Next, make a groove in moistened, sterile rooting medium, insert the cut surfaces (retain polarity for the slices), and lean the cuttings so the undersides of the leaves face the medium (4). The cuttings need high humidity from a plastic dome over a flat or a sweatbox, and gentle heat supplied by an electric heat mat from below (5). Hundreds of baby plants will grow along the edge of the leaf-blade cutting (6).

Below: Leaf cuttings can be made from many gesneriads, such as this Cape primrose (*Streptocarpus* hybrid), as well as the African violet.

Opposite: One more type of Rex begonia cutting is the "leaf wedge." Sections are cut into fan shapes with large veins at the point that will be stuck in medium and from which hefty roots and plants will grow.

LITTLE ONES

A fun project to do with kids uses an African violet leaf-petiole cutting. The leaf stem will be rooted in a clear glass of water, and although we know that roots formed in water are different from those grown in rooting medium or potting soil, the adaptable African violet will survive. The "educational value" justifies the divergence from standard practice.

Take a piece of aluminum foil, trim it into a circle, and shape it over a small jar of water. Poke two or more holes in the foil, and insert a leaf petiole into all but one hole. Each leaf should rest on the rim of the jar, and the petiole should angle underwater. The remaining open hole is for adding water.

It will take about two years to produce a good-size blooming African violet—provided, of course, that the plant isn't raided for more cuttings. Two years is too long to hold a child's interest, but the best parts of the process are discovered early—weekly—along the way. If cuttings of fresh leaves are taken in late winter when the hours of daylight increase, and the indoor environment is warm, roots will start to grow quickly, to be followed, shortly, by tiny plants. When the roots are about 1 inch long, the plantlets should be transplanted to potting medium so that the crown of each new plant (the spot where the roots meet the top growth) is at surface level.

Jacqueline Triggs and Julia and Tracy Landauer (opposite) make African violet cuttings as follows: Select a plant and cut leaves (mind the blade). Fashion a circle of aluminum foil to cover a jar of water. Make holes in the foil so that inserted leaves will rest on the edge of the jar with their cut petioles in the water, and leave an extra hole for adding water when needed. The roots will grow quickly if a young, full-grown leaf is taken in late winter to midsummer. The exciting moment occurs when a miniature plant appears above the roots in the jar—time to transplant the baby to medium. Rest the old leaf on the edge of a pot and position the plantlet at soil level with roots below. The result is shown on page 151.

(1) (2) (3)

(4) (5) (6)

(7) (8) (9)

Slice and dice: Rex begonias are propagated from cuttings of various sizes. In every case, a cut vein will go into the medium and that is where roots and then new plants will grow. Assemble: A leaf ('Fire Flush'), razor blade, hairpins, pane of glass to cut on, and straightedge. For a whole-leaf cutting, turn the leaf over on the glass and make short incisions across the major veins (1). Place the leaf on rooting medium and push hairpins through the leaf, straddling the veins between the cuts (2). Roots will grow, then plants (3, 4). Another leaf ('Iron Cross') is readied for a checkerboard treatment (5). Press the leaf down with the straightedge and cut across the veins (6). Turn the straightedge 90 degrees and continue (7) until 1-inch squares are made (8). Set them with their largest veins in medium to grow roots and plantlets (9).

CUTTINGS OF MONOCOTS

The leaves we've been using for cuttings so far have been from dicotyledons with a branching network of veins. Now, monocotyledons, which have parallel leaf veins, are the subjects. Many rushes, such as papyrus (Cyperus), will supply leaf-petiole cuttings, and some lily family members provide material for making transverse sections of vertical leaves to root.

The lily family is among the largest in the plant kingdom: Asparagus spears are distant cousins of the onion bulbs; giant 10-foot-tall yucca plants are related to tiny snow drops. Plants you might consider trying include hardy hyacinth, tender *Lachenalia*, pineapple lily *(Eucomis)*, and snake plant *(Sansevieria)*.

But do not expect to pass on the lovely variegation of a particular snake plant *cultivar* through leaf cuttings. This anomaly is one exception to the rule that vegetative propagation always produces clones; the chimera that create the variegation are located in the meristem, or growing cells at the plant's growing point, which for *Sansevieria* is the underground stem or rhizome's terminal end. The leaf cutting makes a new rhizome, which is a reproduction of the original species without the variety's characteristics. A snake plant with variegation can only be started from a division of its rhizome (see page 194) that includes the or meristem growth.

There are many species of *Sansevieria*, however, and using leaf cuttings is a great way to make more of those. The procedure for taking leaf cuttings of monocots is similar to that for taking leaf sections of Cape primrose (see page 153). Polarity is essential; the cutting will not grow roots in the medium if set upside down (if the atmosphere is humid enough, roots will actually grow into the air if the cutting is stuck wrong side up). Use a waterproof felt-tipped pen and mark little arrows on the leaves.

Top, left to right: Leaves from monocots, such as ones in the lily family, including the snake plant *(Sansevieria trifasciata),* can be cut and rooted, but polarity must be retained, so arrows are drawn on cuttings with permanent marker. The leaves of many succulents will root at the petiole end: Jade plants *(Crassula argentea* cvs.) drop their fleshy leaves; roots grow, and developing plants absorb the moisture from the old leaves.

Above, left to right: A compound leaf of the aquatic umbrella palm *(Cyperus alternifolius)* roots in nature when a leaf stalk bends to touch the water, or when you cut off the whorl of leaves with a 1-inch-long stalk. Trim the leaf tips if they are frayed. Then the stalk is pushed into moist medium up to its leaves, which is where roots and shoots will grow, as can be seen with the nearby miniature papyrus *(Cyperus profiler)*.

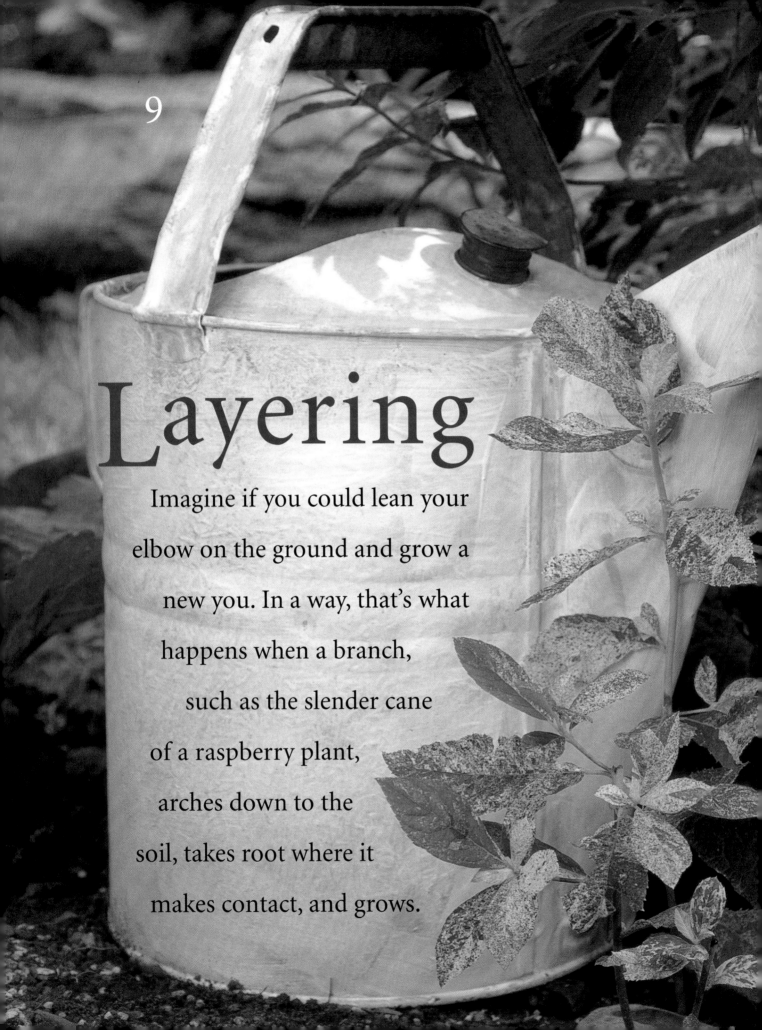

9

Layering

Imagine if you could lean your

elbow on the ground and grow a

new you. In a way, that's what

happens when a branch,

such as the slender cane

of a raspberry plant,

arches down to the

soil, takes root where it

makes contact, and grows.

The contact with moisture and soil stimulates the stem to sprout roots, and then a new stem and leaves. Eventually, a whole new self-sustaining plant develops that can be severed from its parent. Plants evolved this ability to spread and repair themselves to survive, and this tenacity can be exploited by the gardener.

Layering is probably the most elementary kind of vegetative propagation with stems. A layer isn't exactly a "cutting," because nothing is removed until the process is complete. To increase the odds for success, gardeners don't rely on the chance contact of branch to soil.

Instead, we intentionally bend a branch down, "damage" the stem tissue, and place moist medium around it. A callus may or may not form, but roots will be produced.

Many of the plants suitable for layering are shrubs that are difficult to root in other ways, such as camellia, winter hazel, daphne, rhododendron, and English holly. Small trees such as the hybrid London plane, shadblow, and even the rare dove or handkerchief tree can be started by layering. If you can convince someone who has a good candidate for layering to do so, a bargain may be struck.

SIMPLE LAYERING

Simple layering is easy. A stem of a shrub that is up to two years old may be supple enough to be arched to the ground. To keep the stem in place, cover it with a rock or pin it with a U-shaped

piece of wire or a landscape-cloth peg. To ensure success, damage the stem when you secure it. The simplest way to do that is to push on the peg until you feel a "crack." Add the rock to hold the peg in place, keep the spot moist and cool, and make it easy to find later.

Preceding pages: For layering, a branch of a variegated clethra was bent to the ground (to the right of the watering can) and pinned in place.

Opposite: Woody vines, such as *Wisteria floribunda* 'Longissima Alba', are easy to propagate by layering. This method is so successful because the "cutting" is not severed from the source of its support until after roots have formed.

Above right: One technique for vines, called serpentine layering, involves pinning every other node to the soil and yields several clematis plants to cut apart and transplant.

Left: In layering, a stem's adventitious buds produce roots. A philodendron, which produces aerial roots, is an excellent candidate for air layering.

Below: The northeastern U.S. native flowering raspberry *(Rubus odoratus)* can be tip-layered by burying the terminal growth.

(1)   (2)   (3)

(4)   (5)   (6)

(7)   (8)   (9)

Simple layering: To propagate a plant via simple layering, choose a branch of last year's growth in late spring (1), such as this gold-leafed ninebark (*Physocarpus opulifolius* 'Luteus'). Remove flower buds if present (2). Take a landscape-cloth peg or homemade wire pin (3) and press it into the ground with enough force to feel a "crack" (4). Cover the pinned spot with a bit of soil and/or a flat-bottom rock (5) to secure the layer and maintain moisture. Depending on the source and the stage of growth, roots may develop swiftly under the rock (6). Check by poking around the pinned stem for evidence, but replace the rock if roots are few (the layer can remain in place through the winter). If ample roots have formed, remove the layer with a generous root ball (7) and cut the stem free (8). Once transplanted and watered, the plant may produce new growth (9)—a sure sign of success.

Depending on the plant, a layer made in late spring could be ready by late summer. Lift the rock and scratch around the soil surface, and if there are roots, excavate to determine how extensive the root system is. Don't remove the peg too early; the springiness in the branch may lift it right out of the ground.

When it is sufficiently rooted, the offspring should be pruned away from the parent just before the layering point. Then dig up the root ball and surrounding soil, and move the plant.

Herbaceous plants are layered less frequently because stem cuttings work well, but you can still layer these plants in place. If enough roots haven't formed by autumn, leave the stem. In late winter, before shoots on the parent plant have emerged, remove the rock. Soon new growth will come up above the layer.

VARIATIONS ON
THE THEME

Although the simple "damage" described above is usually sufficient, one method to improve the chances for success with less-eager-to-root plants requires a more precise wound. With a sharp blade, make a ½-inch-long diagonal slice a third of the way through the stem where it will meet the ground. Practicing on some expendable twigs will help give you a feel of how this cut can be made without severing the stem or scoring it so deeply that it snaps off when it is bent to the ground. Bury the damaged area under about an inch of soil, and peg it in place before covering it with more soil or a rock, or both. This technique is more exact than the push-and-crunch method, but it will still yield one plant per branch.

Another variation is serpentine layering, frequently used to propagate vines. The method quickly produces several good-size plants. Select a long shoot of the previous year's growth that can be lowered to the ground from spring to the fall (fall-struck layers will have to winter over in place). The clematis will serve as an example here. There are several nodes along its stem. First, remove the leaves at every other node, and wound the stem at these places. Start below each leafless node and cut toward it to create the

diagonal slice. Peg each of the damaged nodes to the ground, where roots will form. If this layering is done in late spring, the results will be evident fairly quickly. New growth may appear above the pegged nodes or as a flush of new leaves at the exposed nodes. Be sure to check for roots before separating the plants. When the plants are cut apart just below each pegged node, there will be a rooted bottom end to plant and a leafy top.

Above: A wound will facilitate rooting. When serpentine-layering a clematis, use a sharp knife to cut into the node that is to be pinned or buried **(left)**. Cut off leaves at the damaged nodes and carefully lay the stem over cleared ground next to the parent plant. Gently pin the leafless nodes or cover with stones **(right)**.

Below: One garden's pearl is another one's peril. While the grass *Arondo donax* runs amok in Los Angeles, the variegated version in a garden where temperatures dip below 0 degrees F (-17.8 degrees C) just staggers by. On the other hand, the golden ghost bramble behind it hops. *Rubus cockburnianus* 'Aureus' travels as is typical of the genus, a habit that can be exploited to generate a new plant with the freshest golden growth and weed out its predecessor. The perpetual juveniles don't have a chance to become aggressive.

A simple procedure called "basketing," which is similar in technique to outdoor layering, can revitalize the kind of leggy indoor hanging plant that everyone seems to own. Plants such as philodendron, pothos *(Scindapsus),* and arrowhead vine *(Syngonium)* are good candidates for this practice. The first step is to repot the plant into a container 2 inches larger than the original one and press fresh medium firmly around the root ball in the new pot *(left).*

After potting, spread out the vines on a table, and pull them one by one into the pot, winding them around the old plant *(center)* and pegging them into the medium with hairpins that straddle the stems. Give a good, hard push at every third node or so *(right).* These vines have adventitious roots—little tan nubs at the leaf nodes that will eventually grow down into the medium. The plant will look better right away *(opposite),* and over the course of the next year, new shoots with leaves will sprout at the nodes to fill the container and make a lush plant several times the size of the original.

TIP LAYERING

Berry-bearing plants are often layered at the terminal ends of their canes to produce new plants. In late summer, the tip of the new growth is cut back by 3 to 4 inches and buried. The tip will branch and root, producing multiple shoots that can be cut off as individual plants. Nurseries usually place "stock plants" in rows for tip layering, but this method can be used with a trailing, biennially fruiting variety such as purple raspberry or boysenberry.

This isn't an activity to perform on the wild *Rubus alleghaniensis;* the wild blackberry species

can be too much of a good thing. However, fruiting varieties that are slow to reproduce or are in need of rejuvenation, as well as some of their ornamental cousins, could be candidates, such as the lanky hybrid *R.* 'Benenden' with 2- to 3-inch single rose-like flowers.

MOUNDING

A third method, called mounding, is useful for certain shrubs that have become too big for their location, which would be better served by younger, smaller plants. This technique allows many new plants to be made year after year. Louis Bauer used a quick version to produce willow whips for a steep slope to retain the soil while slower-growing shrubs took hold. The willows will be weeded out when their job is done.

The first step of the process was to cut the willow back to a stump, an operation known as "coppicing"—essentially, cutting back plants to create a little thicket —or "stooling," because the early result resembles a small stool. (This technique is used on willows to produce a multitude of new, straight stems for making baskets or weaving wattle fence.) In late winter, Louis dumped soil on the bottom of the willow shoots. But a more deliberate procedure could be undertaken with special shrubs, such as smokebush, currant, gooseberry, or quince. Cut these down to just a few inches above ground level. Growers sometimes use moist sawdust, but because this technique takes place in the open, a well-drained loamy soil can be used. When the new shoots are 3 to 6 inches tall, apply loose soil to cover half their height. Repeat the application when the shoots are about 10 inches tall, again halfway up the stems. By late summer, the shoots will be taller still, and additional material may be added to the mound. Mounding is horticultural snake charming, slowly coaxing roots to grow higher and higher through the season.

In autumn, scratch around the surface of the medium to check for roots. In mild climates, the shoots can then be removed if enough roots have formed to support the

Above: A basket willow was propagated to provide rooted stems as needed for a soil stabilization project. Various perennials, shrubs, small trees, and small fruits can be propagated by this method. The first step was to "stool" or "coppice" the adult by cutting or sawing the top growth down to a nub or stump (hence, "stool"). Louis Bauer dumps sandy soil over the stool (any well-drained medium can be used, even sawdust) **(left).** New roots will grow into the medium over time, depending on the species. The willow mounded in late winter had vigorous roots a month later **(right).**

Below: The reason for coppicing is not always utilitarian. Willows with colored bark at Wave Hill are cut back, or coppiced, to encourage young shoots with colorful bark for a brilliant winter display. It is likely that the term *coppicing* shares a derivation with *copse.* Dormant buds at the base of the woody plants grow into a thicket of straight shoots, suggesting a miniature forest.

cuttings. Otherwise, and in colder climates, wait until the following spring. Use a stream of water from the garden hose to wash the roots clean and find the point where the shoots attach to the stool. Cut the stems as low as possible beneath the sprouting point and place them in a nursery bed, or transplant into the garden if they are large enough to thrive without frequent water-

ing. One mound can produce dozens of plants. If that is not enough, you can remound the stool after removing the shoots and more plants will be produced for several seasons.

A LOFTY PURSUIT

Air layering is an ancient practice formerly called "Chinese layering." Perfect in simplicity and ingenuity, air layers are made in midair on plants such as *Dieffenbachia, Monstera,* ficus, citrus, *Mahonia,* rhododendrons, and even magnolias. For centuries, Chinese propagators used two halfpots, placing them on either side of a wound on a vertical branch. They tied the pots together so that the lower end of the branch poked through a hole at the bottom of the pot and the terminal growth stuck out of the top of the container. The pot was then filled with soil. When enough roots had grown to

support the branch, it was cut off the parent— pot and all—to become a new specimen. We now use modern materials, but the process has otherwise changed little.

The allure of air layering is its ease and success rate. The operation lets you observe the project and, as with all layering, produce a cutting without first removing it from the main plant. The classic patient to air-layer is a tall, leggy rubber plant *(Ficus elastica)* that has outgrown its corner of the indoor garden and needs to be rejuvenated as one or more shorter, fuller plants. A sharp tool such as a single-edged razor blade, a toothpick or matchstick, whole sphagnum moss, plastic film, and rubber bands will be needed. Rooting hormone is an optional ingredient that will accelerate results.

To impede the flow of moisture, carbohydrates, and natural hormones, and to initiate roots at the damaged area, there are two approaches you can use to make cuts into the stem. In the first, ring or girdle the stem by etching two shallow cuts through the bark, about ¾ of an inch apart, completely around the stem. Then make a shallow slit to connect the first two cuts, and peel away the bark. Scrape off the green phloem layer, just under the dry bark, and most of the cambium layer beneath that. Powdered rooting hormone or a liquid diluted to softwood-cutting strength may be applied to the cuts with a paintbrush.

The second method is demonstrated on page 168. Cover the wound with a wad of moss centered over the cut point in the stem. (On plants with stems thinner than the rubber plant's, make smaller wounds and consider placing a stake in the pot and tying the wad to it for support. You can also place a splint right up against the stem, straddling the wound, and tie it above and below the cut before mossing and dressing.)

After completely enclosing the stem, wrap a 6-inch-square piece of clear polyethylene

Left: Many plants can be layered in midair— a fact that did not escape the ancient Chinese. Their method of air layering, also called Chinese layering, employed two halfpots bound together and filled with medium. As with all layering procedures, the new plant is sustained while it develops roots and will ultimately be cut off to go it alone.

Right: The last remnant of your first apartment, a towering rubber tree (shown in Polaroid snapshots), is brought down to size by air layering. One stem is shown rooted and ready to be potted. After the air layers are removed, the old topless stems can be cut back further and will eventually sprout one or more shoots (or, nostalgia notwithstanding, the plants can be discarded).

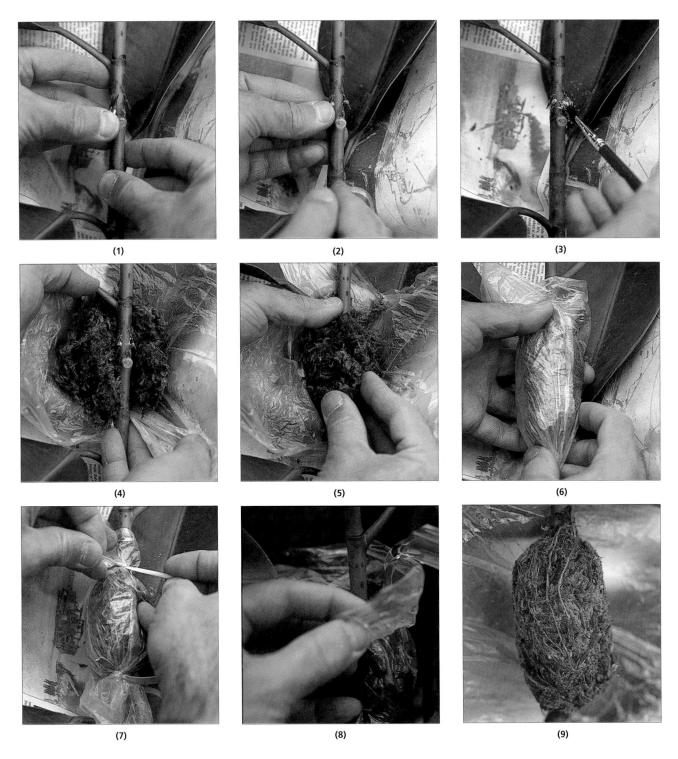

(1)   (2)   (3)

(4)   (5)   (6)

(7)   (8)   (9)

High hopes: Two slits are made by rocking a single-edged razor ½ inch upward and 3/16 inch into the stem (1). Pieces of toothpicks are inserted (2) to keep the wounds open. If hormone is used, either brush the wound with powder (3) or dip a few strands of sphagnum in a solution to pack into the cuts. Ready a square of plastic film. Take a handful of wet moss and squeeze out the water. Place the plastic in one hand with the wad of moss on top (4). Wrap the moss around the wound (5), followed by the plastic (6). Secure above and below with rubber bands (7). If water has to be added, the top band can be stretched open (8). When roots can be seen, the layer is ready (9). Cut below the wad for potting, moss and all.

layered in the autumn, the process will work, but take up to a year. On even older growth of semiwoody plants such as the ficus, rooting will be slow, and fewer roots may develop. Conversely, tall indoor plants that have softer growth, such as those in the genera *Dieffenbachia* (dumb cane) and *Aglaonema* (Chinese evergreen), might show roots on mature trunks in a month or less.

AL FRESCO

After you've tried air-layering tropical or subtropical plants indoors, air-layering outdoors could be the next challenge. Most air layers of woody plants are made in late autumn or spring on the low sections of vertical shoots, or "water sprouts," on shrubs or trees such as magnolias. Use either cutting method. Dust the wound with rooting hormone powder before covering it with a wad of whole sphagnum moss, or soak the moss in liquid hormone. Then wrap with plastic as with indoor air layers.

film (or plastic cut from a clear, heavyweight food-storage bag) around the moss, and secure it at the top and bottom with cut rubber bands tied in a knot. Although other materials such as aluminum foil are also effective, with clear plastic growing roots are visible and you can see if the moss is becoming lighter in color, which means it is too dry. Wire twist-ties are sometimes used to secure the plastic, but rubber bands work best because they can be stretched open at the top to pour a bit of warm water into the moss.

When roots are visible, remove the plastic and cut the rooted stem below the layer. Center the stem's roots and moss in a flowerpot just large enough for the new plant to stand up in when potting medium is added. The original plant will branch at the stub, and when it appears well proportioned again, set it out on the curb on a day when it won't be collected as trash—there's a gardener born every minute, so it will most likely find a nice new home.

As plants grow older, they become more difficult to air-layer, and it takes much longer. Ideally, woody plants with shoots that are one to two years old should be air-layered in the spring. Indoors, with a subtropical woody plant, roots will form in as little as three months. If a shoot of the previous season's growth is air-

During the following growing season, add water to the moss wad and pick off some leaves to reduce moisture stress through hot weather. The layer may have to be left attached to the parent for two growing seasons or longer.

Above: Tender tropicals with visible adventitious buds are easy to air-layer. The buds on a wrapped *Dieffenbachia* stem begin to grow into the moist moss at once. The new plant will be ready in about four weeks.

Below: For the refurbished *Ficus elastica,* short and stocky is a complimentary description befitting its new stature.

10

Grafting

Grafting is botanical fusion.
Few aspects of vegetative
propagation sound so
enigmatic or seem so
daunting. But grafts
readily occur on woody
plants in nature when a
branch or limb presses firmly
against another.

The branches squeeze tighter as they grow, until the cambium layers of both are exposed at the contact point. If the branches remain in place, the cells will knit together and may merge into a single limb. The horticultural process starts with a section of stem, called a scion, that is surgically attached to a growing plant, called the understock or rootstock.

Professionals graft plants mainly because it is the fastest way to get the largest number of salable-size products from the least amount of tissue of the chosen variety. There are other reasons to graft. The understock may impart some disease resistance or winter hardiness to the scion-topped tree, and control its size as well. Nearly every apple you eat comes from a grafted tree. New rose introductions at the garden center are grafted onto readily available rose rootstock. Most hybrid tea roses are propagated by a technique called "budding," in which a few dormant buds of one variety are slipped under the bark of a seedling or cutting propagated to be the understock.

Why would a home gardener want to do such a thing? A beloved old tree—injured or threatened by development—could be grafted and perpetuated for future generations. If a tree is

damaged at trunk level—by foraging animals, for example—it may be repaired with "bridge grafts." A frail sport can be grafted onto a vigorous understock. A cascading plant could be grafted onto a straight trunk to produce a weeping tree. Some varieties cannot be propagated by any other means.

The techniques recommended here utilize hardy woody plants during their dormant season and are illustrated with plants for novice grafters to try.

ALL IN ONE

Gladys Bozenhard, an enthusiastic amateur gardener, became intrigued by the idea of grafting when she heard that several apple varieties could be made to grow on one tree. I thought this was a frivolous novelty, but there, on three small apple trees, Gladys had over a dozen varieties. Each tree had four or five kinds growing on separate branches, which ripened through the entire season, from late summer to late fall. When they flower, the varieties can cross-pollinate for heavier fruit set. Sweet dessert types, tart baking kinds, antique varieties, and experimental new ones grow in a 10- by 20-foot area of the garden.

Grafting is one of the most advanced forms of propagation, but it is not out of the reach of the amateur. Learning to graft is a bit like learning to drive a car—it must be witnessed firsthand and practiced under the eyes of a teacher. But once learned, grafting skills are never forgotten.

Gladys enrolled in a short course in grafting and discovered she had the knack. She would be surprised to hear that a 50 percent success rate is desirable, since her plants nearly always prosper.

The most startling revelation from these ama-

Preceding pages: All apples—apple tree varieties, that is—are grafted.

Opposite: The coloring stems of peach trees and the earliest sign of swelling buds signal the time for grafting fruit trees.

Above: Nearly all perennial fruits are hybrids that can only be propagated asexually. (Consider the seedless orange.) One apple tree grafted with several varieties grows in Gladys Bozenhart's garden.

Below: Tree peony cultivars **(left)** are grafted. Roses can be easily shipped and grown from single grafted buds; in a famous example, stems of *Rosa* 'Madame A. Meilland' **(right)** were sent to the grower Conard-Pyle aboard the last airplane from Paris to the United States as World War II began. Buds were distributed, and on the day Berlin fell to the Allies the superb hybrid tea rose was introduced with a new name: 'Peace'.

teur grafters like Gladys, however, is that they contradicted the accepted practice of grafting when trees and shrubs are completely dormant —in midwinter. Most of these gardeners undertake their projects in late winter to early spring —just before flower buds swell on the plants they are using. These people seemed intuitively to realize that in a few weeks, the plants would begin their most active growth of the year, when they are most determined to persevere.

Opposite: *Magnolia* 'Elizabeth' was bred at the Brooklyn Botanic Garden from *M. acumenata* and *M. denudata*. The chance seedling would be difficult to duplicate but easy to reproduce via grafting.

Above: Among Gladys Bozenhard's essential equipment is a clipboard for recording dates of procedures, variety of scion, and understock.

Below: Rudimentary apical wedge grafting calls for inserting a V-shaped scion into a corresponding cut in an understock of the same diameter **(left).** The inverted saddle graft involves blunting the cut point of the understock and rounding the wedge cut of the scion **(right).** The cambium must line up exactly.

MAKE THE CUT

The key to successful grafting is bringing the cambium layer from one plant into perfect contact with the cambium layer of another. The parts must be compatible—for example, from two species in the same genus. Stem sections must retain polarity—up stays up.

Many of the same tools used for stem cuttings can be adapted to grafting—pruning shears, alcohol for sterilizing, rubber bands, and paper towels. A few others may be called for, such as wax to seal the top of the scion. A sharp knife is indispensable, and professional grafters have special knives for each procedure. For beginners, a snap-blade utility knife is fine, and heavy leather gloves should be worn for protection. A pencil and a notebook are necessary for keeping careful records on the plant sources and the dates of the procedures.

KINDS OF CUTS

To facilitate joining scion and understock, different kinds of cuts have been developed for various plants and stages of growth. The cuts expose the greatest amount of tissue whenever possible and often provide physical stability.

Two equal-size twigs *could* be cut straight across to expose the cambium, but it would be difficult to join these pieces. The grafters' version of this rudimentary cut is a diagonal slice on the top of the understock and on to the bottom of the scion. More area is provided for stability, and more cambium is exposed. When these elements are spliced and bound, a "whip graft" is formed.

In a "saddle graft," the scion is cut into a V shape, and the understock is cut into a corresponding shape. The scion, which will become the leader, is lowered onto the understock, which will become the trunk and roots.

Above: A demonstration of rubber band tying.

Above right: Cleft grafting is recorded in the propagator's sketchbook: wedge-cut scions are inserted, cambium to cambium, into a vertical cut in a sawed stem, and held in place with grafting wax.

Below: With thin-barked Japanese maples, a variation of a T-bud and a splice graft is made by inserting a twig with a diagonal sliver cut from the side opposite a bud into a T-shaped incision through the bark **(left).** The graft is carefully positioned **(center)** and secured with a rubber band **(right).**

A "wedge graft" is similarly straightforward. The scion is cut into a pointed wedge. The understock is cut straight across, and then a perpendicular slit is made. The pointed scion is inserted in the slit and the two pieces are banded together. In a "cleft graft," an understock of a greater diameter than the scion is sawed straight across, and then V-shaped notches are cut into it through the sawed top. The scion or multiple scions are cut to precisely fit into the slotted openings of the understock so that the edges of their left or right side—where their cambium is exposed—come in exact contact with the cambium layer of the understock. Melted grafting wax is painted over the cut areas to seal them and hold the parts in place.

In "side veneer grafts," often used for evergreens and Japanese maples, a long, shallow cut is made in the bark of the understock, and a smaller scion is fashioned with an opposing cut.

In "approach grafting," two plants growing in pots are placed side by side. One gets a V-shaped groove and the other is carved with a corresponding ridge. The two plants, still in their pots, are then bound.

"T-budding" is demonstrated on page 177. "Rind grafting" is similar. A T-shaped slit is made on the bark of the understock. The bark is loosened with the back of the blade. The bottom of the scion is trimmed like a reed and slipped beneath the bark. Like all grafts, the cuts must be kept moist and sealed. After the scion sprouts, the top of the stock is cut away.

Experienced gardeners graft herbaceous plants, and in the laboratory, micrografts are performed on just-sprouted seeds. By now, you are probably recalling that most grafting operations have to be demonstrated, witnessed, and then practiced. But every grafter begins by taking his or her first cut.

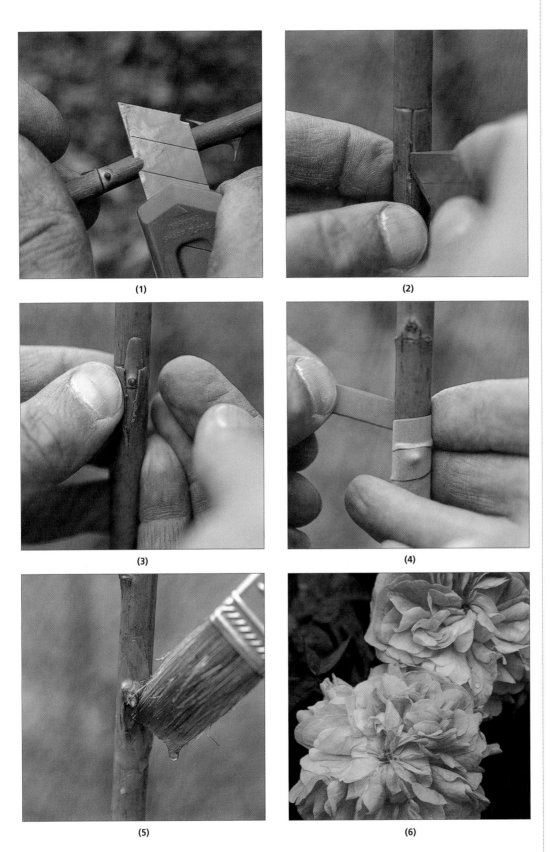

(1)

(2)

(3)

(4)

(5)

(6)

T-budding is a method most often used for ornamental woody plants—especially roses (demonstrated here). Begin by cutting a scion stick, snap off the thorns, and with the bud facing upward make a shallow cut that goes in, passes behind the bud, and comes out again (1). Then peel the wood from behind the bud and bark and discard it. The understock gets a T-shaped cut and the bark is slipped free using the back of the knife blade (2). The bud is eased beneath the flaps of bark (3) and cut flush at the top into a shield shape that fits snugly. The cut and bud are entirely covered by a tied rubber band (4), which will disintegrate by the time the accepted bud begins growth—the following spring if the graft is made in summer. The graft can also be covered with wax (5). Prior to the mass popularization of hybrid tea roses, cultivars such as 'Marie Louise' (1813) (6) were grown from greenwood cuttings, but demand and the fact that many tea roses have feeble root systems made T-budding ubiquitous—until recently. Concerns about hardiness and disease are bringing back the demand for "own-root" roses.

CURIOSITY
CAUSED THE CUT

Gladys Bozenhart's early grafting efforts were made in the field—with her own apple trees. Her technique was performed in midspring with dormant twigs of one variety, grafted onto branches of established trees. From her start as a curious gardener, she has gone on to guide a volunteer effort to build the antique-apple collection at Tower Hill Botanic Garden in Boylston, Massachusetts. Now she is helping Sturbridge Village Historical

Gardens create a collection starting with trees that are bench grafted—the indoor version that uses nursery-supplied rooted dormant understock, and is demonstrated below.

Gladys uses pruning shears, a sharp knife, alcohol for sterilizing the knife between cuts (1), rubber bands, paper towels, and a dab of wax to seal the top of the scion after each graft. She uses the version of the splice or whip graft called a "whip and tongue."

(1)   (2)   (3)

(4)   (5)   (6)

First, Gladys holds the scion and understock side by side to determine the exact point where they are the same thickness (2). The pieces are trimmed 2 inches above the spot on the understock and 2 inches below the spot on the scion (3, 4). The first cut for grafting is a diagonal slice 1½ inches long made to the bottom of the scion (5). This is followed by a diagonal cut of the same size at the top of the understock (6). Gladys checks to see that the cuts match (7), and she retrims only if absolutely necessary, because whittling might distort the sliced sections. A second cut is made into each piece, a third of the way down the scion and a third of the way up the understock (8, 9). The cut should go straight into the stem and penetrate about ¾ inch. The scion and the understock should fit so well that they will hold themselves together once joined (10). The grafted area is secured firmly and kept from drying out using a rubber band to completely cover the area of the joined material (11). The roots of the labeled graft are kept moist in a plastic bag (12) until potting, which should happen soon. The potted plant can be summered in a protected spot outdoors and then planted in a nursery bed or its ultimate spot in the garden.

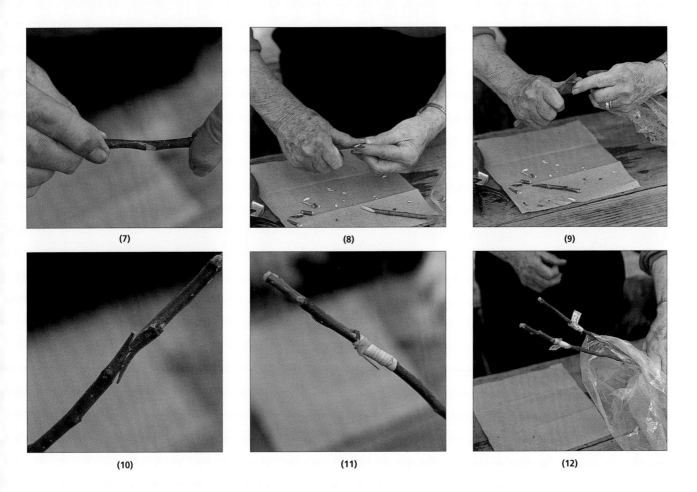

(7)

(8)

(9)

(10)

(11)

(12)

GRAFT AFTERCARE

After connecting cambium to cambium, the key to a successful graft is to keep the plants firmly attached and full of moisture while the cut areas are fusing. Grafting was once popular, but the cut rubber band has become the preferred method. In Great Britain, patches of pure crepe rubber are used to cover smaller grafts, such as those involving buds. The rubber disintegrates before it can squeeze the growing wood, and the covered buds can grow right through the brittle rubber. Some grafters tape a bit of plastic film over the banded area of the graft for a week or two to retain moisture.

Professional growers pot up their grafted plants and place them in shaded greenhouses or plastic-film-covered Quonset-hut-like hoop houses with temperature and humidity controls. In early autumn, the plants can be placed back into the greenhouse, planted in a nursery bed, or wintered over in a cool place such as a mudroom or unheated garage.

Most home propagators, however, improvise to provide a suitable environment for the new grafts—Dick Figlar keeps his newly grafted magnolia trees inside by a sliding glass door for a few weeks until they can go outside to a sheltered spot, while Gladys Bozenhard pots her grafted bare-root saplings in gallon nursery pots and sets them on a chair next to the kitchen table to keep an eye on her projects for a couple of days. She then moves the saplings to the screened porch for a short time before setting the pots in a sheltered garden spot.

The newly grafted plants in pots will sprout leaves and soon heal their joined sections. The dormant may not grow until the following year. Then, the scion should be encouraged to become the only top growth of the plant. If a bud graft was made for a tree variety, any growth from the original understock should be cut off just above the graft so that the bud can grow and become the new leader. Any buds that develop below the graft on the understock should be rubbed off so that the former variety will not overtake the new plant.

You may be intimidated or stimulated by these procedures. Either way, attempt a simple graft. One thing is certain: Rare is the gardener who successfully grafts a plant just once.

Right: To graft magnolias, Dick Figlar uses the chip-bud method in mid-spring, a week before buds swell. His favorite tool is an injector razor blade. He inserts the blade above the bud and cuts beneath and toward it (1). A second angled cut is made below the bud continuing away from it (2). The crosscut frees the chip and bud (3). The chip bud will be inserted into a corresponding cut made to the understock.

Opposite: The chip bud graft is wrapped with a rubber band (1). Then Dick covers it with clear plastic to keep the humidity high for about a week (2). The cells fuse and the graft takes (far right). The graft is well established the following spring (3). The top of the understock seedling will be cut off, and the scion shoot will become the new leader.

(1)

(2)

(3)

(1)

(2)

(3)

11

Division

Sooner or later, everything comes down to the ground: the place where the shoots meet the roots. This spot is known as the crown, and there are many ways to make more plants at this part of a plant. Division, which mostly involves cutting through the crown and down through the roots, is the most frequently used method for reproducing perennials in the garden.

Certain shrubs can be divided through their crowns, as can multistemmed houseplants when they have grown too large for their pots, but for the most part, crown division remains the province of hardy herbaceous perennials.

Many herbaceous flowering perennials *must* be divided from time to time. This rejuvenation results in healthier plants, more foliage, and, of course, many more flowers. And one thrill with division comes when a perennial brought home from the garden center in spring is large enough to divide right then and there—before it is even planted in the garden. Depending upon the species, these divisions may grow to be as large

as the original plant by season's end: more plants for free. Soon, dividing perennials in your garden becomes an annual task, and as one clump becomes a cluster, a drift, or a river of color, you'll find division to be about the most satisfying rite of spring.

There are ways besides division to propagate plants at the crown. Many plants increase in size by continuously forming new plantlets around the circumference of their crowns. These plants produce concentric circles of plantlets each season, and these plantlets can be removed and immediately transplanted individually to grow to maturity.

If the growth around the crown does not form individual plantlets, stem cuttings may be taken instead. Small stems with leaves can be stripped off the outer edge of the crown. These basal cuttings will be placed in the sweatbox until roots grow.

AN INVITATION TO THE BALL

The colloquial term for a plant's mass of roots is *root ball*. When you unpot a plant, the roots and medium often retain the shape of the container. The spherical term derives from when a plant is unearthed from the garden for transplantation, or when a tree or shrub is dug. The conglomeration of the woody plant's roots and soil is often wrapped up in burlap and tied. That's called "balled and burlapped," or "B&B."

Herbaceous perennials with multiple stems arising from the crown and a fibrous root system

composed of wiry thin roots can be cut from top to bottom in line with the stem growth, so that pie-wedge sections are removed and replanted. This is done in very early to mid-spring, when new growth is just showing.

Perennials that bloom in early spring can be divided when they start to enter their dormant period, which in the case of spring ephemerals could be summer to autumn, when the active growing period has ended.

The tools for division are pruning sheets, a knife, a small-toothed saw, a spade, a trowel, and a watering can. If the soil is dry, water the day before division. Some sources recommend plunging a sharp spade into the ground through the crown to divide an established perennial. There are also suggestions for using two garden forks, back to back. Both of these methods crush and tear the perennial, causing quite a bit

Preceding pages: A hosta crown ready for division.

Opposite: The most frequent act of propagation in a garden dependent on herbaceous perennials is division. In spring, plants are renewed by having their crowns cut into sections. The dead centers are discarded and fresh divisions are either replanted or transplanted.

Above: Hardy herbaceous perennials, such as this astilbe **(left)**, are most often propagated by division in early spring by plunging a spade straight through the crown's crowded growth at ground level, lifting and transplanting sections. Offsets that appear at crown level, such as on this hen-and-chicks plant **(right)**, can be pulled free for more plants.

Every third or fourth year, most fibrous-rooted perennials should be divided in earliest spring when new growth is just beginning; but it may not be too late a month later for many plants, such as *Kalimeris mongolica,* as long as flower buds have not formed and the new growth is cut back by at least half (1). The root ball is completely lifted (2). Then it is cut into sections by plunging a serrated knife through the crown (3). As they are cut, each segment is pulled apart and realigned for cutting again (4). Many pieces, even very small ones, can be made, but ones that include a bit of the thick core will recover faster (5). Cutting back the plants delayed flowering and produced more compact growth from these vigorous *Kalimeris*—made from two root balls (6).

(1)

(2)

(3)

(4)

(5)

(6)

of damage. If a perennial is dug out of the ground, there will be less damage and many more divisions can be made. Since it is also a good idea to recondition the soil before setting a section of a perennial back in its original location, lifting the entire plant provides an opportunity to do so.

In late winter to early spring, spring-blooming fibrous-rooted perennials that have not begun their growing season will have little pink buds at the top of the crown. Later, plants that

bloom in summer and may have pushed new growth can also be divided; however, cut the growth on these back by half, so that the crown is clearly in view. Reducing the top growth will also compensate for any loss of roots during division. Consider the arrangement of the eyes on the crown or spread the emerged growth with your hands to find spots where a knife can be threaded between the stems. Use the knife to cut the clump in half and then continue to cut the sections. If you want to see flowers, or want the plants to reestablish quickly, limit the number of divisions so that each new clump includes five or more eyes or stems. Plant the divisions before their roots can dry; if that is not possible because there are too many, wrap or roll them up in moist paper towels or burlap and keep them out of direct sun.

When you are ready to replant the divisions, dig a new hole for each one. Hold each plant in one hand as you fill in with soil around the roots, setting the crown just a bit higher than it

was when originally growing. Push in more soil, and when it is all around the roots, push it hard. Make sure that the crown is now even with the soil surface or at the depth at which it was growing before and that the soil comes in close contact with the roots and there are no air spaces. Water well. When the water has drained away, add a bit more soil to reestablish the surface level if necessary. Smooth the soil surface and water again. In the following weeks, keep an eye on the divisions; active growth should begin soon after transplantation.

Plants with slender roots like spaghetti can often be treated similarly to the ones described above. Hostas, for example, can be lifted and carefully cut apart. The eyes of the hosta are prominent, and in early to midspring, they are very easy to see as points, somewhat like upside-down canine teeth. A hosta plant can be divided into any number of pieces as long as each section has at least one eye, but again, for faster results, include more eyes.

Above: A specimen hosta, 'Krossa Gold', shown in its second summer from one fleshy-root division.

Below: A young hosta is dug up and washed clean to clearly reveal the spaces between the shoots. Spread the roots and carefully thread a knife between them and cut through the crown. Pry the sections apart slowly to untangle the roots without breaking them. The pieces can be cut as small as one eye, but larger ones prevent the loss of too many roots and deliver bigger plants. To accelerate multiplication, hostas can be "topped" in spring. When shoots are 1 or 2 inches tall, the soil is cleared away to expose the crown, which is wiped clean with a moist paper towel. A snap-blade knife is inserted through the base of the shoot and into the dense crown. The wound is dusted with hormone and kept open with a toothpick before the soil is replaced.

PLANTS WITH THICK ROOTS

Many herbaceous perennials grow into clumps but have neither fibrous roots nor stringy ones. Daylilies, with their thick, fingerlike roots, are easy to divide. Dig up a clump of the plants, and separate those individual plants with promising eyes or shoots simply by shaking them while pulling slowly apart. They are so easy to work with that if you bounce the root ball on a garden fork held parallel to the ground, the clump virtually falls into separate plants. The oldest sections should be discarded, along with any dead, hollow, papery remains.

If a clump is very old and thickly matted, some surgery may be necessary to prune away dead material and reveal the healthy young growth. If the plant is still difficult to pry apart, cut down through the crown between groups of eyes, as described for hostas. Divisions of the resilient daylily will recover quickly when replanted.

Back-to-back garden forks could be used as the first step for dividing very old and congested clumps. Lift the entire clump first, if possible, and then plunge the two garden forks into the center of the crown and pry the clump in half.

There are fleshy-rooted herbaceous perennials that have roots so thick and woody that they will never fall apart like a daylily's. The peony, for instance, can live for a century or longer, and division sets it back quite a bit. But a peony might be divided if it has to be moved, or to have more plants to make a herbaceous hedge perhaps, or to plant above a retaining wall where double peony flowers could flop over and be enjoyed at eye level.

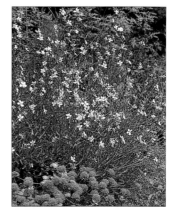

Top: Although many books recommend inserting two garden forks back to back, such an operation would turn a hosta to pulp. The forks can be used for the initial bisection of a large fibrous-rooted perennial, but excavating the entire plant first will prevent crushing it against the sides of its hole. (The burlap tarp makes for neat cleanup.)

Center: Dividing a plant with thick roots is more akin to surgery than simple division. A single *Gaura lindheimeri* is shown after the procedure **(left)** and then again during its second summer in the garden **(right)** when it is covered for months with pinkish white butterfly flowers (above recently divided curly chive, *Allium senescens montanum* var. *glaucum*).

Below: A single Gaura plant is lifted in spring **(left),** and its horseradish-like roots are separated by slowly breaking the point of contact at the crown **(center),** producing three divisions **(right).**

Dig up the large peony root after the foliage has died back in autumn. Split the root with a sharp spade, or saw it into sections with at least three eyes in each. Replant each division with the crown no less than 1 inch and no more than 2 inches deep. Although it is best to replant the divisions as soon as possible, the roots can be covered with damp burlap and placed in a cool, shaded spot for a week or so.

DIVIDING BASAL ROSETTES

Many herbaceous plants produce a ground-hugging disk or rosette of semievergreen leaves that persist during their resting months of dormancy. These dense growths between the roots and the stems are like the foundation of a building, forming a solid transition between what is below the earth and what is to come above it. When the plants awake in the spring, shoots push up from the rosettes, which increase in size during the year.

Biennials often produce basal growth in their first year from seed. The following spring, a flower spike bolts toward the sky. After they are finished flowering and producing seed, plants such as foxglove and verbascum may form tiny secondary rosettes around the parent plant. The original plant will eventually die, but the off-spring may be large enough to be removed in late summer or early autumn, replanted, and watered well. In cold climates, mulch the autumn divisions when the ground freezes. They will often grow large enough to blossom the following spring.

BASAL CUTTINGS

Many herbaceous perennials produce little side shoots from their crowns that are less self-sufficient than secondary rosettes and require some coddling. *Aster, Gentiana, Achillea*, and *Campanula* produce shoots that can be removed in early spring or autumn, but they are treated like stem cuttings.

Above, left to right: The woodlike crown and root of long-lived perennials, such as a peony, may never need dividing, but the process works to reproduce a special variety. A hand saw or sharp spade can be used to split or cut through the crown, taking care not to damage buds. A basal rosette is a flat disk of foliage emanating from a common crown. Just as the period of active growth is beginning in spring, basal side shoots of *Primula* × *bulleesiana* are carefully pried from their parent to include some roots and quickly transplanted.

Below: Small perennials and alpines, such as *Campanula garganica,* produce multiple crowns and roots, which must be divided with precision. Lift a tiny plant in spring or autumn and wash it clean **(left).** Then carefully tease apart separate crowns and roots with a tool **(center).** In spring, the plantlets can be set in a nursery bed; in autumn, rooting medium is recommended **(right).**

AN EYEFUL

A visit with master propagator Kelly Grummons at his Colorado nursery is an education. Every so often, I come upon a magician such as he, who seems to nearly be able to stick a pencil in the ground and grow an oak tree. Kelly plays bee to a succulent figwort by pinching pollen from one plant to bring to another, or pinches the center of a chrysanthemum to produce a dozen more in a few months. Kelly doesn't think there is anything special about these feats. What is his secret? Is it inborn talent, or is he privy to scientific systems known only to the horticultural elite? Maybe, his ability comes from experience, and his ease comes with a willingness to take risks.

This man performs his acts of propagation in what some might consider a less-than-perfect climate. After all, the mountains of Colorado are not known for warmth or high humidity. Undaunted, Kelly just goes about the business of making more plants. His first job in the area was for the retail nursery Paulino's. When he arrived there, the pots of perennial varieties were arranged alphabetically in a 10-foot-deep, 20-foot-long section of the nursery. When he left to start his own business, the A to Z perennial offering was more than 100 feet long.

It is a rather unusual notion that a retailer could lead, and perhaps initiate, a trend rather than following along—trying to keep up with demand. But gardeners from all over the area made the trip to Paulino's and bought perennials as fast as Kelly could propagate them. And this master's supplies never faltered.

Many of the plants Kelly propagates come from his friend Panayoti Kelaidis, the curator of the rock garden at the Denver Botanic Gardens. Some of the plants started from seeds there turned out to be perfect for the conditions of the Mile High City.

I went to see Kelly demonstrate "gouging," a rather unpleasant but descriptive name for the removal of the growing center, or eye, of a perennial. After the operation, the plant sends up many small shoots around the crown. For the demonstration, Kelly chose a single, young chrysanthemum.

In this procedure, which could be compared to coppicing a woody plant (see page 166), the growing point at the center of the plant is cut out with a sharp knife. Gouging can be performed on a plant in the garden or on one still in a pot, and it is a useful technique to use on a well-established young potted perennial in the early spring.

Shortly after the eye has been removed, little plants begin to emerge all around the parent plant. In a few months, these side shoots can be removed and potted individually. Depending on the time of year and the hardiness of the plant, the offspring can be hardened off and planted in the garden or, in fall, left in their pots and wintered over in the cold frame.

(1)　　　　　　　　(2)　　　　　　　　(3)

(4)　　　　　　　　(5)　　　　　　　　(6)

(7)　　　　　　　　(8)　　　　　　　　(9)

Kelly Grummons (**opposite**) demonstrates cutting the growing point of a small potted chrysanthemum with a knife (1) and removing it (2). Soon the gouged plant produces many offsets around the base (3). The plant is slipped out of its pot (4) and the plantlets are pulled apart (5). The side shoot with roots (6) is ready to be potted up (7) as any rooted cutting (8). This economical method has vivid results (9).

If the spring-taken shoots have roots, they can be planted in the garden or potted to grow larger in a shaded cold frame or nursery area. If the side shoots do not have roots, set them in rooting medium in the sweatbox in spring. In a cool greenhouse, shoots can be grown in perlite in the humid environment with a bit of bottom heat. Here, they develop quickly. Once they have rooted, pot them up and harden-off the plants in the cold frame and then move them to a nursery area, or if they are large enough, to a permanent spot in the garden.

If taken in autumn, the basal cuttings can be set in a flat of medium in the cold frame. If you have a cool greenhouse, the flat can be brought there in midwinter, as described above.

OFFSETS

Some plants produce miniature rosettes around larger basal ones. Some produce ever-widening circles of plantlets at their crowns. Other plants give rise to similarly spontaneous generations from extensions that either arch up above the crown, hug the ground, or run just below the surface of the soil. Some of these fortuitous miniatures nestle tightly to their parents, but they all are completely ready to take their places. The horticultural term for these adventitious plants is *offsets.*

The spider plant and the garden strawberry are familiar examples. *Aloe vera* likewise generates young plants on its main stem as the plant

ages. The Boston fern *(Nephrolepis exaltata)* produces long fuzzy strings that can be used for propagation. Some orchids bear offspring called "keikis." Ground covers, such as bugle *(Ajuga),* spread by "runners" or "stolons"— traveling stems. Siberian iris produces row upon row of plantlets around the circumference of an ever-widening crown. Even woody plants, such as lilacs, may produce new shoots, or "suckers," from underground stolons. This behavior is often described in a plant's name —such as *Cornus stolonifera,* the botanical name of a shrubby dogwood that grows into a thicket.

Bromeliads grow small plantlets, "pups," around the central, parent plant. Hen-and-chicks *(Sempervivum)* is a hardy succulent that begins as a flat disk with leaves arranged in concentric rings; as it matures, small plants grow around the original rosette. Bromeliads and hen-and-chicks are monocarpic—the parent flowers once and dies—so they rely on the new plantlets to quickly fill the void.

PROPAGATION VIA OFFSETS

Removing offsets is much like dividing crowns, but this method of propagation takes advantage of the plants' readiness to subdivide. One of my favorite plants, the wonderful alpine or woodland strawberry *(Fragaria),* commonly known by its French name, *Fraise des bois,* is propagated by

offset division. This strawberry bears tiny, aromatic fruits that are usually red—there is also a white-fruited variety that has a fragrance and taste reminiscent of pineapple. Although garden strawberries produce wiry stolons with new plants forming along the lengths of the runners (page 197), wild strawberries create plantlets that cluster around the crown of the mother plant. To remain productive, crops of both types of strawberries should be renewed frequently with young plants.

To divide the *Fraise des bois,* start in early spring before new growth commences in earnest. Dig up a three- or four-year-old clump and shake off the soil. Carefully tear off the plantlets and plant them as soon as possible. If you must keep the plantlets for a while before planting, roll their roots in a moist paper towel, leaving the top growth above the paper. Slip the whole bundle into a plastic bag, root end first, and leave the bag open in a cool shaded spot, or close the bag and store it in the refrigerator for up to a week.

Another plant suitable for this type of division is the Siberian iris. Unlike bearded irises, Siberian irises do not grow from ground-hugging rhizomes but from a massive clump, which can become a congested, woody mat. (For rhizome division, see page 212.) If the iris is not lifted and divided every five years or so, the center will die out and the clump will become a doughnut of grassy iris foliage with few flowers.

Spread a tarp next to a mature plant that has finished blooming so you can keep track of all the iris divisions. A helper may be needed to lift and roll the plant out of its hole and onto the tarp. Snip back the foliage and slice around the clump by plunging a spade into the soil in a circle to its full depth.

You may have to saw old clumps of Siberian iris into wedges. In the most difficult cases, you may need to start while the iris is still in the ground, in order to even be able to lift sections at all. Once the root ball and crown have been excavated, the little individual plantlets around

Above: Dividing offsets is necessary as older, crowded plants decline. After several years, the center of a Siberian iris dies out, bearing fewer flowers and presenting a doughnut of floppy foliage. If the clump is too large and dense to excavate, saw through the center in the ground and lift sections. After the sections are pulled apart **(left)**, a serrated knife may be necessary to cut through the crown's woody tissue. Pry off divisions with one to three "fans" **(center).** The transplants will bloom in two years **(right),** and square in number every season.

Below: Plants such as *Sempervivum* grow into rosettes of petal-like leaves. After the original plant flowers and sets seed, it dies. However, by that time, it has become ringed by plantlets, giving rise to the common name hen-and-chicks. The youngsters can be removed and transplanted. Gently pull off one of the offsets with as much stem as possible. Surround the stem with a wad of moistened sandy soil **(left),** and squeeze the soil into an existing crevice **(center)** or pile up rocks to include the stem and soil. In time, the plant will grow chicks of its own and blossom **(right).**

the clump can easily be pulled away and transplanted, using the method discussed for the woodland strawberry above. Discard the woody center. In as little as two years, the offsets will be blooming and making plantlets of their own.

ONE BORN EVERY MINUTE

Harvesting a chunk of a suckering shrub is about the quickest way to acquire a full-size plant from a cutting. Suckers are straight shoots that arise from underground stolons or slender rhizomes. A number of woody plants produce

some newspaper set on a tarp or in a plastic bag with the edges rolled open. Don't worry if a lot of the soil falls away as the sucker is lifted. Lilacs are typically shipped "bare-root" from mail-order suppliers and will not be killed by a lack of soil at this time of year, because they have no leafy top growth. Moisten the newspaper, pull the bag up tight to hold the roots in place, and close it by tying twine around the base of the woody stem. Keep the newspaper wet and the plant cold until it can be transplanted.

At the site of the lilac's new home, dig a large

Above: Offsets are produced at the ends of short rhizomes in some members of the lily family such as agave **(left).** The new plant can be cut off, as with this *Sansevieria cylindrica* **(center),** with its young roots if possible **(right).** This is the method used to produce a clone of a cultivar.

Right: Sympodial orchids, such as this *Oncidium,* are ones that produce swollen offsets from the base of older plants, called "pseudo-bulbs." In order to grow and bloom again, the pseudo-bulbs must be removed and repotted. The shriveled old plants will not bloom again and should be discarded. (The result in the winter following this summer division can be seen on page 78.)

suckers such as shrub dogwoods. A common lilac, *Syringa vulgaris,* with many stems may have a good-size piece on the outside of the clump that can be propagated for a new place in the garden.

Professionals try to prepare large sections of plants such as the lilac by pruning the roots a year in advance of harvest to encourage the formation of new roots. In that case, a spade is plunged into the ground in a circle around a group of suckers in late winter, cutting some of their roots and causing them to branch. But moving a single suckering stem without this preparation seems to work if the timing is right.

When the lilac is dormant in late winter, as soon as the ground has thawed, select a shoot. Bring a sharp spade, some newspaper or burlap, a plastic bag or tarp, twine, and a watering can. Find the underground stem that leads in a straight line from the center of the clump to the sucker.

Plunge the spade into the ground close to the parent to cut the stolon. Dig up the new plant with as many roots as possible, and lift it onto

plant to get around. The plantlets that sprout from these runners can be cut off and dug up with their roots, ready for transplanting. You can propagate many non-clump-forming grasses, such as big bluestem *(Andropogon gerardii)*, by cutting and digging a section of the stolon with top growth and roots that appear from nodes along the way.

Some special subshrubs and ground covers, such as pachysandra, have fleshy blanched-white stems beneath the ground. Pachysandra can be encouraged to cover an area if you remove a hank of pale rootlike stem with a slim little root and a leaf bud attached. Dr. Richard Lighty of Mt. Cuba Center for the Study of the Piedmont Flora in Delaware showed me how to propagate the notoriously difficult native Allegheny spurge *(Pachysandra procumbens)*. In early spring, he grabs a stem of one of the leafy shoots, giving it a very hard yank. The stem

enough hole for the roots, set them comfortably in the hole, add garden soil and tamp it down so that it comes in contact with all the fibrous roots, and water well. New roots will begin to grow immediately, but if you want to compensate for possible root loss, cut back the top growth after the new plant starts to grow, or simply pick off some of the leaves as they emerge. The lilac may begin to flower the first season, since the buds for those blossoms were produced the year before the move. Cut away the emerging flower stems to redirect the plant's energy toward root growth. Keep the plant well watered for the first year. The lilac may not flower the second spring after planting, but once the offspring is established, it will produce more blooms every spring.

SPRINTERS AND AMBLERS

Herbaceous stoloniferous plants include many of the members of the mint family *(Labiatae)*, such as bee balm *(Monarda)*, spearmint and peppermint *(Mentha)*, and mountain mint *(Pycnanthemum)*. The stolons lie below the surface of the soil, and, as anyone who has grown mint knows, this is a very successful way for a

Above: Stoloniferous plants, such as gray dogwood *(Cornus racemosa)* create thickets of suckers.

Below: New lilac plants can be created from suckers removed from the outer edge of a mature stand. This procedure takes place in late winter when the shrub is dormant. Work a spade or shovel about a foot out from the stem to loosen the soil and find the underground stem that connects it—usually closest to the clump—and plunge the spade into the ground to sever it.

(1)   (2)

(3)   (4)

(5)

Above: Lift the new plant and the roots (1) and place it on moist newspaper (2). This is a dormant, bare-root transplant and the paper should cover the roots to keep them damp (3). Slip the ball into a plastic bag (4). The tall sucker may quickly become a feature in the landscape (5).

Opposite: Garden strawberries and other plants make babies at the ends of runners. Peg the small plants in "daughter pots."

Below: Perennials with runners just below or above the ground may root where leaf nodes touch soil, such as ajuga and moneywort.

breaks off with one little root and then can be replanted, with most of the blanched stem and rootlet laid a few inches underground. The following spring, an entire new and vigorous plant sprouts from the bud near the cut end.

As with so many methods of vegetative propagation, timing is critical, even for species that are less fussy than this spurge. In most gardens, the evergreen ground cover European wild ginger (*Asarum europaeum*) spreads very slowly unless the gardener intervenes. Plants divided in midspring, however, just after flowering, as new growth is beginning, spread quickly.

To propagate this shade lover, knock a new plant out of its pot or dig up a thick clump. The

individual plant stems and roots will practically fall apart. Replant the stems a few inches apart —in a few years, one plant of wild ginger will become a carpet.

12

Geophytes

Most people label all fleshy, subterranean plant growths "bulbs," but some of these rotund, carbohydrate- and sugar-storing modified stems are not bulbs but tubers, corms, and succulent rhizomes. Garden author and plant expert Judy Glattstein refers to all of these by a scientific name, *geophyte*, which translates as "earth-plant."

There may not be a practical reason to propagate an inexpensive, common red tulip, but if the subject is a species tulip with subtle color and delicate form, reproduction might be irresistible. It is also easy, as tulips produce small versions of themselves next to the original. The tulip is a true bulb, as is the lily, with scales joined in a basal plate from which roots also grow, although their bulbs do not look alike. The tulip is *tunicate*, enclosed in a papery cover like an onion. The lily is *nontunicate*,

best solution would be to propagate rare geophytes *in* their homelands and remove the incentive to steal them. (Cyclamen are being raised beneath trees in Turkish orchards.)

To propagate tunicate bulbs more aggressively, commercial growers perform "twin scaling," a propagation technique in which vertical slices of bulbs are taken with as little as two tiny scale sections joined at the basal plate. New bulbs grow in between the scales. A simpler procedure, called "chipping," creates

with scales arranged like the petals of a waterlily flower. As scales on a tunicate bulb grow, they remain attached at the basal plate, but new bulbs begin to separate from each other like the cloves of a head of garlic. These offsets can be pried apart in late summer when they are dormant and then planted separately.

Certain hardy bulbs, such as snowflakes (*Leucojum*), from the Mediterranean region, are threatened in their native habitats. It is imperative that endangered plants be propagated for distribution, not wild-collected. The

larger sections, reminiscent of an orange.

As soon as the plants go dormant in summer, the bulbs are dug and washed clean. Cut the "nose" or pointed tip off the bulb. Then, cut about eight to sixteen parts—like sections of an orange. The pieces are usually treated with fungicide and placed in moist vermiculite in a plastic bag for three months. In autumn, at bulb-planting time, the cuttings are removed. Tiny bulbs will have grown at the base of the scale. The sections are potted and green shoots appear in spring.

Preceding pages: Lily flowers flaunt their sexuality to attract pollinators, set seed, and multiply, but there are many other ways to propagate these plants.

Opposite: Geophytes— plants with modified underground stems (bulbs, corms, rhizomes, tubers)—can be grown from seed. The tuberous cyclamen flower stem coils to pull in its fruit for safekeeping.

Top: Early winter snow drops (*Galanthus*) **(left)** grow from bulbs, as do the subtle flowers of *Tulipa humilis* var. *pulchella* **(center).** The house plant climbing onion (*Bowiea volubulus*) is grown for its ornamental bulb, which also provides sections of scales for reproduction **(right).**

Above: Unusual *Galanthus* varieties have become highly collectible and are propagated by "chipping" or "twin scaling." As soon as all the leaves have yellowed, the dormant bulbs are dug up. The bulbs are cut in half, then quarters **(left),** then finally eighths or smaller, each with a bit of the basal plate **(center).** The pieces are placed in a plastic bag with moist vermiculite, and by autumn have grown tiny bulbs **(right).**

There are other ways to propagate certain hardy bulbs: scooping (or spooning) and scoring. In scooping, the basal plate is completely removed with a specialized tool that is like a wide melon baller. Hyacinths are the primary candidates for this

procedure, along with *Scilla, Leucojum, Lachenalia,* and grape hyacinth *(Muscari).*

Cut a rounded scoop from the base of the bulb with a utility knife, or score the bulb through the basal plate by making two or three wedge-shaped grooves across the bottom *(above left).*

To encourage the formation of bulblets, set the scooped or scored hyacinth on its side to callus in a warm (above 70 degrees F [21 degrees C]), dark place with ample air circulation for a few days. The place above the top light fixture of a floral cart is a good spot. Laying the bulb on an old screen or a wire rack will help improve air circulation. In commercial production, bulbs are treated with fungicide and the temperature is gradually raised above 85 degrees F (29.5 degrees C) and the relative humidity is kept high, about 85 percent.

Your scooped or scored bulb should begin to make tiny bulblets in just a few weeks *(above right).* After two months, pot the original bulb pointy side down in sandy, fast-draining, sterilized potting medium.

In spring, leaves will grow, and by autumn, the hyacinth bulblets will be roughly ¾ inch across, and can be planted in the garden; amend the soil with bonemeal. If a remnant of the old bulb holds onto the little ones, plant the whole thing *(below left).*

The bulbs may take three to four years to reach flowering size. Commercial growers lift and grade the bulbs each autumn, replanting small ones until they reach blooming size. Scooping might have applications for gardeners with large properties or collectors on a budget. But the best reason is for the fun of seeing all this "magic" take place. The bulbs shown here were heirlooms—'City of Harlem' from 1927 and 'Gypsy' *(below right).*

PROPAGATING GARDEN LILIES

Garden lilies from the genus *Lilium* belong to one of the largest families of plants, with members that vary as much as the habitats in which they live. Aloe is kin to asparagus, as are dracaena, trillium, and all the spring-flowering bulbs. Three-inch-tall blue scillas *(Scilla siberica)* color the early-spring garden, and century plants *(Agave americana)* can push their floral spikes 30 feet toward the sky. As you would expect, these plants call for diverse approaches to propagation.

Lilies do reproduce sexually: they are monocots and produce a blade as their seed leaf, like grass. Some species, such as *Lilium formosanum,* sprout in less than three weeks and may bloom in their first year. Others, such as *L. martagon,* are two-step germinators and, unless conditioned by the gardener, take years to germinate and bloom (see "Take Two Steps," page 206).

Vegetative propagation of lilies is even more variable. Several lilies, such as the regal lily *(L. regale),* produce offsets next to their bulbs. The North American native lemon lily *(L. parryi)* produces a slender bulb that resembles a rhizome with bulblets along its length. Several lilies can be propagated from stem cuttings, but these are not like the familiar stem cuttings; the stems do not grow roots or shoots. Instead, bulblets grow at the leaf axils. And still other lilies produce "bulbils," propagules, at their leaf axils.

L. longiflorum is the familiar Easter lily—an easily forced bulb that is sold as a seasonal potted plant and is cold-hardy to about 10

degrees F (−12 degrees C). This lily grows "bulblets" that form underground on its stem and at the base of the bulb. Unpot the parent bulb and carefully rub the medium off. Some bulblets will break free and others can be pulled off. These can be potted individually in a humus-based medium, about 1 inch below the surface, in a 3½-inch pot, or a few could be planted in a 6-inch container and transplanted in a year or two.

The Easter lily also presents an opportunity to try another propagation method. Just after flowering, take the plant out of its pot, remove

Above: Lilies from seed grow in two ways depending on species. Some, like *Lilium formosanum,* sprout quickly and often bloom in their first year; others are two-step germinators (page 206) and may take a year or longer to germinate.

Below: After the flowers of *L. formosanum* fade, the tall stems develop enormous fruits that are held on candelabra-like stems and make exquisite dried arrangements **(left).** The fruits also offer thousands of seeds, which can easily be sown by tossing some in moist vermiculite **(center).** Within weeks, the *epigeal* seeds sprout and can be slipped free of the vermiculite by pinching and pulling their blade leaves **(right).** These seedlings are shown with potted ones that were started three months before.

the potting mix, and hose off the bulb. Peel scales off the parent bulb (as if preparing to eat an artichoke). Set the scales on an old window screen in a dark, humid place with good air circulation and moderate temperature. Bulblets will begin to show in a few weeks, and with the scale attached can be set in perlite in a sweatbox when they are the size of buckshot. When they are the size of peas, the scale will have shriveled,

bulb scales shown were not treated. If you have problems, try a quick dip in topical hydrogen peroxide and pat dry on a clean paper towel.

The progeny resulting from scales varies. Some lilies create a single leaf in the first year. Other species form a rosette of leaves before producing flowering stems, and some species simply produce a dormant bulb.

Propagating lilies is irresistible, and perhaps

Opposite: The fruits of *L. formosanum* can be used for indoor decoration and still provide plenty of seeds for sowing. Thousands are stacked perfectly within the chambers of the dehiscent fruits.

Left to right, top to bottom: Lilies can be propagated vegetatively by various means, for which the familiar Easter lily *(Lilium longiflorum)* serves as a model. Bulblets grow naturally along the stems of this lily and many others and may be encouraged by laying the stem horizontally in medium. Tiny bulblets may also appear below the bulb, growing from its base, and once freed, sprout their own leaves. Most lily bulbs can be propagated from individual scales pulled down and off the base of their mothers—like eating an artichoke. The scales are set on a screen in a humid place out of sunlight, and in a few weeks, tiny bulblets form at the basal end that can be potted. This is one method for producing hundreds of lily bulbs commercially.

and the bulblets can be potted as above.

Many other lily species can be propagated from scales placed in moist vermiculite in plastic bags, but fungal diseases are a common problem. Almost every source you'll encounter isn't shy about using fungicides. One probably can't buy bulbs that haven't been treated, since the potential for disease is high. The Easter lily

unavoidable, as anyone who has grown the tiger lily knows. Collect the bulbils from the leaf axils of *L. lancifolium* (syn., *L. tigrinum,* the tiger lily), *L. bulbiferum,* or *L. sulphureum* to sprinkle where they will all root. As suspected, these are naturalized aliens for thoughtful placement—perhaps along the driveway—and not for casting into the "wilderness" of the back forty.

Many lily seeds germinate very quickly, while others are very slow. The ones that take a long time are "two-step germinators" (see page 74). Step one takes place when, after receiving moisture and warmth, the radicle, or immature root, emerges from the seed, and a tiny bulbil forms. Then the bulbil experiences a period of dormancy through winter. Step two comes with the return of warmth in spring, and light encourages the sprouting

of the first true leaf. Seeds of martagon lilies (*Lilium martagon*) ordered from a catalog will arrive in winter. If the intention is to let nature apply the warmth, moisture, cold, and warmth again, the seeds can't be sown outdoors until the following summer. Try conditioning them indoors. If there are martagons in the garden, harvest fresh seeds for conditioning.

Collect the seeds from the split (dehiscent) fruit of the martagon in late summer. Each bulb will produce a pod for every flower, and there may be a dozen or so, depending on the age of the plant. Each pod holds about a hundred seeds.

As the pods turn brown and begin to split, bend the flower stem carefully and insert the candelabra-like cluster into a paper bag. Cut it free from the plant and let it fall into the bag. When the chambered pods are dry, open them over paper so that the stacked seeds are not lost.

When you are ready to "sow," you'll need paper towels, zipper-lock sandwich bags, a marking pen, and a spray bottle of water or a bulb mister. Arrange the seeds evenly in the middle of a

paper towel, and then fold it so the seeds are covered. Spray the towel until it is just damp, and slip it into the plastic bag. For your records, mark the bag with the harvest and sowing dates. Place the closed bag in a warm spot of about 70 degrees F (21 degrees C), and check it periodically by holding it up to the light. You should see tiny beads of condensation around the edges of the paper. If you suspect the towel may

be drying, open the bag and sprinkle in a little more water.

Another reason to peer through the bag is to see if there is any mold around the seeds. A tiny bit of black mold is not cause for alarm, but if the area of mold is more than twice the diameter of a seed and in colors other than black, remove the towel from the bag, and with the sharp point of a knife, transfer the seeds to a new moist towel.

This first step, bagging the seeds until they develop little bulbils, will take from one to three months, depending on the freshness of the seed and temperature. The fresh seed that I sowed in August showed signs of change in just three weeks.

Once the bulbils have developed, "sow" them in medium in 3-inch-square plastic pots and transfer them to the refrigerator (perhaps in a plastic shoebox. After three months, take them out and place the pots in a warm place again—under a fluorescent light or in a sunny window. Leaves will show quickly (developing bulbs and leaves). In midspring, you'll be able to harden off the little plants (page 97). After hardening, place the plants in a sheltered nursery or in a cold frame.

Opposite: The magnificent martagon lilies (left) are *hypogeal* and form bulbils before sending up a true leaf in their second year. The fruits of this lily are also ornamental (right). **Above:** The process can be accelerated by the home propagator as follows (left to right, top to bottom): Seeds are harvested. They are spread on a paper towel, which is folded into quarters and moistened. The towel is slipped into a plastic zipperlock bag marked with the species name, source, and date of sowing and kept at room temperature. When the bulbils are visible through the bag—in three to eight weeks, depending on freshness—they can be removed. Then they are potted and placed in the refrigerator to simulate winter for twelve weeks. If unpotted, the bulbils would look like the two shown, but brought to light and warmth, they sprout true leaves (right).

Above: A crocus flower from the best-known spring corm. Corms resemble bulbs, but instead of having scales, they are solid.

Below, left to right: Albeit a somewhat subdued example of *Gladiolus,* 'Happy Time' also grows from a corm. New corms appear

CORM AGAIN

The most familiar plants that grow from corms are probably gladioli and crocuses. Unlike bulbs, corms have no scales, just a hard, swollen stem base. Gladioli are sold as dormant corms for planting in spring. Soon leaves grow, and the plant bolts upward with a tall flower stalk. But instead of making an offset on the side, the corm produces a new corm above the old one, as large as or larger than the original. The new corm will be next year's flowering plant.

Just as lilies have their bulblets, gladioli also present dozens of pea-size offsets that grow around the base of the parent corm, called "cormels," which can be used to propagate new plants. In late summer to autumn, dig the tender corms to bring inside to a frost-free place.

degrees F (4.5 degrees C), but do not let the corms freeze.

In spring, soak the hard, dry cormels for two days, changing the water a few times. Then plant the cormels in the rows of a nursery area to be grown on until they are blooming size. The cormels will need to be dug up again in the fall, of course; some of them may be large enough to be planted the following spring and will produce flowers that summer. Others, however, will require another year of storage and planting before they will bloom.

The corms can also be cut into sections, each containing an eye, or growing bud. A large corm may yield two to four cuttings. In early spring, dig up some of the largest corms from the garden. Wash them thoroughly. Use a very sharp knife or a snap-off-blade cutting tool for the

annually beneath the old corms, which are discarded; and cormels—tiny corms—grow around withered corm bases as well. These modified stems can also be sectioned—each piece containing an eye or sprout.

Opposite: After a frost, the gladiola are harvested, dried for a day or two, and the corms and cormels are pulled free to be stored in an airy place in net bags.

Let the entire plant dry for about a week in a warm place. Over newspaper, cut off the stalk, and then pry the new corm from the old one; the cormels will usually fall off, but if they do not, they can be rubbed free.

The corms and cormels will benefit from a "curing" on a screen in a warm place, up to 95 degrees F (35 degrees C), for another week, which protects the harvest from disease. Store the corms and cormels in a place with good air circulation—such as in a fine-mesh recycled onion bag suspended on a hook in a cool, airy spot. The temperature can drop as low as 40

operation, and sterilize it in rubbing alcohol between cuts. Brush the open tissue with hydrogen peroxide, and pat it dry at once with a clean paper towel. Allow the cut sections to dry on a rack until the flesh has completely sealed, three days to a week or more. Then plant the sections in pots of sterilized medium or in a spot in the garden with well-drained soil.

Crocuses and other hardy corm-forming plants are not lifted from the garden for winter protection, but they can be dug up and cut or divided during their dormant period as well (summer for the crocus).

TATER TOTS

Although the potato plant grows above the ground, the part we eat is the swollen end of a stolon, a stem that travels horizontally—usually underground. For gardeners interested in propagating plants for ornamental plantings, other

tuberous plants will be more tempting. Most of the decorative plants with tubers do not have stolons but develop their fat, modified stems directly at the base of the stalks—dahlias, tuberous begonias, elephant's ears *(Colocasia)*, and caladium are good examples. Many of these tubers are not hardy and must be over-wintered indoors.

To store dahlias over winter, dig up the tubers after a killing frost in the autumn and cut the stalks back to 6 inches. Let the bunch dry for a day, and store the tubers in peat moss (if you use it), sawdust, dry sand, or dry leaves in boxes or pails set in a cool place such as a spot in the basement where the temperature hovers around 50 degrees F (10 degrees C).

Ornamental sweet potato vines *(Ipomoea batatas)* have become the rage of the summer garden for their near-black, tri-color green, pink, and white, or chartreuse leaves. The tubers of these plants are stored in the same manner as the dahlias.

If you grow caladium tubers in pots, let the medium dry out completely in the fall. Store the tubers in dry soil mix in their pots.

Dahlia tubers can be divided in spring. Some tubers may break apart when you remove them

Opposite: Tuberous-rooted plants include these tender black-leaved taros (*Colocasia antiquorum* 'Illustris') grown from recently divided offsets.

Above left: Examples of tuberous plants include *Arisaema* species **(left)**. The most comely jack-in-the-pulpit *(Arisaema candidissimum)* **(center)**. A dahlia flower **(right)**.

Below left: After a killing frost, dahlia tubers are dug up and stems are cut back **(left)**. The tubers with labels are wrapped individually or set into nearly dry leaves in a box or basket kept around 50 degrees F (10 degrees C). When the temperature has warmed outside, the tubers can be unwrapped **(center)**. Individual pieces—each with eyes—can be cut or pried apart **(right)**.

Above: Propagation's downside: The caltha look-alike, *Ranunculus auruntiacus,* produces tubercles at its leaf axils that drop and sprout, making this weed difficult to eradicate.

must be dried like gladioli corms (see page 208). Use a sulfur dust if you wish, or try a quick dip in hydrogen peroxide. Sweet potatoes can be cut, dried and potted as well, and placed under light. By the time the weather has warmed outside, the plants will be well on their way to decorating the summer garden.

CREEPING RHIZOMES

Unlike the swollen tubers that form at the base of stalks or as globular growths at the ends of underground stems, the horizontal stems of some plants have themselves modified to become the storehouses of carbohydrates. These rhizomes also have eyes and can be used for propagation. Some plants that have rhizomatous stems use them to travel, and they can

Top: Cannas and the other geophytes have strong wills to survive, and also stored sugars, moisture, and starch to support growth, as this errant piece of tuber attests **(left)**. The rhizome, barely the size of a pinkie finger, fell by the edge of the path, rooted, and produced shoots. *Canna* 'Tropicana Phaison' flower **(right)**.

Above: Canna rhizomes are stored the same way as dahlia tubers are. The unwrapped canna can be broken into sections **(left)** or cut with a serrated knife **(center)**. Each piece must have at least one eye, or growing point **(right)**. In spring, when all danger of frost has passed and the temperatures are above 60 degrees F (15.5 degrees C), the rhizomes can be planted. One canna section may produce a dozen new plants by autumn.

from storage, but as long as each one has an eye, they will grow into new plants. Trim the remnant of last year's stem, then carefully cut the remaining tubers apart, including at least one eye in each piece. The eyes may be hard to see, depending on how developed they are; look for little pink points. Expect to have five or more blooming-size plants for every one planted the previous spring.

Dahlias can also be propagated from stem cuttings. If a tuber is potted in late winter and placed under lights, shoots will emerge that can be treated like herbaceous cuttings (see page 120). If you are lucky, tubers of plants such as caladium, colocasia, or *Amorphophallus* will have produced offsets that can be broken off and potted. The main tubers can also be cut into wedges—each with an eye. The cut flesh

move at quite a clip. A distinction can be made between rhizomatous stems and rhizomes as storage organs. Just think of a bearded iris as one kind. The growth of the iris is always produced at the terminal ends of the rhizomes. A canna rhizome has eyes all over its length and, unlike the iris, presents multiple opportunities for propagation.

Cutting sections of the rhizome in spring— each with at least one eye—is a way to produce more plants. When cannas that have been stored in cool places indoors (50 degrees F [10 degrees C]) are unwrapped in the spring or lifted from the ground in frost-free areas, pieces often break apart. In this way, canna rhizomes practically self-propagate. Unfortunately, not all rhizomes are so prodigious.

Varieties of German bearded iris must be

and lily-of-the-valley. But there are also non-lily plants with rhizomes—even some ferns that have creeping growths, either below or above the ground. The scaly rhizomes of certain gesneriads, such as achimenes, can also be used for propagation. These rhizomes snap apart for potting and new plants. The tender rabbit's-foot *(Davallia)* and bear's-foot fern *(Polypodium)* have fuzzy rhizomes that grow over rock outcrops and tree trunks in nature. These ferns can be propagated from sections of rhizome with several fronds attached. Pin the cut sections to about half their depth in moist perlite in the sweatbox in spring, or at other times of year in a box with bottom heat. After roots form, pot the new plants in a humus-based medium. In time, the creeping rhizomes will completely cover their new pots.

divided every three to four years to renew the plants and increase blooming. But new plants can only be made from the growing points on these rhizomes that grow on top of the soil; the old part of the rhizomes dries up and decays. The time to divide bearded irises is during their midsummer dormancy. Cut the fans of leaves back to about 6 to 8 inches long, and remove the newest parts of the rhizome for replanting. Be sure to cut off or dig out any damaged or diseased material, which usually appears dark brown or black. Because there are several diseases that bother bearded irises, consider dipping the cut sections in a 10 percent bleach solution for ten seconds before replanting.

Many rhizomatous plants are lily relatives, such as the bearded iris, canna, sansevieria,

Top: Hardy plants from rhizomes can also be divided into sections, such as bearded irises, which must be lifted, cut, and replanted to perform their best. Modern hybrids produce so rapidly that this process may have to take place every other summer.

Above: Dig out a clump of iris **(left)** and cut the fans back to about 6 inches **(center).** The old growth is broken or cut away and any diseased or infested spots are cut out. But an additional step is worthwhile. Bearded irises are troubled by disease and the insect iris borer. A simple remedy for both is to dip each rhizome section in a solution of 10 percent household bleach to water for ten seconds **(right).**

Below: Then the fresh sections will be replanted close to the surface so the horizontal rhizome is exposed to baking sunlight—necessary for the best flowering.

13

Roots

Beneath the tree, below the shrub, underneath the herbaceous perennial's crown, and sprouting from the base of a bulb are roots: the last stop from the top of plant propagation to the bottom.

Roots anchor a plant in the soil. They absorb moisture and nutrients and transport them to the outer reaches of the leaves. Every structure of a plant presents ways to grow new roots, and even a section of root itself can be prompted to become a new perennial, shrub, or even a tree for your garden.

Some propagators consider root cuttings the easiest of all ways to reproduce plants. In theory the results are guaranteed, but propagating from tiny root cuttings is not always as

Preceding pages: Oriental poppies are about the easiest root cuttings to make—one can practically use a rototiller.

Opposite: A wonderful nicotiana with violet flowers grew in Mary Anne Griffin's Newport, Rhode Island, garden. Guaranteeing this plant's return from seed is not possible, but in an experiment, root cuttings were taken. Setting them vertically in a pot worked: little plants sprouted.

This page: The nicotiana from root cuttings eventually bloomed—in the same rich color **(right)**. A few plants were kept and a few sent back to their original home. Some unusual plants make candidates for root cuttings; for example, the huge herbaceous native *Aralia racemosa* **(above left)**, and woody trees and shrubs that are stoloniferous, such as the red buckeye, *Aesculus pavia* **(below left)**.

easy as the pros make it sound. An experienced propagator with a commercial greenhouse can have success with cuttings as small as ½ inch long. These cuttings are laid in flats horizontally—like little hash marks on

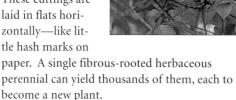

paper. A single fibrous-rooted herbaceous perennial can yield thousands of them, each to become a new plant.

Beginners will have greater success if they try large roots at first. These and nearly all root

cuttings have a better chance for success if set vertically in the medium. However, it is nearly impossible to keep cuttings of wiry roots upright, such as those from late-blooming anemone varieties. Cuttings from these easy-to-root plants can be laid horizontally just below the surface of perlite in a flat. But to be safe, the sections should be more than ½ inch long—2 to 4 inches long depending on the source.

There are many variables in root propagation: success depends on the type of plant, the condition of its roots, the time of year, temperature, the size of the cutting, and the propagator's patience. Some plants are finicky about root propagation, while others require almost no effort. When an Oriental poppy *(Papaver orien-*

tale) is accidentally run over with a rototiller and bits of roots are mixed through the soil, you could end up with a field full of these plants.

The overriding principle is that the cutting must have enough food resources to carry it through the process of making new roots and shoots. That's one reason why tiny cuttings are more difficult. If an herbaceous plant is dug up in the spring for root pruning, roots that form through the summer and that are harvested in autumn will have the greatest chance for success, since they will be young and thick—full of stored nutrition to carry them through the months ahead.

ROOTING ROOTS

Always select the thickest roots from a given plant. Phlox roots will never be pencil-thick, so just choose the largest ones. A preliminary step will make the process go more smoothly. In early spring, dig up the perennial when the ground has thoroughly thawed. Cut back new top growth, if any, and reduce the root system to stumps 1 to 2 inches long. Replant the peren-

species such as old-fashioned bleeding hearts (*Dicentra spectabilis*) and Oriental poppies are taken when the foliage of these plants has faded or died back in midsummer.

Roots from hardy plants in containers can be harvested in late winter if the pots are not frozen and growth is beginning. Slender roots of anemone and phlox could be handled then. The eager roots are set just below the surface of perlite in a flat and placed in a warm greenhouse or

(1)   (2)   (3)

(4)   (5)   (6)

Broad, compound leaves, fuzzy flowers, and rich, ruby fruits are attractions for the North American native *Aralia racemosa*. The procedure for making root cuttings of the aralia starts by digging up a plant when it is dormant and cutting back the top growth (1). The roots are washed clean (2). Thick roots are selected for cuttings (3), and the rest of the plant is returned to the garden. Tiny fibrous side roots are removed (4). The cuttings are made about 3 inches long, and polarity must be retained, so angle cuts are made at the bottom (earth end) of the cuttings (5), straight cuts at the top (skyward) (6).

nial. Although root propagation can be done without this preparation, the rate of success will not be as high, and the plants will take longer to appear above the medium.

Late autumn to early winter, when the plants are dormant, is often the best time to go back to the perennial to harvest root cuttings. The herbaceous plants have disappeared above the soil, and, along with woody plants, they have sent provisions underground for safekeeping. There are exceptions, however; cuttings from

sweatbox in strong light but out of direct sunlight. New roots and shoots will develop at once, and bottom heat will hasten the development. Similarly, very thick roots, such as the horseradish-size ones of *Anchusa*, can also be encouraged to develop quickly if placed on perlite in mid- to late winter soon before growth begins. These large roots are laid horizontally on the medium, and they can even be sectioned to produce multiple plants (page 220).

Most pencil-thick roots are cut into sections

and potted up vertically in containers. Several cuttings can fit into a single container. The size of the pot has to be in scale with the roots. For example, around eight 2-inch-long acanthus roots would be comfortable in a 1-gallon container. Once you have chosen a plant to propagate, prepare a suitable pot by filling it to the top with clean, moistened potting medium. Strike off the surface of the medium by scraping a ruler or homemade striker across the rim, and

it from heaving.) Lay the collected roots on a cutting board, and trim off tiny side feeder roots. Polarity must be retained under all circumstances. New shoots will form at the former top, or proximal end, of the roots sections.

To keep track of polarity (which is harder than one might imagine), start at the proximal end and make sections with a straight cut at the top and a diagonal cut to indicate the bottom; immediately retrim the angled top of the next section

(1) (2) (3)

(4) (5) (6)

A gallon pot is filled with moist medium and tamped down to remove air pockets (1). A pencil drills holes to receive the root sections (2). The cuttings are set into the medium so that they are flush with its surface (3). Grit is poured to the top (4) and skimmed off (5). The pot can be set above bottom heat in a cool greenhouse, but any spot will do as long as the pot will not freeze. And since there is no top growth, direct sunlight is not necessary, nor is extra water usually required until the sprouts appear above the ground (6). Top growth is not a guarantee that new roots have formed, so leave the cuttings for a season.

tamp the medium down to eliminate air spaces. Add more of the mix, if necessary, to bring the level up to ½ to ¼ inch below the pot rim, depending on the size of the root cutting. Thick roots will be set deep, and slender ones will be higher or shallower in the pot.

Dig up the plant and wash its roots clean of soil. Cut off a few roots for propagation, and replant the parent. (Mulch the plant with a loose covering of pine boughs or oak leaves after the soil freezes to keep the ground around

so that it is square again. The length of the cuttings also depends on their thickness—thick roots should be cut into longer sections than thin ones, but always err on the long side. Roots of *Aralia racemosa*, which are nearly as thick as a pencil, yield cuttings 2 to 3 inches long.

Make holes in the medium to receive the cuttings using a pencil, stick, or toothpick, corresponding to the diameter of the roots. Space the cuttings evenly and in proportion to their size. Insert the roots so the tops are flush with the

Opposite: The late-summer-to-fall-blooming anemones will yield hundreds of slender roots for propagation.

Above: The thin-root process begins in late winter by knocking a greenhouse-grown plant out of its pot or harvesting roots from garden plants below mulch. The wiry roots are pulled from the ball **(left).** Dormant buds can be seen as white specks. The root sections are placed horizontally in rooting medium (perlite) **(center);** again, bottom heat will speed the process. In a month or two, green plants appear all over the medium and the little plants can be pulled free **(right)** to be potted individually and watered.

Below: Thick roots, such as those of perennial forget-me-not (*Anchusa azurea*), are like pieces of horseradish and can be prepared in autumn by slicing through a chunk horizontally **(left).** This produces two long halves and exposes the white flesh. The halves are set into rooting medium cut side up **(center)** in a greenhouse or sweatbox (bottom heat is helpful). Roots grow, as do shoots. In spring, pieces of the root cuttings with shoots can be cut apart. The sections are potted individually **(right)** and will be hardened off—along with the seedlings started under lights in the indoor nursery.

surface of the medium. Pour grit over the top, and strike the surface even with the pot rim. Insert a label with the name of the plant and the date that the cuttings were stuck.

The roots of tender perennials can be placed in a cool location with a bit of bottom heat, but hardy root cuttings will not require extra warmth. A great spot for these pots is in the cold frame. There they will be protected from the rain; too much water is the main threat to root cuttings. Lift the pot to judge the weight and, thereby, the moisture content, but don't be surprised if the pot only needs water once again until new growth appears above the grit—which will be your first sign that something is happening below. Do not attempt to uproot the cuttings, as the top growth appears well before the plants have produced enough tiny feeder roots to support a new independent specimen.

The time it takes for root cuttings to produce plants ready for the garden varies—several months or longer. The *Aralia* cuttings spent two winters in the cold frame before they were ready

to be knocked out of their pot and planted in the garden. That was in their second spring, when they made lush top growth.

ROOTS OF WOODY PLANTS

Woody plants that are known to produce suckers and vertical shoots near the main plant, shrubs such as lilac, sumac, buckeye, daphne, and woody aralia, can also be propagated from root cuttings. (Remember that many variegated plants will not pass that characteristic along by this method.) A surprising number of trees can likewise be propagated from root cuttings, but, as you might imagine, harvesting the roots is a challenge. Suckering trees, such as black locust, acacia, catalpa, and *Paulownia* (or empress tree), often have shallow roots that can be uncovered for cuttings. Vines such as passionflower and cross vine can be propagated from their roots, as can trumpet vine (although I can't imagine why one would want more of this athletic creeper).

The Cutting Edge

One thing gardeners are sure of:
the garden is never finished, and we
wouldn't have it any other way.

Micropropagation, meristem propagation, and *tissue culture* are synonyms for the latest method of vegetative propagation. This process entails growing an entire plant from as little as a single cell of the meristem, or growing point, of a plant. After many successes, and many failures, micropropagation has proved to represent the future for commercial propagation.

Although micropropagation holds a powerful allure, the financial and personal commitment necessary is daunting. One of the few books on the subject, *Plants from Test Tubes: An Introduction to Micropropagation,* by Lydiane Kyte and John Kleyn, suggests that tissue culture might be feasible for home gardeners, but then it goes on to list the requirements, including a sterile laboratory with an air-filtration system, body suits, masks, latex gloves, goggles, flasks, dishes, and a microscope.

In micropropagation, the guiding premise is totipotency, the notion that every cell of a plant has the genetic information encoded for every part of the plant. By manipulating hormones, a propagator "tells" a tiny cutting of callus or cells of new tissue to grow roots and shoots in vitro. The cuttings are made with surgical tools and placed on a growing medium, usually gelatinous agar, that has been enhanced with hormones and nutritional chemicals precisely concocted for the specific plant species.

Hundreds of cultivated varieties of expensive plants, such as hostas and orchids, are being reproduced through micropropagation. Tera Nova Labs in Oregon produces little plants of some of the *Pulmonaria* and *Heuchera* discoveries of one of its partners, Dan Heims. Dan's hybrids, such as *Pulmonaria* 'Spilled Milk' and *Heuchera* 'Pewter Veil', are commonly found at garden centers. Tera Nova can make as many as 100,000 copies of one of these hybrids in only two years from its discovery.

Another advantage to tissue culture is that it is often a way to produce disease-free material from an infected plant, which otherwise would pass the pathogen to its progeny. The newest growth of plants either is not diseased or can be partially sterilized by a quick dip in a disinfecting solution of bleach and water.

The most exciting reason to venture into micropropagation is that plants that may be extremely or nearly impossible to reproduce

Opposite: Vials under fluorescent lights hold tiny coleus plants grown from just a few cells of meristem tissue in sterile, nutrient-enriched agar. The process begins with a surgeon's tools and vials of prepared medium.

Top to bottom: After being dipped in a dilute solution of sterilizing bleach that kills surface contaminants but is not strong enough to harm the plant's cells, the cutting is held with tweezers as the scalpel is readied. A tiny piece of the newest tissue is cut out. The cutting is picked up with tweezers to be lowered into the vial and placed onto the medium surface.

through other methods can be propagated in vitro. Orchids are a prime example; this family is notoriously difficult and slow to propagate by sexual means because the seeds resemble spores with no nutritional support. Commercial growers have grown seeds in flasks of nutritional medium for decades, but sexual reproduction of an orchid hybrid by conventional means had been nearly unfeasible for mass marketing. Micropropagation presents a viable method that has revolutionized the orchid industry.

Students at Ryde College of Horticulture in Sydney, Australia, demonstrated simple operations for me on relatively easy-to-root cuttings such as coleus. Half-inch-long pieces of a plant were removed, dunked with tweezers in a 10 percent solution of bleach and water, and placed in a glass dish. Cuttings of the terminal growth, about 1/16 inch long, were sliced away from the sections with a sterilized scalpel. Next, the tiny bits were picked up with the tweezers and dropped onto prepared medium in labeled test tubes. The tubes were sealed and placed under fluorescent lights. Watching the process made micropropagation a little less intimidating to me, and perhaps worth a try in the future. I saw the results of earlier experiments as tiny plants in similar vials.

It is not unreasonable to imagine that someday home gardeners will be practicing tissue culture. As more gardeners want to learn about propagation, someone will undoubtedly find a way to translate this most precise and specialized aspect of making more plants into an accessible technique, and perhaps produce a kit for gardeners to try tissue culture at home.

Growing entire plants from tiny bits of tissue is where the journey ends, for now. That highly specialized propagation technique may seem mind-boggling, but remember that some plants you'll want to grow will sprout from seeds in a week or two, and that coleus cuttings taken in spring will have roots in less than three weeks.

PROMISE

To become a great propagator, you must have patience, but to begin to propagate plants, all you need is curiosity. There will be triumphs, and there will surely be misses in your experience. Even great gardeners have experienced failure. Dan Hinkley of the Heronswood Nursery in Washington State writes of many of his adventures with plants, "Been there, killed that." Bob and Briggita Stewart of Arrowhead Alpines in Michigan say that the measure of the best among elite growers is how many plants they have killed. In propagation, just as in all kinds of parenting, sometimes it is necessary to let go.

But I can truly say that I have never lost a plant without learning something.

A beginner asked me recently about an African violet he had that had grown a long barren "neck" and had leaves only at the end of the trunk. The plant was leaning over the edge of the pot, threatening to topple off the windowsill. He wanted to propagate the plant by cutting off the top and rooting it in water. I explained how the top could be rooted in perlite, but I suggested that a better way to propagate it would be to take three or four leaf cuttings and throw the rest of the plant away. He protested, saying that he didn't want to throw the plant away, he wanted to learn. But the best lesson is to know when to cut your losses. Fresh leaf cuttings will yield better plants than the scraggly African violet top.

Imagine the sense of accomplishment when flowers push up from a beautiful rosette of leaves grown from a single leaf. Picture what it will be like when the mail-order perennial you purchased can be divided in its second year into four, five, or six plants. Consider the thrill of watching a plant be "born" from a seed that you harvested. Dream about taking a little chunk of a plant that isn't even on the market, a towering red-leaved canna for instance, and then in only two seasons, walking through a grove of 6-foot giants.

PLANT PROPAGATION GUIDE

The list on the following pages includes about seven hundred genera of plants. Since a single genus may comprise one, fifty, or hundreds of species and varieties, the list could serve as your guide for propagating thousands of plants. The information is general but usually applies to all of the members of the genus. Special cultural notes accompany genera, such as *Hibiscus*, in which there are hardy, tender, woody, and herbaceous annual and perennial species.

The propagation methods are listed in the same order that they appear in the book: sexual propagation is followed by vegetative practices. The cultural information begins by indicating if the plant may be started from seeds and the necessary procedures, such as conditioning, temperature, and timing (see page 240). The vegetative practices begin with stem cuttings and end with root cuttings.

Many plants that are potentially invasive, and often easy to propagate, are not included in this list. Examples include certain members of the mint family, running bamboo and other grasses, plume poppy, *Perilla*, *Polygonum*, *Ranunculus* (buttercup), and purple loosestrife.

The commercially prepared seed packets for the most common annual flowers and vegetables nearly always include detailed propagation instructions. These easy plants are not included in the list.

Conversions: 50°F=10°C, 60°F=15.5°C, 70°F=21°C, 80°F=26.5°C.

Note: Gibberillic acid (GA_3) is a form of the plant hormone gibberillin, which has been used to overcome physiological germination inhibitors in some species. For example, certain seeds that normally require months of chilling, germinate immediately after soaking in the weakest effective solutions of 100 to 1,000 ppm of GA_3 (12 to 48 hours—until they swell). For more information, consult the works of Norman C. Deno (see Bibliography).

ENTRY PARTICULARS

SEED most often refers to species, since most cultivars will not be true to type from sown seed. Heirloom strains will come true, however, if grown away from other members in the species. In all cases, seeds should be completely clean of fruit (moist or dry).

LIGHT calls for surface sowing and exposure to light.

DARK calls for opaque covers for pots or soil over seeds in situ. Check pots for germination—when covers must be removed.

IN SITU refers to sowing seeds where they are intended to grow outdoors. Plants started this way are often ones that are easy to sow, but in some cases, the plants may resent transplanting, such as ones with long taproots. (Many hardy annuals are sown in situ in winter, while some perennials and biennials can be sown in situ from spring through summer to overwinter in place and bloom the following year.)

OUTDOORS does not refer to the open but to the recommended procedure of placing sown seeds in pots in a prepared screen-covered frame in a sheltered or protected location. Most seeds of hardy plants are sown when ripe or in autumn outdoors. They require little care, but moisture in the medium should be checked. (To accelerate the process, pots of some hardy plants may be brought indoors in spring to a location with high humidity, full sun, and cool temperatures [50°F], or they may be placed in a cold frame.)

SOAK is in room-temperature water (unless otherwise specified) and is followed by number of hours and/or temperature of the water, which means the temperature of the water at the outset. If the water should remain at a specific temperature, that will be noted or, in some cases, simply indicated as "warm soak"—above 70°F. For seeds that soak longer than one day, the water should be changed at least once a day. Nearly all seeds of perennial plants received dry in the mail will benefit from a one-hour soak prior to sowing. Once moistened, all seeds must continue the processes leading to germination: they dry, they die.

MOIST-WARM refers to 70–75°F stratification. Seeds can be placed on moist paper towel or moss, or sown in pots prior to treatment.

MOIST-COLD refers to stratification at 40°F (in the refrigerator).

SCARIFICATION means nicking or filing the seed coat, unless otherwise noted. When the coat of a seed seems rock-hard, you can surmise that it may need scarification.

INDOORS, followed by "(temperature)," refers to heated locations—usually under fluorescent lights inside the home or in a greenhouse—and the temperature range for optimal germination. Means must be provided to raise and maintain high relative humidity levels. Plants appreciate lower temperatures at night and after sprouting.

SPORES need to be surface-sown following instructions on page 98.

GERM. DAYS indicates when the first seedlings can be expected to emerge. A wide range of days often means that germination is erratic. The lowest number of days tells you when to begin checking, and the longest number of days might suggest when to abandon hope and discard the seeds and medium.

HERBACEOUS STEM CUTTINGS are ones taken of soft growth usually in the spring, or from new growth that emerges later on non-flowering parts of herbaceous plants that is soft and roots readily. If special recommendations call for taking stem-tip, nodal, or internodal cuttings (below), that will be noted.

SEMI-RIPE refers to the hardened growth from herbaceous plants in summer to late summer.

SOFTWOOD CUTTINGS are sections of stem taken from woody plants when the new growth has ceased elongating and is turgid but is still pliable and tender.

GREENWOOD refers to the new growth on woody plants as it hardens and the stems begin to take on the color of mature growth.

SEMI-RIPEWOOD is the late-season growth of woody plants and is most often used for cuttings of broad-leaved evergreens.

NODAL CUTTINGS are ones trimmed just below a leaf node, and they may be suggested for plants that are prone to rot, or that have hollow or pithy stems, as these will be closed at the node area.

INTERNODAL CUTTINGS are made with cuts between two nodes.

HEEL, MALLET refer to specific cuts on the distal end of a cutting, some of which include a bit of the older stem along with the new harvested tissue (see page 125).

SECTIONS OF BULBS, CORMS, TUBERS, OR RHIZOMES are cut pieces of geophytes. Bulb sections include a scale and bit of basal plate. The others must have an eye (dormant bud).

DIVISION often refers to cutting through the crown of herbaceous perennials just before or shortly after spring-growth begins. (Where winters are mild and summers hot, perennials can also be divided in autumn, as can very hardy ones in cold climates when mulch is required.) Reference to division via suckers, offets, and runners follows.

BASAL CUTTINGS are ones taken at crown level around the basal rosette of an herbaceous plant—usually late winter or late summer.

ROOT CUTTINGS are taken as described on pages 216–220. (For plants that resent disturbance, such as *Eryngium* [sea holly], roots suitable for harvesting can be encouraged by potting the plants in containers with large drainage holes and setting the pots about 1 inch into a 3- to 6-inch-deep bed of moist sand. Large roots will grow into the medium, which can be harvested.)

GENERIC GUIDE TO PROPAGATING ORNAMENTAL PLANTS

ABELIA: softwood, greenwood, semi-ripewood cuttings

ABIES: fresh seed—soak 30 hours and then moist-cold (30 days), light, sow indoors (50–60°F) (germ. 21–30 days); evergreen hardwood cuttings in mid- to late winter, hormone, bottom heat; grafting

ABUTILON: seed—sow indoors (70–75°F) (germ. 30–90 days); softwood, greenwood, semi-ripewood cuttings

ACACIA: seed—file, hot water and then 24-hour soak, then sow indoors (70–80°F) (germ. 21 days); greenwood cuttings

ACALYPHA: softwood, semi-ripe cuttings; division

ACANTHUS: seed—outdoors, or sow indoors cool (50–55°F) (germ. 21–25 days); herbaceous cuttings in autumn; division; root cuttings

ACER: fresh seed—light, outdoors in autumn, or 48-hour water soak, moist-warm (60 days) followed by moist-cold (60 days) followed by light, sow indoors (65–70°F) (germ. 30–365+ days) (note: A. rubrum, A. saccharinum, sow indoors when ripe in late spring to summer; some maples, such as A. griseum, set very few viable seeds); softwood cuttings; layering; grafting

ACHILLEA: seed—light, outdoors in spring or summer up to 2 months before frost, or light, sow indoors (70–75°F) 8–10 weeks before last frost date (germ. 10 days); division; basal cuttings

ACHIMENES: seed—sow indoors (70–75°F) (germ. 14–21 days); herbaceous stem, leaf cuttings; rhizome (tubercle) division

ACONITUM: seed—light, outdoors in frame, or moist-cold (40 days) and then light, sow indoors (70–75°F) (germination erratic); divide early (slow to reestablish)

ACORUS: rhizome division in late spring

ACTAEA: fresh seed—outdoors in autumn, or moist-warm (90 days) followed by moist-cold (90 days) followed by sow indoors (60–70°F) (germ. 270+ days up to 2 years) (two-step germination, see page 74); rhizome division

ACTINIDIA: fresh (green) seed—clean of pulp, sow indoors (50°F) (germ. 7–14 days); dry seed—moist-cold (90 days) followed by sow indoors (50–60°F) (germ. 14–60 days); greenwood, semi-ripewood, hardwood cuttings; layering; grafting

ADIANTUM: spore—(70–75°F); division

ADONIS: fresh seed—outdoors; division

AECHMEA: fresh seed—clean from berries, light, sow indoors on moist sphagnum, high humidity (germ. 7–90 days) (70°F); offsets (pups)

AEONIUM: very fresh seed—some plants are monocarpic and must be raised from seed, sow indoors (65–75°F) (germ. 30–90 days); semi-ripe cuttings of side shoots; leggy, older plants can have stem and top rosette removed and be rooted as stem cutting (anytime, but spring easiest; allow all cuttings to air-dry at least 24 hours)

AESCULUS: fresh seed—outdoors (some species moist-cold 120 days); hardwood cuttings; layer shrubby kinds; grafting (budding); division of root suckers; root cuttings in winter of some species

AGAPANTHUS: seed—sow indoors (70–75°F) (germ. 30–90 days); rhizome division

AGASTACHE: seed—sow indoors (70–75°F) 6–8 weeks before last frost date (germ. 30–120 days); herbaceous (semi-ripe) cuttings; division

AGAVE: fresh seed—light, sow indoors (70–75°F) (germ. 30–90 days); offset division

AGLAONEMA: division of suckers

AJUGA: divide and transplant plantlets with roots that form along runner (some vigorous varieties are potentially invasive, although easy to weed—keep away from lawn)

ALCEA: seed—sow in situ, or sow indoors (70–75°F) (germ. 10–21 days)

ALCHEMILLA: fresh seed—sow in situ in early spring, or sow indoors (60–70°F) 6–8 weeks before last frost date (germ. 21–30 days); division in spring or through the season with cover

ALLAMANDA: semi-ripewood cuttings

ALLIUM: fresh seed—light, outdoors in autumn for hardiest, but most outdoors in spring (store dry in refrigerator), or moist-cold (30 days), followed by light, sow indoors (50–60°F) (germ. 30–365 days); bulb offsets; bulbils

ALNUS: fresh seed—outdoors in autumn or winter; greenwood cuttings in late spring; grafting

ALOCASIA: rhizome or tuber (by species) division

ALOE: seed—light, sow indoors (70–75°F) (germ. 21–28 days); leaf cuttings; offsets

ALSTROEMERIA: fresh seed—where plants are hardy, soak in warm water, and then sow in situ 1 week before last frost or 1 week before first in mild climates, or sow indoors, keep moist (65–75°F) (germ. 15–365 days, erratic); rhizome division in autumn (difficult)

ALTERNANTHERA: seed—sow indoors (70–75°F) (germ. 1–21 days); herbaceous stem cuttings; division for hardy kinds

ALTHAEA: seed—light, sow indoors (60–70°F) 6–8 weeks before last frost date (germ. 10–14 days); division of suckers sometimes possible, or basal cuttings, but difficult

ALYSSUM: seed—light, outdoors in early spring or early autumn, or light, sow indoors (60–65°F) 8–10 weeks before last frost date (germ. 5–14 days); semi-ripe cuttings (summer)

AMARANTHUS: seed—sow indoors (70–75°F) 6–8 weeks before last frost date (germ. 10–15 days)

AMELANCHIER: fresh seed—outdoors; stored seed, outdoors in spring to germinate following spring, or moist-warm (90 days) followed by moist-cold (90 days) then sow indoors (60–65°F) (germ. erratic); semi-ripewood cuttings; layering; division of suckers

AMORPHA: seed—12-hour warm-water soak, sow indoors (50–60°F) (germ. 30–120 days); division of suckers

AMORPHOPHALLUS: division of offset tubers

AMSONIA: seed—outdoors, or moist-cold (30–42 days)—nicking aids germination (germ. 30–365 days); herbaceous cuttings; division

ANAGALLIS: seed—annuals, sow indoors (70–75°F) (germ. 18–21 days); hardy annuals, sow in situ; perennial kinds, division of rooted layers

ANANAS: division of suckers (pups) from crown and base of fruit; cut leafy top off fruit, allow cut surface to dry 24 hours, root on medium

ANAPHALIS: seed—outdoors, or indoors (55–65°F) 6–8 weeks before last frost date (germ. 30–60 days); division; basal cuttings

ANCHUSA: seeds—sow indoors (70–75°F) 6–8 weeks before last frost date (germ. 7–30 days); division; root cuttings

ANDROMEDA: seed—light, sow indoors (50–60°F; note: keep pot in saucer of water to maintain high moisture) (germ. 30–60 days)

ANEMONE: seed—species, outdoors in autumn (or spring) to germinate following spring; division in spring; root cuttings in winter (A. blanda, division of corms when leaves die down in late spring)

ANEMONELLA: fresh seed—outdoors in summer; division (necessary for double form)

ANGELICA: fresh seed—in situ or moist-cold (14 days) then light, sow indoors (60–70°F) (germ. 20–60 days)

ANTENNARIA: seed—sow indoors (70–75°F) (germ. 30–70 days); spring or autumn division of basal offsets

ANTHEMIS: seed—sow indoors (70–75°F) 8–10 weeks before last frost date (germ. 7–21 days); herbaceous stem cuttings; division in spring; basal stem cuttings of alpine types

ANTHURIUM: fresh seed—sow indoors (75–80°F with high humidity) (germ. 2–30 days); division of offsets with roots

ANTIRRHINUM: seed—light, sow indoors (70–75°F) 8–10 weeks before last frost date (germ. 7–14 days); herbaceous stem cuttings (spring), semi-ripe cuttings (autumn)

AQUILEGIA: seed—light, sow in situ, or moist-cold (21 days), light, sow indoors (70–75°F) (germ. 21–28 days); division of basal growths for rooting in warm climates or in greenhouse or frame

ARABIS: seed—light, sow indoors (70–75°F) 6–8 weeks before last frost date (germ. 21–28 days); herbaceous cuttings after flowering; division of rooted layers of creeping forms

ARALIA: seed—outdoors, or moist-warm (90 days) followed by moist-cold (90 days) and then sow indoors (70–75°F) (germ. 21 days); division of suckers (splice side graft); dormant root cuttings

ARAUCARIA: fresh seed—moist-cold (21–84 days) and then dark, sow indoors (55–60°F) (germ. 14–60 days [hypogeal germination—seed leaves remain below surface as true leaves emerge]); semi-ripewood cuttings

ARBUTUS: seed—moist-cold (60–90 days) followed by light, sow indoors (65–70°F) (germ. 30–120 days); semi-ripewood cuttings; layering; grafting

ARCTOSTAPHYLOS: semi-ripewood cuttings—mist helpful (*A. uva-ursi*, layering as well)

ARCTOTIS: seed—sow indoors (70–75°F) 6–8 weeks before last frost date (germ. 14–21 days); herbaceous cuttings in autumn

ARDISIA: seed—mash pulp and place in water to ferment for 14 days and then rinse, dry, soak (24 hours) followed by sow indoors (70–75°F) (germ. 7–21 days); softwood, semi-ripewood cuttings

ARENARIA: seed—light, sow indoors (55°F) 6–8 weeks before last frost date (germ. 7–30 days); cuttings; division of rooted layers of creeping forms

ARGEMONE: seed—in situ after last frost (germ. 14 days)

ARISAEMA: fresh seed—moist-cold (45 days), then light, sow indoors (55–60°F) (germ. 14–21 days [although easy from freshly cleaned seed, may be difficult from dried seed, which should be soaked before sowing, and may take up 180 days to germinate]); removal of offset tubers from around parent tubers in spring in cold climates, autumn in warm climates

ARISARUM: fresh seed—moist-cold (45 days), then light, sow indoors (60–70°F) (germ. 14–21 days); tuber division

ARISTOLOCHIA: seed hardy kinds: outdoors in spring, or moist-cold (90 days)—tender kinds: soak in warm water 48 hours—followed by sow indoors (65–70°F) (germ. variable by type); softwood (tender species and varieties only), greenwood, semi-hardwood cuttings; division

ARMERIA: seed—soak in warm water 6–8 hours, sow indoors (70–75°F) 8–10 weeks before last frost date (germ. 10–21 days); division

ARMORACIA: division; root cuttings

ARONIA: softwood, greenwood cuttings; layering; division of suckers

ARTEMISIA: seed—light, outdoors, or light, sow indoors (60–65°F) 10–12 weeks before last frost date (germ. 30–180 days);

greenwood stem-tip cuttings, semi-ripe stem-tip cuttings (keep foliage dry or cuttings may rot); division; basal cuttings (less hardy kinds can be taken to overwinter in cold frame)

ARUM: fresh seed—moist-cold (45 days) and then sow indoors (55–65°F) 10–12 weeks before planting out in spring or autumn (germ. 14–21 days); tuber division

ARUNCUS: fresh seed—light, outdoors after last frost, or light, sow indoors (70–75°F) (old seed must be soaked and moist-cold 30–90 days) (germ. 30–90 days); division

ARUNDO: division in spring

ASARINA: seed—light, sow indoors (70–75°F) 10–12 weeks before last frost date (germ. 14–30 days); stem-tip cuttings

ASARUM: fresh seed—outdoors as soon as seed is ripe, or moist-cold (30 days) followed by sow indoors (60–65°F) (germ. 7–21 days); rhizomatous stem division in spring (early autumn for hardiest kinds)

ASCLEPIAS: fresh seed—tender and annual kinds: sow indoors (70–75°F) (germ. 21–28 days); hardy kinds: outdoors, or moist-cold (21 days) and then sow indoors (70–75°F) (germ. 30–90 days); herbaceous cuttings; root cuttings

ASIMINA: fresh seed—moist-cold (60–90 days; radicle forms during moist-cold) (germ. 90–150 days); root cuttings in winter

ASPARAGUS: fresh seed (tender ornamentals)—soak 24 hours, sow indoors (70–75°F) (germ. 28 days); division; tuber division

ASPIDISTRA: division

ASPLENIUM: spores—(70–75°F); division; root "bulbils" (adventitious plantlets) while still attached to fronds by pinning to medium

ASTER: seed—outdoors, or sow indoors (70–75°F) 6–8 weeks before last frost date (germ. 15–20 days [may benefit from moist-cold 14 days]); herbaceous cuttings in spring; basal cuttings

ASTILBE: (species) fresh seed—moist-warm (14 days) and then moist-cold (28 days), sow indoors (60–70°F) 6–8 weeks before last frost date (germ. 21–60 days); division in spring

ASTILBOIDES: seed—sow indoors (70–75°F) (germ. 7–14 days); division

ASTRANTIA: seed—light, outdoors when ripe; selections by division in spring or autumn

ATHYRIUM: spores—(70–75°F); division; root "bulbils" (adventitious plantlets) while still attached to fronds by pinning to medium

ATRIPLEX: seed—outdoors after last frost but while soil still cool

AUBRIETA: seed—light, sow indoors (65–70°F) 6–8 weeks before last frost date (germ. 14–21 days); semi-ripe cuttings in summer; division in early spring

AUCUBA: fresh seed—rub pulp from seeds, outdoors (germ. 540 days), or sow indoors (65–70°F) (germ. 30–90 days); semi-ripewood cuttings (cold frame); layering

AURINIA: seed—light, outdoors in early spring or early autumn, or light, sow indoors (60–65°F) 8–10 weeks before last frost date (germ. 5–21 days); herbaceous cuttings in spring, semi-ripe cuttings in summer to late summer; division in autumn

BABIANA: seed—sow indoors (70–75°F) (germ. 28–56 days)

BACCHARIS: fresh seed—sow indoors (70–75°F) (germ. 7–14 days)

BAPTISIA: fresh seed (just-ripe seed), sow indoors (70–75°F) 6–8 weeks before last frost date (germ. 7–35 days); stored seed must be nicked followed by sow indoors (70–75°F); division

BEGONIA: seed—light, sow indoors (70–75°F) 3–4 months before last frost date for bedding types and tuberous varieties (seed must be on surface) (germ. 14–60 days); by type: herbaceous cuttings anytime (stem, leaf); rhizome cuttings; tuberous: sections of tuber as shoots appear; bulbils in leaf axils of some; shoots with bit of tuber treated as stem cuttings; basal stem cuttings in summer

BELAMCANDA: seed—sow indoors (70–75°F) 8–10 weeks before last frost date (germ. 14–21 days); division in spring

BELLIS: seed—light, sow indoors (70–75°F) 8–10 weeks before last frost date (germ. 1–15 days), in cold frame in late summer for spring bloom; divide special cultivars after flowering

BERBERIS: seed—light, outdoors, or moist-cold (60 days) followed by light, sow indoors (50–65°F) (germ. 60–180 days); softwood, semi-ripewood mallet cuttings (see page 125); semi-ripewood cuttings; grafting; division

BERGENIA: seed—outdoors, or moist-cold (14 days) followed by sow indoors (60–70°F) 6–8 weeks before last frost date (germ. 30–80 days); rhizome cuttings in late winter (bury half deep in perlite with bottom heat); division in spring

BETULA: fresh seed—light, outdoors (if planted as soon as ripe, germination may be immediate), or moist-cold (70 days) followed by light, sow indoors (65–75°F) (germ. 30–90 days); greenwood, semi-ripewood cuttings with mist (difficult); grafting

BIGNONIA: seed—outdoors; semi-ripewood cuttings; layering

BLECHNUM: spores—(70–75°F); offsets from stolons (rhizomes)

BOLTONIA: seed—outdoors, or sow indoors (70–75°F) 6–8 weeks before last frost date (germ. 14–21 days); herbaceous cuttings; division; basal cuttings

BOUGAINVILLEA: softwood, semi-ripewood (bottom heat), hardwood cuttings; layering

BOWIEA: scale seedings; division of offsets

BRACHYCOME: seeds—sow indoors (70–75°F) 6–8 weeks before last frost date (70°F) (germ. 14–21 days); basal cuttings

BRIZA: seed—sow indoors (55°F) 6–8 weeks before last frost date (germ. 1–14 days); division of perennial types

BRODIAEA: seed—sow indoors (55–60°F) (germ. 30–90 days); division of cormels in autumn

BROUSSONETIA: seed—outdoors; softwood cuttings

BROWALLIA: seed—light, sow indoors (70–75°F) 6–8 weeks before last frost date (germ. 14–21 days); herbaceous cuttings

BRUGMANSIA: seed—light, sow indoors (70–75°F) (germ. 21–60 days); softwood, greenwood, semi-ripewood cuttings

BRUNFELSIA: softwood, greenwood cuttings

BRUNNERA: seed—moist-cold (30 days) and then sow indoors (70–75°F) 8–10 weeks before last frost date (germ. 30–90 days), or outdoors in late summer to autumn for cold frame; division; root cuttings in late winter in greenhouse

BUDDLEIA: seed—light, outdoors, or moist-cold (30 days) followed by light, sow indoors (70–75°F) (germ. 20–30 days); softwood, greenwood, semi-ripewood, hardwood cuttings

BULBOCODIUM: seed—outdoors; division after flowering and plants are dormant

BUPLEURUM: seed—sow indoors (70–75°F) (germ. 14–28 days); semi-ripewood cuttings; division in warm climates

BUTOMUS: fresh seed—sow indoors cool (55–65°F), keep medium saturated in bowl of water (germ. 30–60 days, erratic); division in spring; bulbils

BUXUS: seed—outdoors in spring; greenwood, semi-ripewood cuttings

CALADIUM: fresh seed—sow indoors (70–75°F) immediately (germ. 30–90 days); varieties can only be propagated vegetatively; division of tuber offsets; sections of tubers in spring

CALAMINTHA: seed—outdoors in situ when soil warm, or sow indoors (60–70°F) 8–10 weeks before last frost date (germ. 7–14 days); herbaceous stem cuttings in spring; division in spring; transplant self-layered plantlets

CALANTHE: divide rhizome sections with at least two pseudobulbs and growing shoot in early spring

CALATHEA: semi-ripe cuttings; division

CALCEOLARIA: seed—light, sow indoors in autumn (70–75°F) (germ. 5–10 days), keep cool after germination (50–55°F at night)

CALENDULA: seed—dark, outdoors in spring when still cool and frost possible, or dark, sow indoors (70–75°F) 6–8 weeks before last frost date (germ. 1–14 days)

CALLICARPA: seed—clean of pulp, light, sow indoors (70°F) (germ. 7–14 days), outdoors in autumn, or dried in spring; semi-ripewood, hardwood cuttings

CALLIRHOE: seed—light, outdoors where hardy, or light, sow indoors (50–60°F)

(germ. 30–180 days); stem-tip or semi-ripe cuttings of some kinds

CALLISTEMON: seed—light, sow indoors (55–65°F) (germ. 14–60 days); greenwood, semi-ripewood cuttings

CALLUNA: fresh seed—light, outdoors, or moist-cold (30 days) followed by light, sow indoors (65–70°F) (germ. 30–60 days); small softwood cuttings

CALTHA: fresh seed—outdoors best, or sow indoors (55–60°F) (germ. 30–90 days); division in spring after flowering or in late summer

CALYCANTHUS: seed—outdoors in autumn; greenwood, semi-ripewood cuttings; division of suckers

CAMASSIA: seed—sow indoors cool (55–60°F) (germ. 30–180 days); division of offsets in autumn

CAMELLIA: seed—soak in warm water 24–48 hours, sow indoors (70–75°F) (germ. 30–60 days) (may be difficult, try moist-cold 30–60 days); semi-ripewood cuttings (nodal, internodal stem-tip, and leaf cuttings [leaf-bud, split leaf bud] as per evergreen rhododendrons); layering; grafting

CAMPANULA: seed—light, sow indoors (70–75°F) 8–10 weeks before setting out while still cool and light frosts possible (germ. 14–28 days); division in spring; basal stem cuttings; root cuttings of some species

CAMPSIS: seed—moist-cold (60 days) followed by light, sow indoors (70–75°F) (germ. 14–21 days)

CANNA: seed—scarification and soak in warm water 48 hours, sow indoors (70–75°F) (germ. 7–14 [or up to 365] days); rhizome cuttings; division of suckers from base and cutting off rhizome bud nodules (toes) that form on some kinds of cannas

CARAGANA: seed—24–48-hour soak in warm water followed by light, outdoors, or light, sow indoors (65–70°F) (germ. 14–21 days); greenwood cuttings

CARDAMINE (DENTARIA): fresh seed—outdoors, or sow indoors immediately to grow cool; herbaceous cuttings in late spring (leaf cuttings of *C. pratensis*); division of rhizomes

CARDIOCRINUM: seed—outdoors where temperature does not drop below 15°F, or (two-step germinator, see page 206) moist-warm followed by moist-cold and sow indoors (70–75°F) (germ. 90–700 days); division of offsets (plant is monocarpic)

CAREX: fresh seed—light, sow indoors (70–75°F) (germ. varies by species, 7–60 days); division

CARPINUS: fresh seed—light, outdoors, or if seed has dried, scarify followed by moist-warm (30 days) followed by moist-cold (120 days) and then light, sow indoors (60–70°F) (germ. 30–365 days); greenwood cuttings; grafting (whip)

CARYOPTERIS: seed—sow indoors (65–70°F) (germ. 30–90 days); softwood,

greenwood, semi-ripewood, hardwood cuttings

CASSIA: seed—hardy herbaceous perennial: scarification followed by sow indoors (70–75°F) 6–8 weeks before last frost date (germ. 7–90 days); stem cuttings; division in spring

CATALPA: seed—light, sow indoors (60–70°F) (germ. 14–30 days; note: stored seed germinates readily); greenwood cuttings with heel; grafting (chip-budding); root cuttings

CATANANCHE: seed—sow indoors (70–75°F) 6–8 weeks before last frost date (germ. 14–21 days); division when in active growth; root cuttings in winter

CATHARANTHUS: seed—dark, sow indoors (70–75°F) 12–14 weeks before any possible frost danger has passed (germ. 14–21 days); semi-ripe cuttings in late summer to early autumn

CATTLEYA: division of pseudobulbs

CAULOPHYLLUM: division in spring or early autumn; sections of rhizome

CEANOTHUS: seed—24-hour soak followed moist-cold (14 days) and then light, sow indoors (65–70°F) (germ. 30–60 days); softwood, semi-ripewood, hardwood cuttings; root cuttings in autumn

CEDRUS: fresh seed—germinates readily (3-hour soak followed by moist-cold, 14 days, helpful), light, sow indoors (60–65°F) (germ. 7–60 days, erratic); evergreen hardwood cuttings (in October or later, hormone and bottom heat); grafting (to *C. deodara*)

CELOSIA: seed—light, sow indoors (70–75°F) (germ. 7–14 days)

CENTAUREA: seed—(annuals in situ); dark, sow indoors (60–70°F) 6–8 weeks before last frost date (germ. 7–30 days); (perennials: division in spring; root cuttings in winter)

CENTRANTHUS: fresh seed—outdoors, or sow indoors (60–70°F) 8 weeks before last frost date (germ. 21–30 days); division in spring

CEPHALANTHUS: seed—outdoors in autumn, or sow indoors (70–75°F) (germ. 7–14 days); semi-ripewood, hardwood cuttings

CEPHALARIA: seed—outdoors, or moist-cold (40 days) followed by sow indoors (55–60°F) (germ. 21–60 days); basal stem cuttings in midspring

CEPHALOTAXUS: seed—(recommendations vary; my attempt with only cold stratification failed) outdoors, or moist-cold (90 days) followed by moist-warm (90 days) followed by moist-cold (90 days), sow indoors (60–65°F); semi-ripewood cuttings (hormone, wounding perhaps, helps—mist accelerates rooting); grafting

CERASTIUM: seed—sow indoors (65–75°F) 6–8 weeks before last frost date (germ. 5–10 days); herbaceous stem-tip cuttings spring; division in spring

CERATOSTIGMA: seed—moist-cold (40 days) prior to sow indoors (60°F) (germ. 30–90 days); softwood cuttings; division; root cuttings

CERCIDIPHYLLUM: fresh seed—sow indoors (70–75°F) (germ. 7–14 days) (note: store clean and dry seed in refrigerator followed by above)

CERCIS: seed—hot water (170°F) and then 24-hour soak followed by light, outdoors, or moist-cold (6–90 days) and then light, sow indoors (70–75°F) (germ. 30–90 days); greenwood cuttings; grafting (apical-wedge)

CEROPEGIA: seed—sow indoors (75–90°F) (germ. quickly, fresh seed in less than a week); stem cuttings, runners while attached in daughter pots; division of tubers; tubercles

CESTRUM: seed—light, sow indoors (70–75°F) (germ. 70 days); softwood, greenwood, semi-ripewood cuttings

CHAENOMELES: fresh seed—pick seeds out of cut fruit and then light, outdoors, or moist-cold (60–70 weeks) followed by light, sow indoors (55–65°F) (germ. 70–90 days); softwood, greenwood, hardwood cuttings; layering (mounding); root cuttings

CHAMAECYPARIS: seed—harvest in autumn and store moist-cold (60 days) followed by light, sow indoors (50–60°F) (germ. 30–60 days); evergreen hardwood cuttings in late summer to midautumn; grafting

CHAMAEDOREA: seed—soak 24–48 hours, sow indoors (70–75°F) (germ. 30–120 days); offsets

CHASMANTHIUM: seed—light, outdoors; division; basal offsets

CHEILANTHES: spores; division of rhizomes

CHELONE: seed—moist-cold (40 days) followed by sow indoors (55–65°F) (germ. 14 days); stem cuttings in late spring; division in spring

CHIMONANTHUS: fresh seed—when fruits are green, light, sow indoors (70–75°F) (germ. 60 days), or ripe and stored seed, moist-cold (90 days) followed by moist-warm (90 days), sow indoors (germ. 60–90 days); softwood cuttings (heel); layering

CHIONANTHUS: seed—light, outdoors (germ. 2 years), or moist-cold (30 days) followed by light, sow indoors (60–70°F) (germ. 30–180 days or longer [note: germ. may not occur until second spring]); alternative method for seed—moist-warm (90 days) followed by moist-cold (90 days), light, sow indoors (60–70°F); layering

CHIONODOXA: fresh seed—outdoors in situ, or sow indoors (50°F) (germ. 30–90 days); division of offsets in autumn

CHLOROPHYTUM: division; peg offsets to medium while attached to parent (daughter pot), or separate and root in medium

CHOISYA: semi-ripewood cuttings, mist helpful

CHRYSANTHEMUM: seed—sow indoors (70–75°F) 6–8 weeks before last

frost date (germ. 1–21 days), perennial species appreciate lower temperatures at night; stem cuttings (bottom heat helpful) anytime—easiest in spring— (overwinter in cold frame); division in spring

CHRYSOGONUM: fresh seed—outdoors, or sow indoors (60–70°F) (germ. 21–30 days); division in spring

CIMICIFUGA: fresh seed—outdoors, or moist-cold (60–380 days), or sow indoors (55–60°F) (germ. slow—90–380 days); division in spring (best) or autumn (apply loose mulch)

CISSUS: seed—sow indoors (70–75°F) (germ. 30–180 days); tender species—stem cuttings (bottom heat helpful) in spring; hardy kinds—semi-ripewood to semi-ripewood cuttings (mist helpful); layering

CISTUS: seed—light, sow indoors (65–70°F; medium must be very moist at all times, cover pot with pane of glass, or pre-germinate on moist paper towel in plastic bag) (germ. 7–30 days); softwood to semi-ripewood cuttings

CITRUS: semi-ripe cuttings in summer (hormone and mist helpful); grafting; air layering

CLADRASTIS: seed—dry-stored should be steeped in warm water (120°F—gas oven with pilot light, perhaps—replenish water a few times) 2–3 days until swollen and sow indoors (70–75°F) (germ. 14–21 days); root cuttings

CLAYTONIA: fresh seed—collect ripe seed and sow immediately outdoors

CLEMATIS: seed—moist-cold (2–6 months depending on species), sow indoors (70–75°F) (germ. 30–365 days depending on species); cuttings variable by type, include softwood and semi-ripe leaf-bud cuttings, semi-ripewood stem cuttings; layering (serpentine, see page 163); specialized grafting onto *C. vitalba* seedling understock

CLEOME: seed—8–10 weeks before last frost date, moist-cold (14 days) and then light, sow indoors (70–75°F) (germ. 1–14 days), or sow in situ in spring

CLERODENDRUM: seed—hardy species, moist-cold (30–90 days) followed by light, sow indoors (65–70°F) (germ. 30–90 days); softwood, semi-ripewood cuttings; division; root cuttings

CLETHRA: fresh seed—moist-cold (90 days) followed by moist-warm (90 days), light, sow indoors (70°F) with high humidity or even under mist (germ. 21 days); greenwood cuttings (softwood and semi-ripewood cuttings of evergreen varieties possible under mist); layering; division of suckers

CLINTONIA: fresh seed—outdoors, or sow indoors in late winter (55–60°F) (germ. 30–90 days), cold frame first winter; division

CLIVIA: fresh seed—sow indoors (70–80°F) (germ. 7–21 days, dry-stored seed takes longer); division of offsets

COBAEA: seed—sow indoors (70–75°F) 6–8 weeks before last frost date (germ. 14–30 days); semi-ripe cuttings

CODONOPSIS: fresh seed—light, sow indoors (60–70°F) (germ. 7–42 days)

COFFEA: seed—soak in warm water 48 hours followed by light, sow indoors (70–75°F) (germ. erratic—42 days or longer); semi-ripewood cuttings under mist with bottom heat

COLCHICUM: seed—outdoors; divide cormels during summer

COLEUS (SOLENOSTEMON): seed—light, sow indoors (70–75°F) 8–12 weeks before last frost date (germ. 1–15 days); stem cuttings (bottom heat helpful) anytime, but fastest in late winter to early summer

COLOCASIA: in late winter to spring, cut sections of tuber to include at least one eye, allow divisions to air-dry for several days before planting; division of tuber offsets with eyes; basal stem cuttings with section of tuber

COLUMNEA: seed—light, sow indoors (70–75°F) (germ. 30–300 days); stem cuttings (bottom heat helpful) anytime

COMPTONIA: (propagation difficult) division—separation of good-size plants—from suckers; root cuttings in late winter to early spring

CONSOLIDA: seed—dark, sow in situ in late winter to spring

CONVALLARIA: fresh seed—light, outdoors; division of rhizomes (pips)

CORDYLINE: seed—soak hot water, sow indoors (70–75°F) (germ. 30–90 days); stem-section cuttings; air layering

COREOPSIS: seed—light, sow indoors (annuals: 6–8 weeks before last frost date, 70–75°F; perennials: 8–10 weeks before last frost date, 55–70°F) (germ. 2–25 days); perennial kinds: division; basal stem cuttings in spring

CORNUS: seed—light, outdoors, or moist-warm (60 days) followed by moist-cold (90 days) and then light, sow indoors (50–60°F) (germ. 90–730 days); shrubby species: softwood, greenwood, semi-ripewood cuttings with mist, or hardwood cuttings (often easiest); tree types (difficult): softwood cuttings under mist (note: do not remove cuttings from medium once rooted; devote a flat to the cuttings and allow them to go through winter dormancy before repotting [try Oasis or rock wool blocks]); grafting; division of suckers from shrub types

CORYDALIS: fresh seed—light, best sown in situ (it is easy to germinate seeds indoors, but seedlings have long taproots that are easily damaged—consider paper pots, light [50–60°F] [germ. 30–60 days]); rhizome-forming species: division in autumn or early spring while dormant

CORYLOPSIS: seed—outdoors (2 years), or moist-warm (6 months) followed by moist-cold (6 months); softwood cuttings (wound, see page 142—Oasis cubes or rock wool may be helpful); layering; grafting

CORYLUS: fresh seed—moist-cold (90

days), or seed stored dry up to a year, (70°F) (germ. 30 days); softwood stem cuttings under mist very successful (note: do not remove from medium once rooted—set in pots of medium or devote a flat to these and allow cuttings to go through winter dormancy before repotting); layering, including stooling or mounding

COSMOS: seed—outdoors after danger of frost is past, or sow indoors (70–75°F) 4–5 weeks before last frost (germ. 5–10 days)

COTINUS: fresh (near-ripe "green") seed—outdoors (dry-stored seed difficult: nick and 12-hour soak followed by moist-cold [42–63 days] and then sow indoors [55–60°F] [germ. 30–90 days]—or moist-warm [180–270 days] followed by moist-cold [6–9 months]); softwood cuttings (hormone necessary) (note: do not remove from medium once rooted—try Oasis cubes, or devote a flat to these and allow cuttings to go through winter dormancy before repotting, or set a pot of rooting medium into a larger container of potting medium and overwinter in cold frame); layering in late winter to early spring (easiest method)

COTONEASTER: seed—clean of pulp, often acid-etched (sulfuric acid etch may be replaced by stratification), moist-warm (120–270 days) followed by moist-cold (90 days) and then light, sow indoors warm (70°F) (germ. 180–365 days), or outdoors in spring; softwood, greenwood cuttings (semi-ripewood cuttings with hormone in cold frame); layering; grafting

COTULA: seed—sow indoors (50°F) 6–8 weeks before last frost date, or outdoors after danger of frost is past (germ. 14–42 days); division of perennial kinds in spring

CRAMBE: fresh seed—best sown in situ, or sow indoors cold (40°F) (germ. 21–180 days); division; root cuttings (material should be heavy—pencil-thick)

CRASSULA: stem or leaf cuttings (allow to callus at least 24 hours)

CRATAEGUS: seed—acid-etch nearly impenetrable seed coat followed by moist-cold (90 days) (germ. 60+ days); or as substitute for acid, moist-warm (120–270 days) followed by moist-cold (90 days) and then light, sow indoors cool (50–65°F) (germ. 180–730 days); grafting (budding); root cuttings in early spring may work

CRINUM: fresh seed—outdoors in warm climates, or sow indoors (60–70°F) 6–8 weeks before last frost date (germ. 7–21 days); division of offsets from bulbs in spring

CROCOSMIA: fresh seed—sow indoors (55–60°F) 6–8 weeks before last frost date (germ. 60–90 days); division of thick mats—saving cormels and discarding oldest corms in early spring or after flowering; sections of corms

CROCUS: fresh seed—outdoors in spring (germ. 30–180 days); division of corms

CRYPTOMERIA: seed—store seeds dry, then moist-cold (21 days) and sow indoors with gentle bottom heat (65°F) (germ. 30–60 days—erratic); semi-ripewood cuttings; grafting

CUPHEA: seed—light, sow indoors (70–75°F) 10–12 weeks before last frost date (germ. 8–10 days) (note: plants used as summer annuals take a long time to develop, so early indoor sowing is recommended); herbaceous stem cuttings; root cuttings

CUPRESSUS: seed—light, outdoors in late winter or early spring, or moist-cold (30 days) followed by light, sow indoors (70–75°F) (germ. 30–90 days—erratic); evergreen-hardwood cuttings in late winter to early spring, hormone and mist; grafting

CYCAS: seed—(fresh if possible), sow indoors (70–75°F) (germ. 30–90 days or longer); division of offsets

CYCLAMEN: seed—dark, sow indoors (50–60°F) (germ. 21–180 days); hardy species may be sown outdoors following hot-water soak in autumn or spring, moist-cold (21 days) and then dark, sow indoors, shade and high humidity as seedlings emerge; corms can be divided in late summer, but seed is preferable

CYDONIA: seed—as *Chaenomeles*, varieties are all grafts onto species seedling (whip-and-tongue, chip-bud, T-bud)

CYMBALARIA: seed—outdoors in rock crevices anytime when seed is available (spring to late summer)

CYMBIDIUM: divisions of pseudobulbs; rooting "backbulbs"—aged pseudobulbs that can be removed and rooted in medium to produce shoots

CYNARA: seed—sow indoors (50–55°F) (germ. 14–30 days); division in early spring, but seed preferable

CYNOGLOSSUM: seed—cover seeds in situ in spring, or dark, sow indoors (70–75°F) (germ. 5–10 days); division in spring where hardy

CYPERUS: seed—sow indoors (70–75°F) 6–8 weeks before last frost date (germ. 25–30 days); leaf-petiole (rosette) cuttings (cut entire leaf umbel with 1-inch stem—peg to medium or float on water); division

CYPHOMANDRA: seed—sow indoors (70–75°F) (germ. 20–25 days); softwood cuttings

CYRILLA: fresh seed—outdoors; semi-ripewood cuttings, hormone; root cuttings

CYTISUS: seed—hot-water soak followed by light, sow indoors (70–75°F) (germ. 25–30 days); semi-ripewood (side shoot with heel, hormone), hardwood (hormone) cuttings

DAHLIA: seed—sow indoors (70–75°F) 10–12 weeks before last frost date (germ. 5–10 days); stem cuttings (bottom heat helpful); spring tuber division with at least one eye

DAPHNE: fresh seed—clean of pulp, light, sow indoors (50–60°F) (germ. 150–365 days), or in frost-free place, cold frame per-haps; stem cuttings vary by species: greenwood and semi-ripewood nodal stem cuttings (note: do not remove cuttings from medium once rooted—try Oasis or rock wool blocks]; with bottom heat, roots may form in 6 weeks; cuttings that lose their leaves before rooting should be discarded); layering; grafting (splice veneer, whip-and-tongue, wedge); root cuttings

DARMERA: seed—sow indoors (55–60°F) (germ. 30–90 days); division in spring

DATURA: seed—sow indoors (55–65°F) 8–12 weeks before last frost date (germ. 21–42 days); softwood cuttings (from side shoots)

DAVALLIA: spores; rhizome sections pinned or pegged to medium, bottom heat

DAVIDIA: fresh seed—clean (two-step germinator, see page 74), moist-warm (90 days or until emergence of radicle) then pot up and refrigerate (90 days); softwood (wounding and hormone), leaf-bud cuttings best (use hormone and try Oasis cubes as all resent transplanting)

DELOSPERMA: seed—light, sow indoors (70–75°F) (germ. 1–40 days)

DELPHINIUM (SEE ALSO CONSOLIDA): fresh seed—dark, sow indoors (50–55°F) 8–10 weeks before last frost date (germ. 14–28 days), or outdoors in spring to late summer in time to germinate before frost; division in spring; basal cuttings in spring (take cuttings low at base of plant so hollow stems are closed)

DENDROBIUM: stem cuttings laid horizontally on medium; division of plantlets

DENNSTAEDTIA: spores; division of rhizomes in spring

DENTARIA: see *Cardamine*

DESCHAMPSIA: seed—light, outdoors; division in spring or autumn

DEUTZIA: seed—outdoors, or moist-cold helpful (42–56 days), sow indoors (65–70°F) (germ. 30–60 days); stem cuttings easy—softwood, greenwood, semi-ripewood, hardwood

DIANTHUS: Annual varieties: seed—sow indoors (60–70°F) 8–10 weeks before last frost date (germ. 5–10 days); semi-ripe cuttings. Biennials, such as sweet William: seed—outdoors in spring to summer for blossoms the following year, or sow indoors (70–75°F) 6–8 weeks before last frost date (germ. 10 days) 42–60 days before setting out; root cuttings. Perennials: seed—sow indoors (under lights, 60–70°F; or outdoors after danger of frost is past) 8–10 weeks before last frost date (germ. 10 days); semi-ripe cuttings; division in spring

DICENTRA: fresh seed—outdoors, or if not fresh, dry-stored seed requires moist-warm (6 weeks), moist-cold (6 weeks), moist-warm (6 weeks) followed by sow indoors (55–60°F) (germ. 30 days or longer);

division in late winter to early spring; root cuttings in summer. Note: Asian *D. spectabilis* germinates following moist-cold (6 weeks) followed by sow indoors (50–55°F); and also yields stem cuttings after flowering

DICTAMNUS: seed—outdoors, or moist-cold (42 days) followed by sow indoors (55–60°F) (germ. 30–180 days); division possible, but plants resent disturbance; root cuttings of dormant plants

DIERAMA: seed—light, outdoors in warm climates, in autumn or spring, or light, sow indoors (60–65°F) (germ. 30–180 days); division of cormels

DIGITALIS: seed—light, outdoors in spring through summer, or light, sow indoors cool (60–70°F) 8–10 weeks before last frost date (germ. 10–20 days); division of basal rosettes in spring (or autumn in warm climates)

DISPORUM: seed—light, outdoors, or moist-cold (42 days) followed by light, sow indoors cool (55–65°F) (germ. 30–180 days or longer); division easy in spring

DODECATHEON: seed—outdoors in late autumn, or moist-cold ([some sources recommend freezing] 21 days) and sow indoors (60–70°F) (germ. 90–365 days); division of side rosettes in autumn

DOLICHOS: seed—soak 24 hours, sow indoors (70–75°F) 6–8 weeks before last frost date (germ. 14 days)

DORONICUM: seed—light, sow indoors (70°F) (germ. 15–20 days); division after flowering (late summer to autumn in mild climates, mulch)

DRABA: seed—outdoors in spring, or sow indoors (55–70°F) 8–10 weeks before last frost date (germ. 30–90 days); division in spring

DRACAENA: seed—clean seeds of flesh, light, sow indoors (70–80°F) (germ. 30–42 days); stem-tip cuttings, semi-ripe sections of stem; air layering

DRYOPTERIS: spores; division

ECHEVERIA: seed—light, sow indoors (70–75°F) (germ. 15–30 days); semi-ripe stem cuttings, leaf cuttings, leggy older plants can have stem and top rosette removed and rooted as stem cutting

ECHINACEA: seed—outdoors in spring to late summer, or sow indoors (70–75°F) 8–10 weeks before last frost date (germ. 10–21 days); division in spring easy from root cuttings in late winter

ECHINOPS: seed—outdoors in spring to midsummer, or sow indoors (60–70°F) 2–3 weeks before last frost date (germ. 15–60 days); division in spring; fast from root cuttings taken in spring

ECHIUM: seed—sow in situ (in autumn in warm climates), or sow indoors (60–70°F) 6–8 weeks before last frost date (germ. 7–21 days); stem cuttings

ELYMUS: division in spring or autumn

ENKIANTHUS: seed—light, sow indoors (70–75°F; under mist—high humidity

necessary) (germ. 14–21 days); softwood, greenwood cuttings under mist very successful—do not remove from medium once rooted, set in pots of medium or devote a flat to these and allow cuttings to go through winter dormancy before repotting

EPIMEDIUM: seed—outdoors; division in spring in cold climates and in autumn in mild climates; rhizome sections can be taken and rooted on medium in winter

EPIPACTIS: division of rhizomes while dormant in early spring

EPIPHYLLUM: flat stem cuttings (see page 135), branches or sections

EPISCIA: as for *Saintpaulia.*

ERANTHIS: fresh seed—outdoors (germ. erratic, 30–365 days); division of tubers immediately after flowering

EREMURUS: seed—light, sow indoors (55–65°F) (germ. 30–365 days); division in summer or autumn (note: carefully dig and transplant sections of crown with eyes, spread roots—place on sand in poorly drained sites)

ERICA: seed—light, sow indoors warm (60–70°F) (30–120 days); softwood, semi-ripewood cuttings (two cuttings per 4-inch stem, pinch flower buds from tip, strip needles, no side shoots); layering, mounding

ERIGERON: seed—outdoors, or sow indoors (55°F) 8–10 weeks before last frost date (germ. 15–20 days); cuttings in spring; division in autumn

ERODIUM: fresh seed—in cold frame or outdoors in mild climates; semi-ripe tip cuttings; division; basal cuttings in spring; root cuttings in late winter

ERYNGIUM: seed—light, sow in situ in spring through summer, or light, sow indoors (70–75°F) (germ. 5–10 days [some take longer—may need 30 days moist-warm followed by moist-cold]); division possible but difficult due to taproot; thick root cuttings in autumn (lay horizontally on medium and just cover) (note: material for root cuttings can be encouraged by potting plants in containers with large drainage holes and setting the pots about 1 inch into a 3- to 6-inch-deep bed of moist sand— roots will grow into the medium)

ERYSIMUM: seed—biennial kinds, outdoors in late summer, or sow indoors (55–65°F) (germ. 7 days); semi-ripe stem-tip cuttings (overwinter in cold frame); established perennials can be divided in spring

ERYTHRONIUM: fresh seed—outdoors, germination may take 9 months or longer; division of corm offsets

ESCHSCHOLZIA: seed—in situ in winter, or sow indoors (70–75°F) 2–3 weeks before last frost date (germ. 14 days)

EUCALYPTUS: seed—sow indoors (70–75°F) (germ. 14–90 days depending on species) (note: 4-week moist-cold might be helpful, as is a 10°F temperature drop at night)

EUCOMIS: seed—sow indoors (70–75°F) (germ. 20–25 days); easy from leaf cuttings; division

EUONYMUS: Species require individual treatments (most kinds offered at nurseries are varieties—vegetatively propagated). General: seed—moist-cold (3 months) followed by sow indoors (70–75°F). Deciduous varieties: softwood, greenwood, semi-ripewood (in cold frame) cuttings. Evergreen varieties: (note adventitious roots) softwood, semi-ripewood (in cold frame) cuttings. (Note: greenwood and semi-ripewood cuttings may take 6 months or more to root, hormone useful.) Layering; grafting

EUPATORIUM: seed—outdoors in autumn as seed ripens, or moist-cold (30–42 days) and sow indoors (55°F) 8–10 weeks before last frost date (germ. 30–90 days); stem cuttings in spring; divide established clumps in spring or autumn (mulch)

EUPHORBIA: Seed—tender kinds: sow indoors (70–75°F) (6–8 weeks before last frost date for garden annuals) (germ. 10–15 days); hardy species: moist-cold (30–42 days) followed by cool to sow indoors (65–70°F) (germ. 15–30 days [may take longer]). Tender species: semi-ripewood cuttings—allow cut end to callus for 1 to 2 days before setting in medium; bottom heat helpful. Hardy species: greenwood cuttings (bottom heat helpful in areas with cool summers); division of established hardy perennials

EXACUM: seed—light, sow indoors (70–75°F) (germ. 15–20 days)

EXOCHORDA: seeds—outdoors in autumn; softwood cuttings, semi-ripewood cuttings with hormone

FAGUS: fresh seed—light, outdoors immediately, or store in refrigerator (dry) until winter and light, sow indoors (50°F) (germ. 30–365 days); cuttings nearly impossible, but sometimes layering possible; grafting

X FATSHEDERA: semi-ripewood stem cuttings (bottom heat helpful); grafting of *Hedera* to top

FATSIA: seed—sow indoors (60–70°F) (germ. 10–20 days); semi-ripewood stem cuttings (as with tender *Hedera* varieties, at any season; bottom heat helpful)

FELICIA: seed—outdoors after last frost, or moist-cold (30 days) followed by sow indoors (60–70°F) 6–8 weeks before last frost date (germ. 30 days)

FESTUCA: seed—light, sow in situ; cultivars—division

FICUS: seed—light, sow indoors (70–75°F) (germ. 15–20 days); softwood, greenwood, leaf-bud, semi-ripewood cuttings (hardwood for hardy types—take in midwinter and refrigerate, or try later and treat as semi-ripewood cutting); air layering

FILIPENDULA: fresh seed—outdoors, or purchased seed moist-warm (30–42 days) followed by moist-cold (30–42 days) followed by sow indoors (55–60°F) 8–10 weeks before last frost date (germ. 30–90 days); division; root cuttings

FORSYTHIA: seed—(most kinds grown are cultivars; however, sowing could yield new selections and is easy) outdoors, or moist-cold (30 days minimum) and sow indoors (55°F) (germ. 30–90 days); softwood, greenwood, semi-ripewood, hardwood cuttings; layering, tip layering; division of suckers

FOTHERGILLA: softwood, semi-ripewood cuttings (hormone) (note: do not remove from medium once rooted—set in pots of medium or devote a flat to these and allow cuttings to go through winter dormancy before repotting); layering

FRAGARIA: seed—(collect fruits of alpine types and allow them to dry completely, hold dried fruits over a bowl, and rub between fingers—seeds will fall off) outdoors in autumn or spring, or sow indoors (55°F) (germ. 30 days); division of offsets (alpine varieties) or runners (garden strawberries)—peg to medium, soil, or in daughter pots

FRANKLINIA: fresh seed—keep moist, sow outdoors, or sow indoors (60°F) (germ. 14 days with fresh seed) or moist-cold (30 [to 90] days), sow indoors (50–60°F) (germ. up to 3 years); greenwood, semi-ripewood cuttings (hormone) (note: cuttings root readily but dislike transplanting; consider Oasis or rock wool cubes)

FREESIA: seed—outdoors in frost-free climate, or soak in warm water (24 hours), sow indoors (65–75°F) (germ. 25–30 days); division of offsets in autumn

FREMONTODENDRON: fresh seed—outdoors in indigenous climates; semi-ripe, hardwood cuttings

FRITILLARIA: seed—outdoors, germination may take 1–2 years; division of bulblets from mature plants; scaling and chipping, scooping and scoring

FUCHSIA: seed—light, sow indoors (70–75°F) (fresh seed, germ. 21 days; dry seed, 21–90 days); softwood (very small cuttings may be taken; try Oasis cubes), semi-hardwood (mist helpful), hardwood cuttings (best with hardy kinds)

GAILLARDIA: seed—light, sow indoors (70–75°F) (annuals: 4–6 weeks before last frost date, perennials: 6–8 weeks before last frost date) (germ. 21 days); perennial kinds by division; root cuttings

GALANTHUS: seed—outdoors (germ. erratic); division of clumps; chipping or twin scaling

GALIUM: division in spring or autumn

GALTONIA: seed—sow indoors (70°F) 6–8 weeks before last frost date (germ. 15–20 days); offsets, but few are produced

GARDENIA: fresh seed—sow indoors (70–75°F) (germ. 25–30 days); greenwood, semi-ripewood cuttings (hormone and mist helpful) (note: do not remove cuttings from medium once rooted—best to root in single cells in flats)

GAULTHERIA: fresh seed—(collect from fruits in autumn through winter) moist-cold (30 days) followed by light, sow indoors (55–65°F) (germ. erratic); semi-ripewood cuttings; division of rooted (naturally layered) horizontal stems

GAURA: seeds—sow indoors (70–75°F) 4–6 weeks before last frost date (germ. 14–30 days); semi-ripe stem cuttings in summer with heel; division (dig deep so as not to damage thick root); basal cuttings in spring

GILLENIA: see *Porteranthus*

GELSEMIUM: seed—outdoors where hardy; semi-ripewood (with hormone under mist), hardwood cuttings

GENISTA: seed—(acid scarification in trade) file (sandpaper) and soak in hot water (12 hours) and then cool to sow indoors (65–70°F) (germ. 14–21 days); softwood, greenwood with some varieties, semi-ripewood stem for most with hormone, hardwood cuttings in climates with mild winters

GENTIANA: seed—moist-cold (2 months) followed by dark, sow indoors (70–75°F) (germ. 14–180 days depending on species); stem-tip cuttings taken from spring bloomers; division after flowering; basal cuttings in autumn from autumn-flowering kinds

GERANIUM: fresh seed—(varies by species) tender: sow indoors (70–75°F) (germ. 3–21 days), hardy: sow indoors (50°F) (germ. 3–90 days) or outdoors in late autumn; division in spring or autumn of hardy varieties; basal cuttings when spring growth slows; root cuttings of some, including alpine species

GERBERA: fresh seed—light, sow indoors (70–75°F) 10–12 weeks before last frost date (germ. 7–14 days); semi-ripe cuttings in summer; division in summer or autumn

GEUM: seed—outdoors in spring or summer, or sow indoors warm (65–85°F [10°F drop at night beneficial]) 8–10 weeks before last frost date (germ. 21–28 days); division in spring, but autumn preferable

GINKGO: fresh seed—light, outdoors, or moist-warm (30–60 days) followed by moist-cold (30–60 days) then light, sow indoors (70–75°F) (germ. 30–60 days); semi-ripewood cuttings root well—even from mature trees (hormone and mist); grafting

GLADIOLUS: seed—sow indoors (70–75°F) (germ. 20–40 days, keep in pots: cormels form first year below grassy foliage); division of cormels, corm; corm cutting producing sections with at least one eye

GLAUCIDIUM: fresh seed—outdoors (note: may take 2 years or longer to germinate; leave initial seedlings in pot until third year to allow for stragglers; seeds treated with gibberellic acid-3 sprout quickly), or sow indoors (50–55°F) (germ. 30–90 days or up to 2 years); division in late winter, early spring of peony-like woody rootstock with dormant buds

GLAUCIUM: seed—sow in situ in spring

GLEDITSIA: seed—hot-water soak (170°F) followed by sow indoors (70–75°F) (germ. 7–14 days) (moist-cold [60–90 days] recommended but not necessary in test with fresh seed); grafting

GLORIOSA: seed—sow indoors (70–75°F) (germ. 30 days); division of tubers

GLOXINIA: seeds—light, sow indoors (70–75°F) (germ. 15–21 days); stem cuttings (bottom heat)

GOODYERA: nodal stem cuttings (allow to callus 48 hours); division in spring

GREVILLEA: seed—soak 48 hours (or moist-cold 30 days), light, sow indoors (70–75°F) (germ. 20–25 days)

GUNNERA: seed—sow indoors (60–70°F) 6–8 weeks before last frost date (germ. 14–60 days); leaf cuttings in spring; division in spring

GYMNOCLADUS: seed—(extremely hard seed coat, sulfuric acid soaks for up to 2 days) try file, hot water, and then 24-hour soak; greenwood, hardwood cuttings

GYPSOPHILA: seed—sow indoors (60–70°F) (sow annual types in situ in spring after all danger of frost is past) (germ. 10 days); basal cuttings; division of perennial types can be done, but all resent root disturbance and for that reason grafting is used for *G. paniculata*

HABENARIA: division of young tubers with pointed shoots in spring

HAEMANTHUS: seed—sow indoors (60–65°F) (germ. 7–42 days); offsets

HAKONECHLOA: division

HALESIA: seed—outdoors (may not germinate until second spring), or moist-warm (6–9 months) followed by moist-cold (6–9 months); softwood, semi-ripewood, hardwood stem cuttings (all with hormone)

HAMAMELIS: (varieties propagated vegetatively, but seed is difficult in any event—best [light] outdoors [germ. in second spring]); softwood stem cuttings (early hormone and gentle bottom heat), semi-ripewood possible with hormone and mist, but rooted cuttings must overwinter without disturbance; layering; grafting for hybrids to *H. virginiana* understock

HAWORTHIA: seed—light, sow indoors (60–65°F) (germ. 21–60 days); offsets

HEBE: softwood, semi-ripewood cuttings (cuttings small, like those of *Calluna* and *Erica*—hormone and mist helpful, but mildew may attack cuttings)

HEDERA: softwood, semi-ripewood, hardwood cuttings; layering (note adventitious roots); grafting

HEDYCHIUM: seed—sow indoors (70–75°F) 6–8 weeks before last frost date (germ. 20–25 days); section of rhizome while still dormant in early spring

HELENIUM: seed—outdoors in situ in early spring or early autumn, or sow indoors (70–75°F) 8–10 weeks before last frost date (germ. 7–10 days); division in spring

HELIANTHEMUM: seed—outdoors in situ in spring to summer, or sow indoors (70–75°F) 6–8 weeks before last frost date (germ. 14–21 days); semi-ripe cuttings

HELIANTHUS: seed—outdoors in situ after all danger of frost is past, or sow indoors (75–85°F) 2–3 weeks before last frost date (germ. 5–14 days); perennials only—division in spring or autumn

HELICHRYSUM: seed—light, sow indoors (70–75°F) 6–8 weeks before last frost date (germ. 7–10 days); semi-ripe cuttings in summer for flowering kinds; foliage types—stem-tip cuttings from mid- to late summer (keep foliage dry); division in spring where plants winter-over

HELICTOTRICHON: division in spring or autumn

HELIOPSIS: seed—(species) outdoors in spring to summer, or sow indoors (70–75°F) 8–10 weeks before last frost date (germ. 10–15 days); cultivars: cuttings; cultivars: division

HELIOTROPIUM: seed—sow indoors (70–75°F) 10–12 weeks before last frost date (germ. 14–42 days); greenwood, semi-ripewood cuttings (benefit from bottom heat); root cuttings in autumn with bottom heat

HELLEBORUS: fresh seed—outdoors (many species and hybrids may need two winters before germination), or try moist-warm (56–70 days) followed by moist-cold (56–70 days) sow indoors (60–65°F) (germ. 30–545 days), sowing very fresh seed may bypass long conditioning period; division in spring—carefully pry plantlets apart at crown

HEMEROCALLIS: seed—(species or to create hybrids) outdoors, or moist-cold (42 days) followed by sow indoors (60–70°F) 6–8 weeks before last frost date (germ. 15–60 days); sections of fresh flower scapes may sometimes root at leaf-sheath nodes; division (of established hybrid plants)

HEPATICA: seed—light, outdoors, or moist-cold (30 days) followed by light, sow indoors (50–55°F) (germ. 30–365 days, erratic)

HEUCHERA: seed—(species) light, sow indoors cool (55–70°F) 8–10 weeks before last frost date (germ. 10–60 days); leaf-petiole cuttings; division in spring or autumn

X HEUCHERELLA: division in spring

HIBISCUS: seed—hardy woody species: outdoors, herbaceous kinds: nick and soak 12 hours and then sow indoors (70–75°F) (annuals: 6–8 weeks before last frost date) (germ. 15–30 days, may take longer); herbaceous cuttings in late spring to midsummer; tender woody evergreens: semi-ripewood cuttings, layering; hardy *H. syriacus* very easy from hardwood, but may be rooted as softwood, greenwood, and semi-ripewood cuttings; grafting

HIPPEASTRUM: fresh seed—sow indoors (70–75°F) (germ. 30–45 days, older seeds take longer); division; chipping

HOSTA: seed—seed can be sown indoors as soon as ripe (sow fresh indoors (50–70°F) (germ. 15–90 days), or dried for spring sowing indoors 6–8 weeks before last frost date; division (note: hostas can be encouraged to produce multiple eyes or buds at crown level by "topping": in spring, clear away soil at the base of a new shoot to expose the eye at its base from which it sprang; clean the area with a damp paper towel, and make a cut with a snap-blade knife or similar tool through the bud and about ½ inch into the crown; dust with hormone and insert a toothpick into the wound; by autumn, many buds will have formed and the following spring several more shoots than would normally have been produced will appear); root cuttings

HOYA: semi-ripewood cuttings; layering

HUMULUS: seed—herbaceous perennial species: sow indoors (70–75°F) 6–8 weeks before last frost date (germ. 30–90 days, can be erratic), annual types: in situ after all danger of frost is past and soil is warm; leaf-bud cuttings; layering (simple and serpentine) easy in late spring

HYACINTHOIDES: fresh seed—sow outdoors in situ, in flats or drills in nursery bed; division of deep-rooted bulbs (invasive in England, rarely in U.S.)

HYACINTHUS: (difficult from seed, and varieties must be vegetatively propagated); leaf cuttings; division; twin scaling; chipping; scooping; scoring

HYDRANGEA: fresh seed—sow indoors (50°F) (high humidity) (germ. varies depending on species—as short as a few weeks for fresh *H. quercifolia*); softwood, semi-ripewood (as small as split stem leaf-bud cuttings [see page 150]), hardwood cuttings; serpentine layering of climbing hydrangea; division of suckers of *H. macrophylla*

HYPERICUM: seed—outdoors, or sow indoors (50–55°F) 8–10 weeks before last frost date (germ. 30–90 days, may take longer); softwood, semi-ripewood, hardwood cuttings; division

HYPOESTES: seed—sow indoors (70–75°F) (germ. 10–12 days); herbaceous stem cuttings in spring, semi-ripe cuttings in summer; ground-cover types can be layered

IBERIS: seed—sow indoors (70–75°F) 6–8 weeks before last frost date (germ. 10–15 days), sow in situ after all danger of frost is past (sow indoors annual kinds consecutively for continuous bloom every 10 days from last frost date until mid-July); division of perennial kinds after flowering

ILEX: seed—clean, outdoors, or moist-warm followed by moist-cold and then sow outdoors or indoors (germ. very slow—may take years); softwood, semi-ripewood, hardwood cuttings with hormones (and patience); layering; grafting

ILLICIUM: seed—(dry-stored seed) sow indoors (70–75°F) or in situ when soil warm (germ. 14–30 days, varies); semi-ripewood cuttings; root cuttings

IMPATIENS: seed—light, sow indoors (70–75°F) 8–10 weeks before last frost date (germ. 7–30 days, can be erratic); herbaceous cuttings

INCARVILLEA: seed—outdoors, or sow indoors cool (55–65°F) 8–10 weeks before last frost date (germ. 25–30 days); root cuttings

INDIGOFERA: seed—hot-water soak 24 hours, sow indoors cool (50°F) (30–90 days); semi-ripewood, hardwood cuttings

INULA: seed—outdoors in situ while soil cool, sow indoors (55–65°F) 6–8 weeks before last frost date (germ. 14–42 days); division in spring (in autumn in mild climates)

IPOMOEA: seed—nick seeds and/or 24-hour warm-water soak and then sow in situ, or sow indoors in paper pots or cells (70–75°F) 3–4 weeks before last frost date (germ. 7–10 days)

IRIS: seed—(variable by species) outdoors in spring (except autumn-sow indoors for bulbous types), or moist-cold (90 days) followed by sow indoors (50–65°F) (germ. 30–365 days); division rhizomatous kinds when semidormant in mid- to late summer, Siberian and similar types with offsets in early spring or in midsummer), divide bulbous types (e.g., *I. reticulata*) when leaves disappear in autumn—these may also be chipped in late summer

ITEA: seed—light, outdoors; evergreen types from semi-ripewood, deciduous kinds from softwood and greenwood cuttings

JACARANDA: seed—file, hot water and then 24-hour soak followed by sow indoors (70–75°F) (germ. 10–15 days); greenwood cuttings

JASMINUM: seed—(some species) sow indoors (70–75°F) (germ. 20–25 days); softwood, semi-ripewood cuttings (hormone), hardwood cuttings in frost-free regions; layering

JUGLANS: seed—light, outdoors in autumn, or moist-cold (90 days) followed by light, sow indoors (50°F) (germ. 30–180 days); edible cultivars grafted to saplings

JUNCUS: ripe seed—outdoors on constantly moist medium; division in early spring

JUNIPERUS: seed—light, outdoors (germ. 2–5 years); evergreen hardwood cuttings in winter are treated as semi-ripewood—wounding and hormone, under mist or with high humidity with bottom heat

JUSTICIA: seed—sow indoors (70–75°F) (germ. 20–25 days); semi-ripewood cuttings

KALANCHOE: seed—light, sow indoors (70–75°F) (germ. 10 days); leaf, semi-ripewood stem cuttings; removal of adventitious leaf growths

KALIMERIS: division in early to mid-spring

KALMIA: seed—light, outdoors, or moist-cold (90 days) followed by light, sow indoors (70–75°F) (germ. 30 days or longer); greenwood and semi-ripewood cuttings (wound); layering in spring

KERRIA: softwood, greenwood, semi-ripewood, hardwood cuttings; divisions of suckers

KIRENGESHOMA: seed—sow indoors (55–65°F) (germ. 30–365 days); division

KNAUTIA: seed—best in situ; basal stem cuttings; division in spring

KNIPHOFIA: seed—light, outdoors in spring to summer, or light, sow indoors (70–75°F) 6–8 weeks before last frost date (germ. 10–20 days); division (transplant large sections, pot small pieces for cold frame)

KOELREUTERIA: seed—nick and soak 48 hours followed by light, sow outdoors, or moist-cold (90 days) followed by light, sow indoors (50–60°F) (germ. 30–60 days or longer); root cuttings

KOLKWITZIA: seed—light, outdoors, high humidity; stem cuttings easy—softwood, greenwood, semi-ripewood, hardwood

LABURNUM: seed—24-hour hot-water soak followed by sow indoors (55–70°F) (germ. 30–60 days); hardwood cuttings; most kinds are varieties propagated by grafting

LACHENALIA: fresh seed—sow indoors (spring) (55–65°F) (germ. 30–120 days); division: scooping; bulbils in late summer

LAGERSTROEMIA: seed—light, sow indoors (70–75°F) 6–8 weeks before last frost date (germ. 15–20 days), or light, outdoors after danger of frost is past; hardwood cuttings

LAMIUM: seed—outdoors in situ, or sow indoors (65–70°F) 8–10 weeks before last frost date (germ. 30–60 days); herbaceous cuttings; division

LANTANA: seed—soak in warm water 24 hours, sow indoors (70–75°F) 6–8 weeks before last frost date (germ. 45–65 days, erratic); greenwood, semi-ripewood cuttings

LARIX: fresh seed—light, outdoors, or light, sow indoors with gentle bottom heat (65–70°F) (germ. 30–90 days), older seed may require moist-cold (60 days); grafting

LATHYRUS: seed—nick and soak in cold water followed by dark, sow indoors cool (55–65°F) 6–8 weeks before last frost date (germ. 10–30 days); perennial species can be divided in spring

LAURUS: seed—(as per *Ilex*); semi-ripewood cuttings; layering

LAVANDULA: seed—sow indoors (55–65°F) 6–8 weeks before last frost date (germ. 21–90 days, erratic); softwood, semi-ripewood, hardwood cuttings; layering (mounding) in spring

LAVATERA: seed—sow indoors (70–75°F) 6–8 weeks before last frost date (germ. 15–20 days); softwood, greenwood cuttings

LESPEDEZA: seed—nick or soak followed by sow indoors (70–75°F) (germ. 10–14 days); softwood, greenwood cuttings

LEUCOJUM: seed—fresh when ripe outdoors, or stored in sand in the refrigerator until sowing indoors (55–65°F) (germ. may be erratic); division when variety is dormant

LEUCOTHOE: seed—outdoors, light, acidic medium (peat), or light, sow indoors (60–70°F) (germ. 14–49 days, erratic), seedlings must be left undisturbed for a year or more; greenwood and semi-ripewood stem cuttings

LEWISIA: seed—light, outdoors (germ. 1 or more years); division of basal suckers

LEYCESTERIA: seed—outdoors in autumn where hardy; hardwood cuttings

LIATRIS: seed—sow indoors (55–75°F [temperature reduction at night beneficial]) 6–8 weeks before last frost date (germ. 20–30 days); basal stem cuttings; division in spring

LIGULARIA: seed—sow indoors (55–65°F) 6–8 weeks before last frost date (germ. 14–40 days, erratic); basal stem cuttings; division in spring

LIGUSTRUM: fresh seed—clean and outdoors, or dry seed—moist-cold (42 days) before spring sowing outdoors; softwood, semi-ripewood, hardwood cuttings; layering

LILIUM: seed—fresh seed germinates more readily, but lilies may germinate in weeks (epigeal) or up to years (hypogeal) after producing a little bulb in the medium (for example, *L. candidum, L. henryi, L. martagon*); also depending on species: division of offsets; scales; stem cuttings in trench; a few varieties will even root from leaf cuttings (*L. longiflorum*), and others produce bulbils on stem (place lily seeds in vermiculite in plastic bag for 4–12 weeks—check for leaf or bulblet formation; pot leaf seedlings and grow in light, pot bulblets in medium and refrigerate for 3–6 months, then bring to light and warmth); some lilies' stems will produce bulbs if laid horizontally in a trench or medium—lift bulbs and stem, bury with just tip exposed

LINARIA: seed—in situ after danger of frost is past, or sow indoors (55–60°F) (21 days of moist-cold may be helpful) (germ. 10–15 days)

LINDERA: fresh seed—clean of fruit and outdoors, or moist-warm (30 days) followed by moist-cold (90 days) then sow indoors (60°F) (germ. 30–60 days); greenwood cuttings with hormone and mist (difficult)

LINUM: seed—best in situ, spring to summer; herbaceous stem cuttings

LIQUIDAMBAR: seed—light, outdoors, or moist-cold (60 days) followed by light, sow indoors (55–65°F) (germ. 30–45 days);

greenwood cuttings; layering; grafting for varieties

LIRIODENDRON: fresh seed—light, outdoors, or moist-cold (60 days) followed by light, sow indoors (55–65°F) (germ. 60–90 days); greenwood cuttings; grafting of varieties

LIRIOPE: seed—24-hour soak followed by sowing outdoors in summer, or sow indoors (70–75°F) 6–8 weeks before last frost date (germ. 30 days); division

LISIANTHUS: seed—light, sow indoors (70–75°F) (germ. 10–21 days); division

LITHOPS: seed—light, sow indoors (70–75°F) (germ. 10–40 days)

LOBELIA: seed—annual types light: sow indoors (70–75°F) 6–8 weeks before last frost date (germ. 15–21 days), perennial species: light, outdoors in autumn for spring germination, or moist-cold (90 days) then light, sow indoors (70–75°F) 8–10 weeks before last frost date (germ. 15–20 days); herbaceous cuttings in summer; division

LOBULARIA: seed—light, in situ early spring, or light, sow indoors (55–75°F) 4–6 weeks before setting out while soil still cool and light frost possible (germ. 10–15 days)

LONICERA: softwood, semi-ripewood, hardwood cuttings; layering

LUDISIA: nodal stem cuttings (allow to callus 48 hours); division in spring

LUNARIA: seed—best in situ in summer, or sow indoors (70°F) 6–8 weeks before last frost date (germ. 10–14 days)

LUPINUS: seed—24-hour warm-water soak, nick, dark outdoors in early spring, or sow indoors (55–70°F) (germ. 14–60 days); woody types: softwood or greenwood basal cuttings

LYCHNIS: seed—moist-cold (14 days) followed by light, sow indoors (70–75°F) 6–8 weeks before last frost date (germ. 21–30 days); herbaceous cuttings; division in spring

LYCORIS: fresh seed—outdoors; division of bulblets after flowering

LYSICHITON: fresh seed—outdoors, or sow indoors cool (55–65°F) 10–12 weeks before last frost date, keep medium saturated in bowl of water (germ. 30–60 days, erratic); division in spring

LYSIMACHIA: seed—outdoors best, or sow indoors (55–65°F) (germ. 30–90 days, erratic); herbaceous cuttings; layering (*L. nummularia* only); division

MAGNOLIA: fresh seed (species are very variable—in some, embryo matures during storage, in others inhibitors may develop with ripening—experiment with near-ripe and stored fruits)—soak seeds 48 hours in warm water with liquid detergent, then clean of all pulp, light outdoors (germ. in following spring), or moist-cold (120 days) followed by light, sow indoors (50°F) (germ. 120 days or longer); softwood, greenwood, semi-ripewood cuttings (wound); layering, air layering; grafting varieties on seedlings

MAHONIA: fresh seed—clean, light, outdoors or moist-cold (21 days) light, sow indoors (acidic medium) (50°F) (germ. 90–120 days); leaf-bud, semi-ripewood cuttings; division

MAIANTHEMUM: fresh seed outdoors

MALUS: seed—clean fruits, outdoors, or moist-cold (60 days), sow indoors (65–70°F) (germ. 30–60 days); grafting

MALVA: seed—outdoors in spring to summer, or sow indoors (70–75°F) 6–8 weeks before last frost date (germ. 5–10 days)

MANDEVILLA: seed—(70–75°F) (germ. 14–30 days); softwood, greenwood cuttings (bottom heat)

MARRUBIUM: seed—sow indoors (50°F) (germ. erratic); basal stem cuttings in summer

MATTEUCCIA: spores—sow indoors cool (65–70°F); divide offsets around crown in early spring

MECONOPSIS: seed—sow indoors (55–65°F) 6–8 weeks before last frost date (germ. 14–28 days) (the blue poppies are notoriously difficult to grow, orange or yellow *M. cambrica* is easier and best from fresh seed); division (very carefully) early spring

MELIANTHUS: seed—sow indoors (70–75°F) (germ. 30–180 days, erratic); basal cuttings in spring; division

MELISSA: seed—light, sow indoors (70°F) 8–10 weeks before last frost date (germ. 14–21 days); stem cuttings; division in early spring (potentially invasive mint-family member)

MERTENSIA: fresh seed—outdoors; carefully divide after flowering

MESEMBRYANTHEMUM: seed—dark, sow indoors (65–75°F) 8–10 weeks before last frost date (germ. 15–20 days); cuttings in spring

METASEQUOIA: fresh seed—sow indoors (50–60°F) (germ. 5–20 days); softwood cuttings (mist, bottom heat), hardwood cuttings (store autumn-collected twigs a minimum of 45 days in refrigerator and then hormone dip and move to mist with bottom heat, or plant outdoors in spring)

MICROBIOTA: evergreen hardwood cuttings

MILIUM: fresh seed—light, sow in situ outdoors; division

MILTONIA: rooting of backbulbs (as per *Cymbidium*)

MIMULUS: seed—moist-cold (21 days) and then light, sow indoors (70–75°F) 10–12 weeks before last frost date (germ. 7–21 days) (or outdoors in spring, light, 45–55°F); herbaceous: stem-tip cuttings, division; woody: softwood, greenwood, semi-ripewood cuttings

MINA: see *Ipomoea*

MIRABILIS: seed—light, sow indoors (70–75°F) 6–8 weeks before last frost date (germ. 7–21 days); tuber sections in spring in mild climates

MISCANTHUS: seed—outdoors; division in spring (invasive, discourage seed release in warm climates, do not grow near meadows)

MITCHELLA: seed—in situ in autumn; semi-ripe cuttings; division in spring; sections of runners

MONARDA: seed—in situ in early spring through summer, or sow indoors (50–65°F [temperature reduction at night beneficial]) (germ. 15–20 days); herbaceous cuttings; division in early spring (potentially invasive mint-family member)

MONSTERA: semi-ripewood, stem section horizontally placed on medium or leaf-bud cuttings anytime; layering, air layering

MORUS: seed—clean fruits, light outdoors, or moist-cold (30–90 days), light, sow indoors (65–75°F) (germ. 14–30 days); hardwood cuttings; grafting

MUSA: fresh seed—file, soak in hot water and then cool 24 hours, sow indoors (75°F) (germ. 21–30 days); division of offsets

MUSCARI: fresh seed—outdoors; division; chipping

MYOSOTIS: seed—in situ in early spring to winter, or dark, sow indoors cool (65–70°F) 8–10 weeks before last frost date (germ. 14–30 days) (potentially invasive from seed)

MYRICA: seed propagation difficult—wax must be removed from seeds—outdoors in autumn; greenwood cuttings with bottom heat; layering; division of suckers; root cuttings

MYRRHIS: seed—sow in situ, or sow indoors (55–65°F) (germ. 14–40 days)

MYRTUS: seed—soak 48 hours, sow indoors (55–65°F) (germ. 30–90 days, erratic); softwood, semi-ripewood cuttings

NANDINA: fresh seed—clean seed from fruit in autumn and sow indoors cool (65–70°F) (irregular germ. times due to embryo development and storage); greenwood, semi-ripewood cuttings (hormone for both); division of basal offsets

NARCISSUS: fresh seed—outdoors as available (varieties can only be propagated vegetatively, of course, and many hybrid daffodil fruits are barren); division of offsets; twin scaling, chipping

NECTAROSCORDUM: fresh seed—outdoors in protected spot; division of offsets when dormant

NELUMBO: seed—file side of seeds, and then soak in 100°F water 48 hours, remove seed coat and place seed in a bowl of warm water (75–85°F) with another bowl keeping seeds submerged, change water once or twice a day until seeds germinate (germ. 14–30 days), then plant in pot of heavy soil standing in a bowl of water; sections of rhizome in spring (bottom heat helpful); division

NEMESIA: seed—sow indoors (55–70°F) 8–10 weeks before last frost date (germ. 7–21 days)

NEMOPHILA: seed—dark, in situ after danger of frost, or dark, sow indoors (55°F) 6–8 weeks before last frost (germ. 7–21 days)

NEPENTHES: fresh seed—sow on moist sphagnum with high humidity (75–85°F) (germ. 30–90 days); semi-ripe cuttings; air layering

NEPETA: seed—outdoors in situ when soil warm, or sow indoors (60–70°F) 8–10 weeks before last frost date (germ. 7–14 days); herbaceous cuttings in spring; division in spring

NEPHROLEPIS: spores—warm (germ. erratic); division; runners (roll up and pin stringy stolons to daughter pot)

NERINE: seed—sow as soon as harvested in autumn (germ. immediate); division of bulbs in spring before dormant; chipping in summer

NERIUM: seed—light, outdoors in spring, or light, sow indoors (70–75°F) (germ. 30–90 days); greenwood, semi-ripewood cuttings (late summer or any time proper material is available, bottom heat helpful); layering

NICOTIANA: seed—light, sow indoors (70–75°F) (germ. 10–20 days); root cuttings

NIEREMBERGIA: seed—outdoors in situ in early spring or early autumn, or sow indoors (70–75°F) 8–10 weeks before last frost date (germ. 15–30 days)

NIGELLA: seed—in situ or sow indoors repeatedly for continuous blooming (65–70°F) beginning 6–8 weeks before last frost date (germ. 10–15 days)

NUPHAR: division in spring

NYMPHAEA: fresh seed—hardy kinds: sow indoors (55–65°F), tropical varieties: sow indoors (70–75°F)—keep medium saturated in bowl of water (germ. 30–60 days, erratic); leaf cuttings; offsets in spring; root cuttings; division in spring

NYSSA: seed—light, outdoors or moist-cold (90 days) followed by light, sow indoors (50–60°F) (germ. 90–365 days); softwood cuttings sometimes possible; layering; grafting

OCIMUM: seed—light, sow indoors (60–70°F) 4–6 weeks before last frost date (germ. 7–42 days); stem cuttings

OENOTHERA: seed—light, sow indoors (65–70°F [temperature reduction at night beneficial]) 8–10 weeks before last frost date (germ. 15–30 days); stem cuttings; division in spring

OLEA: seed—clean raw seed, crack coat, sow indoors (70–75°F) (germ. 30–120 days); semi-ripewood cuttings

OMPHALODES: seed—sow indoors (65–70°F) 10–12 weeks before last frost date (germ. 14–42 days); division in spring

ONCIDIUM: seed—(very difficult) light, sow indoors (65–75°F) (germ. 90–365 days); division of offset pseudobulbs after flowering; rooting of backbulbs (as per *Cymbidium*)

ONOCLEA: spores—sow indoors in winter (55–65°F) (germ. 90+ days, erratic); division of rhizomes

ONOPORDUM: seed—sow indoors (55–60°F) (germ. 30–60 days)

ONOSMA: seed—sow indoors (50°F) 10–12 weeks before last frost date (germ. 30–60 days); semi-ripe cuttings in summer

OPHIOPOGON: seed—soak 24 hours in warm water, sow indoors (65–70°F) 6–8 weeks before last frost date (germ. 30–42 days); division in early spring

OPUNTIA: fresh seed—clean seed from fruit, dark, sow indoors (70°F) (germ. 21 days—varies by species); stem pad cuttings (allow to callus)

ORIGANUM: seed—outdoors after frost, or sow indoors (55–65°F) 6–8 weeks before last frost date (germ. 10 days); cuttings in spring; division in spring

ORNITHOGALUM: seed—hardy species: outdoors in autumn, or moist-cold (21 days) and then sow indoors (55–60°F) (germ. 30–180 days); division of bulblets in autumn

ORONTIUM: fresh seed—sow indoors cool (55–65°F), keep medium saturated in bowl of water (germ. 30–60 days, erratic); division in late spring

OSMANTHUS: seed—sow indoors in pots in autumn and place in cool frost-free place; semi-ripewood nodal tip cuttings or with heel if possible (bottom heat, Oasis or rock wool blocks may work well)

OSMUNDA: ripe spores—outdoors in late spring in covered saucers in bright light, or indoors (see page 98); division

OSTEOSPERMUM: seed—light, sow indoors (60–65°F) (germ. 10–15 days); softwood, greenwood, semi-ripewood cuttings whenever available

OXALIS: seed—sow indoors (55–70°F) (germ. 14–60 days); tuber sections in spring (hardy) or after flowering (some species are potentially invasive)

OXYDENDRUM: fresh seed—light, sow indoors (60–70°F) under mist; tissue culture

OXYPETALUM: seed—sow indoors (70–75°F) 6–8 weeks before last frost date (germ. 30–90 days); cuttings in spring

PACHYPODIUM: seed—light, sow indoors (70–75°F) (germ. 30–180 days)

PACHYSANDRA: division of stolons (horizontal stems) in spring

PACHYSTACHYS: softwood, greenwood nodal cuttings in summer

PAEONIA: fresh seed—light, outdoors, or moist-warm (90 days) followed by moist-cold (90 days) followed by light, sow indoors (60–70°F) (germ. 270+ days) (two-step germination, see page 74); division of thick rootstock in autumn; grafting for tree peonies, which are shrubs

PANICUM: seed—outdoors; division of perennial kinds in spring

PAPAVER: seed—sow in situ when seeds available or winter (germ. 10–30 days once temperatures are above 55°F); root cuttings of hardy herbaceous perennial varieties

PARDANCANDA: seed—moist-cold (7 days) prior to sow indoors (70–85°F) 8–10 weeks before last frost date (germ. 14 days); division in spring

PARROTIA: fresh seed—outdoors in autumn, or soak 48 hours, moist-cold (70 days), and sow indoors (germ. erratic); layering in early summer or midautumn; grafting

PARTHENOCISSUS: seed—soak 24 hours followed by moist-cold (42 days) and then light, sow indoors (60–70°F) 8 weeks before last frost date (germ. 60–180 days); softwood, semi-ripewood, hardwood cuttings; layering (simple and serpentine)

PASSIFLORA: seed—(if harvested: let ripe fruit sit for 14 days, then smash and leave for 2 more days, wash seeds in sieve under running water, dry) soak seeds for 24 hours in hot water and then sow indoors (70–75°F) (germ. 30 days, but older seed may take up to 365 days); softwood, semi-ripewood cuttings; layering

PAULOWNIA: seed—nick, soak 48 hours in hot and then warm water (may be pre-germinated on moist paper towel in plastic bag in sunlight), light, sow indoors (55–70°F) (germ. 30–60 days); root cuttings

PELARGONIUM: seed—sow indoors (70–75°F) 8–10 weeks before last frost date (germ. 3–21 days); greenwood, semi-ripe stem cuttings, expose cut 24 hours to promote callus (see page 135); some kinds have tubers that can be removed and potted

PENNISETUM: seed—sow indoors (70°F) 6 to 8 weeks before last frost date (germ. 15–21 days); division in spring

PENSTEMON: seed—light, outdoors, or light, sow indoors (55–60°F) 8–10 weeks before last frost date (germ. 18–21 days); stem cuttings in spring or autumn for cold frame; division of basal offsets and basal cuttings of some

PEPEROMIA: seed—sow indoors (70–75°F) (germ. 15–30 days); stem-tip, leaf-petiole cuttings; division

PEROVSKIA: softwood cuttings in spring (subshrub)

PERSEA: seed—soak cleaned seed in hot water (120°F) for half an hour, sow indoors (70–75°F); grafting to disease-resistant understock

PETASITES: seed—light, sow indoors (55–60°F) (germ. 30–90 days); division in spring

PHACELIA: seed—dark, sow indoors (55–60°F) (germ. 12–30 days)

PHALAENOPSIS: remove rooted offsets or promote keikis—in near-sterile environment, cut away bracts covering dormant buds along underside of flower spikes with sterile blade or scalpel, then smear special hormone and vitamin paste over bud; small plantlets or keikis will be produced soon after that can be pegged to medium to produce roots

PHILADELPHUS: seed—outdoors, or moist-cold helpful (42–56 days), sow indoors (65–70°F) (germ. 30–60 days); stem cuttings easy—softwood, greenwood, semi-ripewood, hardwood

PHILODENDRON: seed—sow indoors (70–75°F) (germ. 30–120 days); leaf-bud, softwood, semi-ripewood stem cuttings; layering (easy—simple, serpentine, air layering—note aerial roots)

PHLOMIS: seed—sow indoors (70–75°F) 8–10 weeks before last frost date (germ. 30–90 days); herbaceous: division in spring; woody: semi-ripe (keep leaves dry, may be rooted in cold frame), hardwood cuttings

PHLOX: seed—annual varieties—dark, sow indoors (55–65°F) 6–8 weeks before last frost date (germ. 10–21 days), summer-flowering perennials: dark, outdoors in autumn, or moist-cold (30 days) followed by sow indoors (70–75°F) (germ. 25–30 days); perennials: stem cuttings in early spring; division in spring (autumn in mild climates); summer-blooming perennials from root cuttings

PHORMIUM: seed—sow indoors (60–65°F) 10–12 weeks before last frost date (germ. 30–180 days); division in spring

PHOTINIA: most types from greenwood or semi-ripewood cuttings (do well with hormone treatment and in rock wool or Oasis cubes [plugs])

PHUOPSIS: seed—light, outdoors in autumn best, or light, sow indoors (50–65°F) (germ. 30–40 days); stem cuttings or sections of runners in summer; division in spring before flowering (may be invasive if happy)

PHYGELIUS: seed—outdoors in spring or summer, or sow indoors (70–75°F) 6–8 weeks before last frost date (germ. 10–14 days); softwood basal cuttings in spring, semi-ripe cuttings in late summer; division in spring (in autumn in mild climates)

PHYSALIS: seed—light, sow indoors (70–75°F) (germ. 10–30 days); division in early spring

PHYSOCARPUS: softwood, greenwood, semi-ripewood cuttings

PHYSOSTEGIA: seed—sow indoors (60–65°F [temperature reduction at night beneficial]) 8–10 weeks before last frost date (germ. 30–180 days); division in spring (potentially invasive mint-family member)

PICEA: seed—moist-cold (21 days) followed by light, sow indoors (55°F) (germ. 30–60 days); semi-ripe cuttings; evergreen hardwood cuttings require bottom heat

PIERIS: seed—light, sow indoors (65–70°F) (germ. 30–70 days); greenwood, semi-ripewood cuttings; layering

PILEA: seed—light, sow indoors (50–65°F) (germ. 30–40 days)

PINUS: seed—soak 24 hours and then moist-cold (42 days) followed by light, sow indoors (55–65°F) (germ. 30–60°F); grafting

PITTOSPORUM: seed—pour boiling

water over seed in sieve and then light, sow indoors (55°F) (germ. 30–60 days); semi-ripewood cuttings; layering; grafting

PLATANUS: fresh seed—outdoors; hardwood cuttings

PLATYCODON: seed—light, sow indoors (70°F) 6–8 weeks before last frost date (germ. 15–30 days); semi-ripe cuttings in summer; division in spring

PLECTRANTHUS: seed—light, sow indoors (70–75°F) 8–12 weeks before last frost date (germ. 1–15 days); stem cuttings (bottom heat helpful) anytime, but fastest in late winter to early summer

PLUMBAGO: seed—sow indoors (70°F) (germ. 25–30 days); softwood, greenwood, semi-ripewood cuttings

PLUMERIA: seed—24-hour soak, sow indoors (65–75°F) (germ. 30–180–30 days); hardwood cuttings, dry ends in cool dark place and then insert in medium at 70°F

PODOCARPUS: seed—outdoors in climates where plants are hardy; semi-ripewood cuttings

PODOPHYLLUM: fresh seed—light, outdoors best, or moist-cold (30 days) followed by light, sow indoors (65–70°F) (germ. 35–180 days); division of rhizomes after blooming

POLEMONIUM: seed—sow indoors (70–75°F [reduce temperature at night]) 8–10 weeks before last frost date (germ. 20–25 days); division in spring

POLYGALA: seed—hardy types: light, outdoors in autumn, less hardy and tender species: light, sow indoors (70°F) (germ. 25–30 days); softwood, greenwood, semi-ripewood nodal cuttings

POLYGONATUM: seed—outdoors in autumn, or moist-cold (30 days) and then sow indoors or cold frame (50°F) (germ. 30–545 days); division spring (in autumn in mild climates)

POLYPODIUM: spores—sow indoors (65–70°F); divide sections of rhizome with leaves in early spring

POLYSTICHUM: spores—sow indoors (65–70°F); divide offsets around crown in early spring; root "bulbils" (adventitious plantlets) while still attached to midrib of frond, pin to medium

PONCIRUS: seed—moist-cold (30–90 days), sow indoors (65–70°F) (germ. 30 days); semi-ripewood cuttings (hormone, mist, and bottom heat)

PONTEDERIA: fresh seed—sow indoors cool (55–65°F), keep medium saturated in bowl of water (germ. 30–60 days, erratic); division in late spring

POPULUS: ripe seed—lay seed and fluff on medium in pots, cover with grit, and set in cold frame (at 50°F, germ. rapid); hardwood cuttings in late autumn to late winter; grafting; division of suckers in late winter

PORTERANTHUS (GILLENIA): seed—outdoors; division in spring or autumn

POTENTILLA: seed—herbaceous perennials: outdoors in autumn or early spring, or sow indoors (65–70°F) 8–10 weeks before last frost date (germ. 14–30 days); woody: greenwood, semi-ripewood, hardwood cuttings; division

PRIMULA: varies by species, in general for hardy perennials: seed—light, sow outdoors in appropriate climates, from autumn to late winter, or moist-cold (30 days) and then light, sow indoors (60–65°F) 8–10 weeks before last frost date (germ. 21–40 days); division after flowering for early-spring blooming, in early spring for late-spring flowering, gouging in early spring

PRUNUS: seed—wash of all pulp, then outdoors in protected place, or moist-cold (90 days or longer) followed by sow indoors (65–70°F) (germ. 30–60 days); semi-ripewood, hardwood cuttings; (some shrub types—layering); grafting

PULMONARIA: seed—sow indoors (60–65°F) 7–9 weeks before last frost date (germ. 30–42 days); division in late winter; root cuttings

PULSATILLA: fresh seed—outdoors best, dry seed—nick, sow indoors (60–70°F) (germ. 30–180 days); tip cuttings; division

PUNICA: seed—soak 24 hours followed by light, sow indoors (70–75°F) (germ. 30–40 days); softwood, greenwood, hardwood cuttings

PYRACANTHA: seed—(squash berries and wash over sieve in running water) moist-cold (42–90 days) followed by light, sow indoors (50°F) (germ. 40–180 days); greenwood, semi-ripewood, hardwood cuttings

PYRUS: seed—clean seed, outdoors, or moist-cold (90 days) (if seeds germinate in refrigerator, surface-sow indoors with fine covering of grit or vermiculite); grafting to seedlings—varieties are vegetatively propagated

QUERCUS: seed—light, outside in protected place, or soak 24 hours followed by moist-cold (90 days minimum, radicle may emerge under refrigeration) and then light, sow indoors (50°F) (germ. 120–365 days); semi-ripe cuttings in rock wool or peat and perlite, bottom heat; grafting

RAMONDA: seed—light, outdoors 2 weeks before last frost date, or light, sow indoors (55–60°F) 6–8 weeks before last frost date (germ. 30–60 days); leaf cuttings; division of offsets in summer

RATIBIDA: seed—sow indoors (70–75°F [reduce temperature at night]) (germ. 21–42 days); division

RHEUM: seed—sow indoors (60–65°F) 8–10 weeks before last frost date (germ. 21–42 days); division of thick rootstock

RHIPSALIS: seed—clean from berries, sow indoors (65–75°F)(germ. 30–90 days); semi-ripe stem cuttings, allow to callus overnight (flat stem, see page 135)

RHODOCHITON: fresh seed—(soak if dry) sow indoors (65–70°F) 6–8 weeks before last frost date (germ. 14–60 days); stem cuttings in spring to summer

RHODODENDRON: fresh seed—outdoors, light (but shaded from direct sunlight), high humidity, acidic medium (peat-based), or light, sow indoors (50–60°F) (germ. 50–90 days); deciduous: softwood cuttings in early spring with hormone, cool location with high humidity or mist; small-leaved evergreen: nodal greenwood cuttings; large-leaved evergreen: semi-ripewood, leaf-bud or stem cuttings with leaf area reduced by trimming, wound, hormone—bottom heat helpful in outdoor frame (55–60°F), or Nearing frame (see page 139); layering; grafting

RHUS: seed—nick or soak 24 hours, sow indoors (65–70°F) (germ. 30–90 days); division in late winter; root cuttings in winter

RIBES: softwood, semi-ripewood, hardwood cuttings; layering; grafting

RICINUS: seed—nick, or soak in warm water 24 hours and then sow indoors (70–75°F) 6–8 weeks before last frost date (germ. 14–21 days)

ROBINIA: seed—light, outdoors, or soak in hot water 24 hours followed by light, sow indoors (70–75°F) (germ. 7–30 days); division; root cuttings

RODGERSIA: seed—light, outdoors, or light, sow indoors (55–60°F) 6–8 weeks before last frost date (germ. 14–60 days); division in spring

ROHDEA: seed—species: fresh, clean, sow outdoors; cultivars: division in spring

ROSA: seed—light, outdoors, or moist-cold (90 days) followed by light, sow indoors (55°F) (germ. 30–365 days or longer, erratic)

ROSMARINUS: semi-ripewood, evergreen hardwood cuttings

RUBUS: softwood, semi-ripewood, leaf-bud, hardwood cuttings; layering (simple, serpentine, tip layering, mounding); division

RUDBECKIA: seed—light, sow indoors (70–75°F) 6–8 weeks before last frost date (germ. 5–21 days); stem cuttings in spring; division in spring

RUTA: seed—sow indoors (60–65°F) (germ. 30–42 days); greenwood, semi-ripewood cuttings (note: plant parts can cause skin reaction in sunlight—wear gloves, cut in shade)

SABAL: fresh seed—soak 48 hours in warm water (change once or twice), wash seed, sow on moist paper towel in plastic bag (70°F), pot in medium and fertilize once germinated; division

SAGINA: seed—outdoors in spring while still cool, or sow indoors (55°F) 6–8 weeks before last frost date (germ. 10–25 days); division in spring

SAGITTARIA: fresh seed—sow indoors cool (55–65°F), keep medium saturated in bowl of water (germ. 30–60 days, erratic); division of basal suckers and tubers in spring

SAINTPAULIA: seed—light, sow indoors

(70–75°F) (germ. 30–60 days); stem, leaf cuttings, leggy older plants can have stem and top rosette removed and rooted as stem cutting; division of basal rosettes

SALIX: fresh seed—sow indoors (60–65°F) at once, as viability very short (germ. 1–2 days); shrub willows and alpine kinds: root readily from softwood and semi-ripewood cuttings, which appreciate high humidity; tall types: easiest from hardwood cuttings in late winter; grafting

SALVIA: seed—tender and annual varieties: light, sow indoors (70–80°F) 6–8 weeks before last frost date (germ. 7–21 days); hardy perennials: moist-cold (30 days) followed by light, sow indoors (65–70°F) 6–8 weeks before last frost date (germ. 14–30 days); hardy herbaceous perennials: semi-ripe stem cuttings in late summer, division of clump-forming types; tender woody plants: softwood, semi-ripewood nodal cuttings, green to semi-ripe cuttings in late spring to late summer (to carry over indoors under lights or in greenhouse)

SAMBUCUS: fresh seed—clean and outdoors (germ. first or second spring); softwood, semi-ripewood (nodal), hardwood (with heel cuttings); grafting

SANGUINARIA: seed—sow indoors (50–55°F) 8–10 weeks before last frost date (germ. 30–90 days); division; rhizome sections in early spring or late summer when dormant

SANGUISORBA: seed—outdoors in early spring or autumn, or sow indoors (50–55°F) 10–12 weeks before last frost date (germ. 30–60 days); division in spring

SANSEVIERIA: leaf cuttings are possible, but varieties must be vegetatively reproduced by cutting of "suckers" or new growths via rhizomes

SANTOLINA: seed—moist-cold (30 days) followed by sow indoors (65–70°F) 8–10 weeks before last frost date (germ. 15–30 days); semi-ripewood cuttings

SARCOCOCCA: seed—sow indoors (55–65°F) (germ. 30–120 days)

SARRACENIA: seed—moist-cold (7 days) followed by light, sow indoors (60–70°F) 8–10 weeks before last frost date (germ. 30–90 days), sow on moist paper towel or whole sphagnum moss kept constantly moist; division in spring or autumn in mild climates

SASSAFRAS: fresh seed—clean seed of flesh, outdoors; root cuttings in winter

SAXIFRAGA: seed—outdoors or in cold frame in autumn, or moist-cold (30 days) and sow indoors (55–60°F) (germ. 14–60 days); division; division of basal offsets in spring to root in medium (*S. stolonifera* and varieties have runners like those of strawberries, *S. granulata* has "bulbils" in leaf axils to "sow" as seeds in spring)

SCABIOSA: seed—sow indoors (70–75°F) (germ. 10–15 days), annuals: 4–5 weeks

before last frost date, perennials: 8–10 weeks (65–70°F) (germ. 10–15 days); division; basal stem cuttings in midspring

SCHEFFLERA: seed—clean of fleshy pulp, sow indoors (75°F) (germ. 20–30 days); semi-ripewood, leaf-bud cuttings; layering, air layering

SCHIZOPHRAGMA: seed—moist-cold (90 days) followed by sow indoors (60–65°F) (germ. variable); greenwood (nodal) cuttings; serpentine layering

SCHLUMBERGERA: flat stem cuttings, at least one segment long

SCILLA: seed—outdoors in autumn, or moist-cold (21 days) and then sow indoors (50°F) (germ. 30–180 days); division of offsets in autumn; chipping in late summer

SCROPHULARIA: division of variegated form; basal stem cuttings in spring

SEDUM: seed—hardy types: outdoors in autumn, or moist-cold (30 days) followed by sow indoors (60–65°F) (germ. 14–180 days); semi-ripe cuttings, leaf cuttings of tender kinds (thick stems may need exposure to air for 24 hours to callus before sticking); division in spring

SEMPERVIVUM: seed—sow indoors (70° F) (germ. 14–42 days)—not true from seed; division of offsets

SENECIO: seed—light, sow indoors (65–75°F) 8 weeks before last frost date (germ. 10–21 days); greenwood, semi-ripewood cuttings; division of perennial types

SENNA: seed—scarification followed by sow indoors (70–80°F) (germ. 7–30 days)

SEQUOIA: seed—(store refrigerated if necessary) light, sow indoors (65–70°F) (germ. 7–60 days, erratic)

SEQUOIADENDRON: seed—(store refrigerated if necessary) light, sow indoors (65–70°F) (germ. 7–60 days, erratic); greenwood tip cuttings

SHORTIA: fresh seed—outdoors, or moist-cold (21 days) followed by sow indoors (60–65°F) 6–8 weeks before last frost date (germ. 30–60 days); division in early spring

SIDALCEA: seed—sow indoors (50°F) 6–8 weeks before last frost date (germ. 14–42 days); division in autumn

SILENE: seed—sow indoors (70–75°F) 8–10 weeks before last frost date (germ. 15–20 days); perennials: stem cuttings in spring

SILPHIUM: fresh seed—nick, outdoors in autumn; division in spring

SINNINGIA: seed—light, sow indoors (70–75°F) (germ. 10–21 days); leaf cuttings (sections or petiole); sections of tuber in spring; basal cuttings (as for tuberous begonia)

SINOCALYCANTHUS: seed—outdoors in autumn; greenwood, semi-ripewood cuttings; division of suckers

SISYRINCHIUM: seed—outdoors in autumn, or moist-cold (21 days) and then

sow indoors (60–65°F) (germ. 30–180 days); division in spring

SKIMMIA: seed—soak 24 hours followed by moist-cold (30 days) and then light, sow indoors (50–60°F) (germ. 30–180 days); greenwood, semi-ripewood cuttings

SMILACINA: seed—light, outdoors best, or moist-cold (30 days) followed by light, sow indoors (60–65°F) (germ. 30–180 days)

SOLANUM: seed—light, sow indoors (70–80°F) (germ. 14–21 days); softwood, semi-ripewood cuttings (easy to root, but nodal stem cuttings taken of compact growth are less prone to disease)

SOLDANELLA: fresh seed—light, outdoors, or moist-cold (30 days) and then light, sow indoors (55–60°F) (germ. 30–180 days)

SOLENOSTEMON: see *Coleus*

SOLIDAGO: seed—outdoors in early spring, or sow indoors (50°F) 6–8 weeks before last frost date (germ. 14–42 days); division

SOPHORA: seed—soak in hot water 24 hours followed by light, sow indoors (70–75°F) (germ. 7–30 days); semi-ripewood cuttings of evergreen types; grafting

SORBARIA: seed—outdoors in autumn; softwood, greenwood, semi-ripewood, hardwood cuttings; layering; division

SORBUS: fresh seed—just-ripe seed may be germinated at once, clean seed of pulp, sow outdoors in autumn—otherwise, moist-cold (120 days—check seeds; if any germinate, pot at once) and then light, sow indoors (65–70°F) (germ. 120–180 days); grafting

SPARAXAS: seed—sow indoors (50–55° F) 8–10 weeks before last frost date (germ. 30–90 days); division of offsets

SPATHIPHYLLUM: division

SPIGELIA: seed—light, outdoors, cold frame, or moist-cold (30 days) followed by light, sow indoors (60–70°F) (germ. 30–60 days); division in late winter

SPIRAEA: seed—sow indoors (55–65°F) (germ. 30–40 days); softwood, semi-ripewood, hardwood cuttings; division

STACHYS: seed—light, sow indoors (70–75°F [reduce temperature at night 10°F]) 8–10 weeks before last frost date (germ. 14–30 days); division; basal cuttings to root

STACHYURUS: seed—outdoors in autumn; greenwood nodal or heel cuttings; layering

STAPELIA: seed—light, sow indoors (65–70°F) (germ. 7–30 days); greenwood, semi-ripewood cuttings—let cut end dry for a day or two to callus before setting in medium (as per succulents)

STAPHYLEA: fresh seed—outdoors, or moist-warm (120 days) followed by moist-cold (90 days) and then sow indoors (65°F) (germ. 30 days); greenwood cuttings with heel

STEPHANANDRA: fresh seed—outdoors, or moist-warm (90 days) followed by, moist-cold (90 days) and then sow indoors (65°F) (germ. 21–30 days); nodal or internodal greenwood cuttings; layering

STEPHANOTIS: seed—72-hour soak (wash and change water) followed by sow indoors (75–80°F) (germ. 30–180 days); semi-ripewood cuttings; layering

STEWARTIA: seed—moist-cold (84 days), sow outdoors or indoors as long as temperature remains above 50°F at night (germ. up to 3 years); softwood cuttings

STIPA: seed—outdoors in spring, or sow indoors (70°F) 6–8 weeks before last frost date (germ. 21–30 days); division in spring

STOKESIA: seed—sow indoors (70°F) 8–10 weeks before last frost date (germ. 20–30 days); division in early spring

STRELITZIA: seed—sow indoors (70–75°F) (germ. 14–60 days); division of rooted offsets

STREPTOCARPUS: seed—light, sow indoors (55–65°F) (germ. 15–30 days); stem cuttings of some, leaf cuttings; division

STROBILANTHES: stem-tip cuttings in spring; division in spring; basal cuttings in spring

STYRAX: seed—sow indoors (55–65°F) (germ. 30–90 days or longer); softwood cuttings; layering of shrubby kinds

SYMPHORICARPOS: seed—moist-warm (90 days) followed by moist-cold (90 days) to sow indoors or out in spring (germ. the following spring); softwood, semi-ripewood, hardwood cuttings; division

SYMPHYTUM: division; root cuttings (variegated types will not carry that characteristic through root cuttings)

SYMPLOCARPUS: fresh seed—outdoors, or moist-cold (90 days) followed by moist-warm (90 days) and then sow indoors (55–65°F—keep medium saturated) (radicle emerges 7–21 days), leaf emerges after second moist-cold and moist-warm treatments

SYNGONIUM: semi-ripe stem cuttings; layering

SYRINGA: seed—(species only—most are cultivars) moist-cold (21 days) followed by light, sow indoors (70°F) (germ. 14–60 days); softwood cuttings taken from new growth as blossoms fade; layering; division of suckers while dormant in late winter; root cuttings in autumn

TANACETUM: seed—sow in situ in spring; division in spring; basal cuttings in spring

TAXODIUM: seed—moist-cold (30 days) and then light, sow indoors (70°F) (germ. 14–60 days); softwood (under mist), hardwood cuttings

TAXUS: seed—clean (wash hands), moist-warm (90 days) followed by moist-cold (90 days) and then moist-warm again (90 days) followed by light, sow indoors (70°F) (germ. 365 days or longer); semi-ripewood cuttings (hormone, wounding perhaps, helps—mist accelerates rooting); grafting

TELLIMA: seed—outdoors, or moist-cold (60 days) followed by sow indoors (55–60°F) (germ. 30–90 days); division in spring or autumn in mild climates

TEUCRIUM: seed—outdoors, or sow indoors (70–75°F) 6–8 weeks before last frost date (germ. 25–30 days); softwood, greenwood, semi-ripewood (nodal) cuttings; division in spring

THALICTRUM: fresh seed—outdoors best (germ. 15–21 days [erratic, however, up to 735 days]); division in early spring

THERMOPSIS: seed—nick or 24-hour soak followed by sow outdoors in early spring, or indoors (70–75°F) 6–8 weeks before last frost date (germ. 15–30 days); division in spring

THUJA: seed—moist-cold (30 days) followed by light, sow indoors (55°F) (germ. 14–60 days)

THUNBERGIA: seed—sow indoors (70–75°F) 6–8 weeks before last frost date (germ. 14–21 days); greenwood (nodal) cuttings

THYMUS: seed—light, outdoors 2–3 weeks before last frost date, or light, sow indoors (55–65°F) 6–8 weeks before last frost date (germ. 15–30 days); division

TIARELLA: seed—outdoors in autumn, or sow indoors (50°F) (germ. 14–90 days); division in early spring, division of offsets from runners of some

TIBOUCHINA: seed—light, sow indoors (60–70°F) (germ. 30–90 days); greenwood, hardwood cuttings in frost-free areas

TILIA: just-ripe seed—collect before inhibitors develop, outdoors; layering; grafting (budding)

TILLANDSIA: seed—light, sow fluffy seeds over medium and cover with grit indoors (60–70°F) (germ. 30–90 days); division of offsets (pups)

TITHONIA: seed—light, sow indoors (70°F) 6–8 weeks before last frost date (germ. 5–14 days)

TOLMIEA: peg leaves with viviparous growths; division in spring

TRACHELOSPERMUM: greenwood and semi-ripewood cuttings (bottom heat); layering, serpentine layering where hardy outdoors

TRADESCANTIA: seed—light, sow indoors (70–75°F [reduce temperature 10°F at night]) 6–8 weeks before last frost date (germ. 30–40 days); nodal cuttings; division in spring (hardy species may be invasive)

TRICYRTIS: seed—light, sow indoors (65–70°F) 6–8 weeks before last frost date (germ. 30–90 days); division in spring

TRILLIUM: fresh seed—outdoors, or moist-warm (90 days) followed by moist-cold (90 days) followed by sow indoors (50–60°F) (germ. 365+ days) (see page 52, sowing "Green"); division of rhizomes after bloom

TROLLIUS: fresh seed—outdoors best in late summer, or with dry seeds moist-cold (30 days) followed by sow indoors (spring) (50°F) (germ. 30–365 days); division after flowering

TSUGA: seed—prior to sowing, expose dry-stored seeds to moist-cold (21 days) and sow in spring, light, outdoors, or light, indoors (60°F) (germ. 7–60 days); semi-ripewood cuttings in autumn (bottom heat)

TULIPA: seed—outdoors best for species, or moist-cold (30–60 days) followed by sow indoors (50°F) (germ. 60–90 days)

TYPHA: division in spring

ULMUS: fresh seed—outdoors; softwood, greenwood cuttings; grafting (budding)

UVULARIA: fresh seed—outdoors best when ripe in late summer; division in spring

VACCINIUM: (blueberry) seed—clean seeds of pulp and then light, outdoors in protected spot, acidic medium (high percentage of peat as per rhododendron) (germ. 365 days or longer); highbush and commercial blueberries: softwood cuttings, evergreen types: semi-ripewood, deciduous types: hardwood cuttings; cranberry: layering; lowbush blueberry: cuttings of rhizome in perlite with bottom heat; division

VALERIANA: seed—outdoors in early spring, or sow indoors (70°F) 10–12 weeks before last frost date (germ. 21–25 days); division in spring or autumn in mild climates; root cuttings

VANCOUVERIA: division

VANDA: sections of stems with or without aerial roots can be removed, wrapped with damp sphagnum, and encouraged to root

VELTHEIMIA: seed—sow indoors (55–65°F) 8–10 weeks before last frost date (germ. 30–90 days); leaf cuttings; bulblets in spring

VERATRUM: seed—outdoors best, or moist-cold (30 days) followed by sow indoors (55–60°F) (germ. 90–365 days); division in early spring

VERBASCUM: seed—outdoors in spring while still cool, or sow indoors (55–60°F) 6–8 weeks before last frost date (germ. 14–30 days); root cuttings in early spring

VERBENA: seed—dark, sow indoors (65°F) 8–10 weeks before last frost date (germ. 14–90 days); cuttings in spring or semi-ripe in autumn to overwinter in cold frame

VERNONIA: seed—light, outdoors when fresh, or store dry in refrigerator followed by light, late-winter sow indoors (55–60°F) (germ. 21–40 days); division in spring or after flowering in autumn

VERONICA: seed—light, sow indoors (70°F) 8–10 weeks before last frost date (germ. 15–30 days); semi-ripe cuttings in summer; division after flowering

VERONICASTRUM: seed—light, sow indoors (55–60°F) (germ. 21–40 days); semi-ripe cuttings in summer; division after flowering

VIBURNUM: seed—squash ripe fruits,

sow indoors together, cover with grit to go outdoors in protected spot, or clean, moist-warm (90 days) followed by moist-cold (90 days) and then moist-warm again (90 days) prior to light, sow indoors (70°F) (germ. 365 days or longer); greenwood, semi-ripewood, hardwood (deciduous) cuttings; layering; grafting

VINCA: seed—dark, sow indoors (70–75°F) (germ. 15–30 days); greenwood, semi-ripewood internodal cuttings; layering; division

VIOLA: seed—most, including pansy types: moist-cold (14 days) followed by dark, sow indoors (65–75°F) 8–10 weeks before last frost date (germ. 14–21 days). *V. odorata:* outdoors only, in autumn; division in spring. *V. tricolor* (seed only): best dark, outdoors in autumn or dark, indoors (65–75°F) 10–12 weeks before last frost date (germ. 14 days); stem-tip cuttings; layering (mounding) may work with low-growing species, use well-drained medium

VITEX: seed—outdoors in spring or autumn outdoors in protected spot in mild climates or cold frame; greenwood, semi-ripewood cuttings

VITIS: softwood, semi-ripewood nodal (reduce leaf area), hardwood cuttings (may be as small as to include one node, wound above and below dormant buds) (hormone for all cuttings); layering (serpentine); grafting

WALDSTEINIA: seed—outdoors or cold frame in autumn, or moist-cold (30 days) followed by sow indoors (55–60°F) (germ. 14–60 days); layering (serpentine); offsets via runners

WASHINGTONIA: fresh seed—soak 48 hours in warm water (change once or twice), wash seed, sow on moist paper towel in plastic bag (70°F), pot in medium and fertilize once germinated

WEIGELA: seed—outdoors in spring; most cultivars: softwood, semi-ripewood, hardwood cuttings

WISTERIA: seed—(seed-grown plants are useful for grafting, but rarely as varieties and take years to flower) nick and soak in hot water, sow indoors (55–65°F) 6–8 weeks before last frost date (germ. 30–60 days); softwood (side shoots with close nodes), hardwood cuttings; layering (serpentine); root cuttings taken in late winter will sprout readily if potted and placed over bottom heat

XANTHORHIZA: seed—outdoors in autumn; greenwood cuttings; division in early spring or autumn

YUCCA: seed—outdoors in spring, or soak 24 hours followed by sow indoors (70–75°F) (germ. varies by species, up to 365 days); softwood cuttings; division of suckers, rhizomes and swollen buds on rhizomes (toes) in early spring; root cuttings

ZANTEDESCHIA: seed—light, outdoors in warm climates, or light, sow indoors (70–80°F) (germ. 30–90 days); sections of tubers with eyes

ZAUSCHNERIA: seed—light, outdoors in spring only where hardy, light, sow indoors (60–65°F) (germ. 30–60 days); stem cuttings in autumn; division in spring

ZEBRINA: nodal stem cuttings; layering, basketing; division

ZELKOVA: seed—moist-cold (14 days) followed by light, sow indoors (50–70°F) (germ. 14–60 days); grafting

ZENOBIA: fresh seed—outdoors, light but shaded from direct sunlight, high humidity, acidic medium (peat-based), or sow indoors (50–60°F) (germ. 50–90 days); semi-ripewood nodal cuttings

SOWING SUMMARY

Most seeds of hardy plants are sown outdoors from autumn to winter, when the garden is quiet and the task can be relaxed—even welcome. But seeds preconditioned indoors* and those of warm-weather annuals and perennials are sown in a flurry of activity beginning in late winter. To avoid becoming overwhelmed, start slowly, perhaps with only three pots and three varieties. Having an area devoted to this activity will make the experience more comfortable. Here is a synopsis of procedures described in Chapter 5, "Sowing."

Outdoor Sowing of Winter-Hardy Seeds:
1. Harvest fruits when ripe. Clean seeds from dry fruits of extraneous material and wash seed from moist fruits of all pulp following soaking.
2. Assemble clean 3½-inch square pots for each species, or flats for mass sowing.
3. Fill containers with moistened medium, strike off the excess and tamp gently. Add more medium to bring it up to the pot rim and tap on the potting bench to level the mix. (For tiny seeds and those requiring light for germination, see step 5.)
4. Distribute seeds uniformly. Press large ones into the medium to a depth that equals their thickness. Add medium up to the pot rim and tap gently.
5. Cover the surface with a thin layer of grit or very coarse sand. Use fine grit for small seed, coarser for larger ones. The layer should be just thick enough to obscure

the medium. Tiny seeds and ones requiring light may be sown on top of the grit layer.
6. Place pots or flats in trays with 1 to 2 inches of water until the grit darkens—about a half hour.
7. Place containers in the screen-covered box outdoors.

Indoor Sowing of Tender Perennials, Annuals, and Preconditioned Seeds:*
1. Determine the sowing date, often included on commercial packets and in the Generic Guide to Propagation. Follow steps 2 through 6, above.
2. Bring pots or flats to your indoor germination location: sunny window, greenhouse bench, or indoor light set-up. If using fluorescent lights, place pots 3 inches below the tubes. Set a timer for 18 hours of light per day. Or provide a window with as much sunlight as possible or a bright area in the greenhouse. Seeds that require darkness for germination must be covered with an opaque card or aluminum foil. Most seeds appreciate gentle heat from below, and the recommended temperature range should be maintained until true leaves appear. (Check seeds in darkness religiously and remove cover once sprouted.)
3. If seeds are allowed to dry once they have absorbed water, they will die. Maintain moisture in the medium. Lift pots to judge weight and become familiar with properly moistened pots.
4. Keep the relative humidity high (above 40

percent). Flats may be draped with loose-fitting plastic film or rigid domes set ajar. Individual pots can be set into open plastic zipper bags or on pebbles kept moist in a tray. The floral cart can be draped in a plastic-film tent. The greenhouse may require a humidifier or misting unit.
5. Once seedlings emerge, the distance from the top of the leaves to the fluorescent tubes must be kept around 3 inches by raising the lights or lowering pots. The medium can be slightly drier and temperatures lower. A 5–10°F drop at night or when the lights are off is helpful.

Packaged Seed of Hardy-Plants from Societies; Mail-Order Sources; or Gathered from the Garden, Cleaned, and Stored Dry:
1. Determine the sowing date.
2. Soak dried seeds that originated in moist fruits in water overnight (change water a few times). Condition if necessary.* Follow steps 2 through 6 for Fresh Seeds, above.
3. Place containers outdoors or indoors as required.

* Research conditioning requirements (such as soaking, nicking, cold-moist or warm-moist stratification) and determine the date to begin treatments. Seeds may be stratified on moistened paper towel, vermiculite, or whole sphagnum moss in plastic bags. Tiny seeds may be sown first (above) and treated in their pots prior to being brought to warmth and light for germination.

COMMON NAME CROSS-REFERENCE

A

Abelia, *Abelia*
Achimenes, *Achimenes*
Adam's needle, *Yucca*
African daisy, *Arctotis*
African violet, *Saintpaulia*
Alder, *Alnus*
Allium, *Allium*
Almond, *Prunus*
Aloe, *Aloe*
Aluminum plant, *Pilea*
Alumroot, *Heuchera*
Amaranth, *Amaranthus*
Amaryllis, *Hippeastrum*
Angel's fishing rods, *Dierama*
Angel's trumpet, *Brugmansia*
Anise, *Myrrhis*
Anise tree, *Illicium*
Apple, *Malus*
Apricot, *Prunus*
Aralia, *Aralia*
Arborvitae, *Thuja*
Archangel, *Angelica*
Arrowhead, *Sagittaria*
Arrowhead vine, *Syngonium*
Arrowwood, *Viburnum*
Arum lily, *Zantedeschia*
Asian bellflower, *Codonopsis*
Asiatic poppy, *Meconopsis*
Asparagus fern, *Asparagus*
Aspen, *Populus*
Autumn crocus, *Colchicum*
Avens, *Geum*
Avocado, *Persea*
Azalea, *Rhododendron*

B

Baboon flower, *Babiana*
Baby-blue-eyes, *Nemophila*
Baby's breath, *Gypsophila*
Bachelor's button, *Centaurea*
Balloon flower, *Platycodon*
Balm, *Melissa*
Balsam, *Impatiens*
Banana, *Musa*
Baneberry, *Actaea*
Barberry, *Berberis*
Barren strawberry, *Waldsteinia*
Barrenwort, *Epimedium*
Basil, *Ocimum*
Basket-of-gold, *Aurinia*
Basswood, *Tilia*
Bayberry, *Myrica*
Bearberry, *Arctostaphylos*
Beard tongue, *Penstemon*
Bear's breeches, *Acanthus*
Beautyberry, *Callicarpa*
Beautybush, *Kolkwitzia*
Bee balm, *Monarda*
Beech, *Fagus*
Begonia, *Begonia*
Bellflower, *Campanula*

Bellwort, *Uvularia*
Bergamot, *Monarda*
Bergenia, *Bergenia*
Betony, *Stachys*
Big tree, *Sequoiadendron*
Birch, *Betula*
Bird-of-paradise, *Strelitzia*
Bishop's hat, *Epimedium*
Bitterroot, *Lewisia*
Blackberry, *Rubus*
Blackberry lily, *Belamcanda*
Black-eyed Susan, *Rudbeckia*
Black-eyed Susan vine,
    Thunbergia
Blanket flower, *Gaillardia*
Blazing star, *Liatris*
Bleeding heart, *Dicentra*
Blood lily, *Haemanthus*
Bloodroot, *Sanguinaria*
Bluebeard, *Caryopteris*
Bluebell, *Scilla*
Bluebells, *Mertensia*
Blueberry, *Vaccinium*
Bluebonnet, *Lupinus*
Blue buttons, *Knautia*
Blue cohosh, *Caulophyllum*
Blue-eyed grass, *Sisyrinchium*
Blue poppy, *Meconopsis*
Blue star, *Amsonia*
Bog rosemary, *Andromeda*
Boltonia, *Boltonia*
Boneset, *Eupatorium*
Boston ivy, *Parthenocissus*
Bottlebrush, *Callistemon*
Bowman's root, *Porteranthus*
    (Gillenia)
Boxwood, *Buxus*
Brass buttons, *Cotula*
Brazilian plume, *Justicia*
Brodiaea, *Brodiaea*
Broom, *Cytisus, Genista*
Brunnera, *Brunnera*
Buckeye, *Aesculus*
Bugbane, *Cimicifuga*
Bugleweed, *Ajuga*
Bugloss, *Anchusa*
Bulrush, *Typha*
Burnet, *Sanguisorba*
Burning bush, *Euonymus*
Bush clover, *Lespedeza*
Bush violet, *Browallia*
Busy Lizzie, *Impatiens*
Butcher's gold, *Columnea*
Butter-and-eggs, *Linaria*
Butterbur, *Petasites*
Butterfly bush, *Buddleia*
Butterfly weed, *Asclepias*
Butternut, *Juglans*
Buttonbush, *Cephalanthus*
Buttonwood, *Platanus*

C

Caladium, *Caladium*
Calamint, *Calamintha*
Calanthe, *Calanthe*
California bluebell, *Phacelia*
California fuchsia, *Zauschneria*
California poppy, *Eschscholzia*
Calla lily, *Zantedeschia*
Campion, *Lychnis, Silene*
Candy lily, *Pardancanda*
Candytuft, *Iberis*
Canna lily, *Canna*
Canterbury bells, *Gloxinia*
Cape cowslip, *Lachenalia*
Cape fuchsia, *Phygelius*
Cape jasmine, *Gardenia*
Cape primrose, *Streptocarpus*
Cardinal climber, *Mina*
Cardinal flower, *Ipomoea, Lobelia,*
    Sinningia
Cardiocrinum, *Cardiocrinum*
Cardoon, *Cynara*
Carnation, *Dianthus*
Carolina allspice, *Calycanthus*
Carolina lupine, *Thermopsis*
Cassia, *Senna*
Cast-iron plant, *Aspidistra*
Castor bean plant, *Ricinus*
Catchfly, *Lychnis, Silene*
Cathedral bells, *Cobaea*
Catmint, *Nepeta*
Catnip, *Nepeta*
Cat's foot, *Antennaria*
Cattail, *Typha*
Cattleya, *Cattleya*
Cedar, *Cedrus*
Century plant, *Agave*
Cephalaria, *Cephalaria*
Chamomile, *Anthemis*
Chaste tree, *Vitex*
Checkerbloom, *Sidalcea*
Checker mallow, *Sidalcea*
Chenille plant, *Acalypha*
Cherry, *Prunus*
Cherry pie, *Heliotropium*
Chilean jasmine, *Mandevilla*
Chinese evergreen, *Aglaonema*
Chinese lantern, *Physalis*
Chokeberry, *Aronia*
Christmas cactus, *Schlumbergera*
Christmas cheer, *Sedum*
Christmas fern, *Polystichum*
Christmas rose, *Helleborus*
Cigar tree, *Catalpa*
Cineraria, *Senecio*
Cinnamon fern, *Osmunda*
Cinquefoil, *Potentilla*
Citrus, *Citrus*
Clock vine, *Thunbergia*
Cockscomb, *Celosia*
Coffee, *Coffea*
Cohosh, *Cimicifuga*

Coleus, *Coleus (Solenostemon)*
Columbine, *Aquilegia*
Comfrey, *Symphytum*
Compass plant, *Silphium*
Coneflower, *Echinacea, Rudbeckia*
Coralbells, *Heuchera*
Coralberry, *Ardisia*
Cornflower, *Centaurea*
Corokia, *Corokia*
Cosmos, *Cosmos*
Cotoneaster, *Cotoneaster*
Cottonwood, *Populus*
Crab apple, *Malus*
Cranberry, *Vaccinium*
Cranberry bush, *Viburnum*
Cranesbill, *Geranium*
Crape myrtle, *Lagerstroemia*
Creeping gloxinia, *Asarina*
Creeping Jenny, *Lysimachia*
Crinum lily, *Crinum*
Crossvine, *Bignonia*
Crosswort, *Phuopsis*
Crown fern, *Blechnum*
Crown of thorns, *Euphorbia*
Cucumber tree, *Magnolia*
Culver's root, *Veronicastrum*
Cup-and-saucer vine, *Cobaea*
Cup fern, *Dennstaedtia*
Cupflower, *Nierembergia*
Cupid's dart, *Catananche*
Cup plant, *Silphium*
Currant, *Ribes*
Cymbidium, *Cymbidium*
Cypress, *Cupressus, Taxodium*

D

Daffodil, *Narcissus*
Dahlia, *Dahlia*
Dancing lady orchid, *Oncidium*
Daphne, *Daphne*
Darmera, *Darmera*
Datura, *Datura*
Dawn redwood, *Metasequoia*
Day jessamine, *Cestrum*
Daylily, *Hemerocallis*
Dead nettle, *Lamium*
Delphinium, *Delphinium* (see
    also *Consolida*)
Dendrobium, *Dendrobium*
Desert candle, *Eremurus*
Deutzia, *Deutzia*
Devil's backbone, *Kalanchoe*
Devil's tongue, *Amorphophallus*
Dogtooth violet, *Erythronium*
Dogwood, *Cornus*
Donkey's tail, *Sedum*
Dove tree, *Davidia*
Draba, *Draba*
Dragon tree, *Dracaena*
Dropwort, *Filipendula*
Dusty miller, *Senecio*

Dutchman's breeches, *Dicentra*
Dutchman's pipe, *Aristolochia*

E

Elder, *Sambucus*
Elderberry, *Sambucus*
Elecampane, *Inula*
Elephant's ear, *Alocasia, Colocasia*
Elm, *Ulmus*
Empress tree, *Paulownia*
English daisy, *Bellis*
Enkianthus, *Enkianthus*
Evening primrose, *Oenothera*
Everlasting, *Anaphalis*

F

Fairy bells, *Disporum*
False castor oil plant, *Fatsia*
False cypress, *Chamaecyparis*
False dragonhead, *Physostegia*
False hellebore, *Veratrum*
False indigo, *Baptisia*
False lily-of-the-valley,
    Maianthemum
False lupine, *Thermopsis*
False Solomon's seal, *Smilacina*
False spirea, *Astilbe, Sorbaria*
False sunflower, *Heliopsis*
Feather grass, *Stipa*
Felt brush, *Kalanchoe*
Fennel flower, *Nigella*
Fescue, *Festuca*
Fetterbush, *Leucothoe*
Feverfew, *Chrysanthemum*
Fig, *Ficus*
Figwort, *Scrophularia*
Filbert, *Corylus*
Fir, *Abies*
Firecracker plant, *Cuphea*
Firethorn, *Pyracantha*
Five fingers, *Syngonium*
Flag, *Iris*
Flannel bush, *Fremontodendron*
Flax, *Linum*
Flax lily, *Phormium*
Fleabane, *Erigeron*
Flowering maple, *Abutilon*
Flowering quince, *Chaenomeles*
Flowering rush, *Butomus*
Foamflower, *Tiarella*
Forget-me-not, *Myosotis*
Fountain grass, *Pennisetum*
Four-o'clock, *Mirabilis*
Foxglove, *Digitalis*
Foxtail lily, *Eremurus*
Frangipani, *Plumeria*
Franklin tree, *Franklinia*
Freemontia, *Fremontodendron*
Freesia, *Freesia*
Friendship plant, *Pilea*
Fringe-bell, *Shortia*
Fringe cup, *Tellima*
Fringed orchid, *Habenaria*
Fringe tree, *Chionanthus*
Fritillary, *Fritillaria*
Fuki, *Petasites*

Fumewort, *Corydalis*

G

Gas plant, *Dictamnus*
Gaura, *Gaura*
Gayfeather, *Liatris*
Gentian, *Gentiana*
Geranium, *Pelargonium*
Germander, *Teucrium*
Giant hyssop, *Agastache*
Giant redwood, *Sequoiadendron*
Giant reed, *Arundo*
Giant rhubarb, *Gunnera*
Ginger lily, *Hedychium*
Glaucidium, *Glaucidium*
Globe flower, *Trollius*
Globe thistle, *Echinops*
Gloriosa daisy, *Rudbeckia*
Glory bower, *Clerodendrum*
Glory bush, *Tibouchina*
Glory lily, *Gloriosa*
Glory-of-the-snow, *Chionodoxa*
Gloxinia, *Sinningia*
Goatsbeard, *Aruncus*
Gold dust plant, *Aucuba*
Golden bells, *Forsythia*
Goldenchain tree, *Laburnum*
Golden club, *Orontium*
Golden drop, *Onosma*
Golden moss, *Sedum*
Goldenrain tree, *Koelreuteria*
Goldenray, *Ligularia*
Goldenrod, *Solidago*
Golden trumpet, *Allamanda*
Goldfish plant, *Columnea*
Good luck plant, *Sansevieria*
Gooseberry, *Ribes*
Grape, *Vitis*
Grape hyacinth, *Muscari*
Grape ivy, *Cissus*
Green-and-gold, *Chrysogonum*
Green ebony, *Jacaranda*
Groundsel, *Senecio*
Groundsel bush, *Baccharis*
Guernsey lily, *Nerine*
Guinea hen flower, *Fritillaria*
Gum tree, *Eucalyptus*

H

Hair grass, *Deschampsia*
Hakonechloa, *Hakonechloa*
Handkerchief tree, *Davidia*
Hardy ageratum, *Eupatorium*
Hardy gloxinia, *Incarvillea*
Harlequin flower, *Sparaxis*
Harry Lauder's walking stick,
    Corylus
Haworthia, *Haworthia*
Hawthorn, *Crataegus*
Hay-scented fern, *Dennstaedtia*
Hazelnut, *Corylus*
Heath, *Erica*
Heather, *Calluna*
Heavenly bamboo, *Nandina*
Hebe, *Hebe*
Heliotrope, *Heliotropium*

Hellebore, *Helleborus*
Helleborine, *Epipactis*
Hemlock, *Tsuga*
Hen-and-chickens, *Sempervivum*
Hen-and-chicks, *Echeveria*
Heron's bill, *Erodium*
Holly, *Ilex*
Hollyhock, *Alcea*
Holy flax, *Santolina*
Honesty, *Lunaria*
Honeybush, *Melianthus*
Honey locust, *Gledetsia*
Honeysuckle, *Lonicera*
Hop, *Humulus*
Horehound, *Marrubium*
Hornbeam, *Carpinus*
Horned poppy, *Glaucium*
Horse chestnut, *Aesculus*
Horsemint, *Monarda*
Horseradish, *Armoracia*
Hortensia, *Hydrangea*
Hound's tongue, *Cynoglossum*
House leek, *Sempervivum*
Huckleberry, *Vaccinium*
Hyacinth, *Hyacinthus*
Hyacinth bean, *Dolichos*

I

Ice plant, *Delosperma,*
    Mesembryanthemum
Indian bean tree, *Catalpa*
Indian poke, *Veratrum*
Indigo, *Indigofera*
Ironweed, *Vernonia*
Ivy, *Hedera*

J

Jack-in-the-pulpit, *Arisaema*
Jacob's ladder, *Polemonium*
Jade plant, *Crassula*
Japanese cedar, *Cryptomeria*
Japanese hydrangea vine,
    Schizophragma
Japanese pagoda tree, *Sophora*
Japanese painted fern, *Athyrium*
Japanese rose, *Kerria*
Jasmine, *Jasminum*
Jelly bean plant, *Sedum*
Jerusalem sage, *Phlomis*
Jessamine, *Jasminum*
Jewel orchid, *Ludisia*
Joe Pye weed, *Eupatorium*
Johnny-jump-up, *Viola*
Jonquil, *Narcissus*
Joseph's coat, *Alternanthera*
Juniper, *Juniperus*
Jupiter's beard, *Centranthus*

K

Kaffir lily, *Clivia*
Kalimeris, *Kalimeris*
Katsura tree, *Cercidiphyllum*
Kenilworth ivy, *Cymbalaria*
Kentucky coffee tree,
    Gymnocladus
Kingfisher daisy, *Felicia*

Kiwi, *Actinidia*
Knapweed, *Centaurea*

L

Lady fern, *Athyrium*
Lady-of-the-night, *Brunfelsia*
Lady's mantle, *Alchemilla*
Lady's smock, *Cardamine*
    (*Dentaria*)
Lady's teardrops, *Fuchsia*
Lamb's ears, *Stachys*
Larch, *Larix*
Larkspur, *Consolida*
Laurel, *Laurus*
Lavender, *Lavandula*
Lavender cotton, *Santolina*
Lead plant, *Amorpha*
Leadwort, *Ceratostigma,*
    Plumbago
Leatherwood, *Cyrilla*
Lenten rose, *Helleborus*
Leopard's bane, *Doronicum*
Licorice plant, *Helichrysum*
Lilac, *Syringa*
Lily, *Lilium*
Lily-of-China, *Rohdea*
Lil-of-the-valley, *Convallaria*
Lilyturf, *Liriope*
Linden, *Tilia*
Lip fern, *Cheilanthes*
Lisianthus, *Lisianthus*
Live-forever, *Sempervivum*
Liverleaf, *Hepatica*
Living stones, *Lithops*
Locust, *Robinia*
Loganberry, *Rubus*
Lollipop plant, *Pachystachys*
London plane, *Platanus*
Loosestrife, *Lysimachia*
Lords-and-ladies, *Arum*
Lotus, *Nelumbo*
Love-in-a-mist, *Nigella*
Love-lies-bleeding, *Amaranthus*
Lungwort, *Mertensia, Pulmonaria*
Lupine, *Lupinus*

M

Madagascar palm, *Pachypodium*
Madwort, *Alyssum*
Maidenhair fern, *Adiantum*
Maidenhair tree, *Ginkgo*
Maki, *Podocarpus*
Mallow, *Lavatera, Malva*
Mandrake, *Podophyllum*
Manzanita, *Arctostaphylos*
Maple, *Acer*
Marjoram, *Origanum*
Marsh mallow, *Althaea*
Marsh marigold, *Caltha*
Masterwort, *Astrantia*
Mayapple, *Podophyllum*
Meadow rue, *Thalictrum*
Meadowsweet, *Filipendula*
Merrybells, *Uvularia*
Mexican orange, *Choisya*
Mexican sunflower, *Tithonia*

Michaelmas daisy, *Aster*
Milkweed, *Asclepias*
Milkwort, *Polygala*
Millet grass, *Milium*
Mock orange, *Philadelphus*
Mondo grass, *Ophiopogon*
Money plant, *Lunaria*
Monkey flower, *Mimulus*
Monkshood, *Aconitum*
Montbretia, *Crocosmia*
Moon flower, *Ipomoea*
Morning glory, *Ipomoea*
Moses on a raft, *Rhoeo*
    (*Tradescantia*)
Moth orchid, *Phalaenopsis*
Mother-in-law's tongue,
    Sansevieria
Mother-of-thousands, *Kalanchoe*
Mountain ash, *Sorbus*
Mountain flax, *Phormium*
Mountain laurel, *Kalmia*
Mourning widow, *Geranium*
Mouse plant, *Arisarum*
Mulberry, *Morus*
Mullein, *Verbascum*
Mum, *Chrysanthemum*
Myrrh, *Myrrhis*
Myrtle, *Myrtus, Vinca*

N
Navelwort, *Omphalodes*
Nectorescordum, *Nectorescordum*
Needle grass, *Stipa*
Nemesia, *Nemesia*
New Jersey tea, *Ceanothus*
New Zealand flax, *Phormium*
Nightshade, *Solanum*
Ninebark, *Physocarpus*
Norfolk Island pine, *Araucaria*
Northern sea oats,
    Chasmanthium

O
Oak, *Quercus*
Obedient plant, *Physostegia*
Oconee bells, *Shortia*
Old maid, *Catharanthus*
Oleander, *Nerium*
Olive, *Olea*
Orach, *Atriplex*
Orchid cactus, *Epiphyllum*
Oregon grape, *Mahonia*
Orpine, *Sedum*
Osteospermum, *Osteospermum*
Ostrich fern, *Matteuccia*
Oswego tea, *Monarda*

P
Palmetto, *Sabal*
Panda plant, *Philodendron*
Panic grass, *Panicum*
Pansy, *Viola*
Pansy orchid, *Miltonia*
Paper flower, *Bougainvillea*
Paper mulberry, *Broussonetia*
Papyrus, *Cyperus*

Pardancanda, *Pardancanda*
Parlor palm, *Chamaedorea*
Partridgeberry, *Mitchella*
Pasqueflower, *Pulsatilla*
Passionflower, *Passiflora*
Pawpaw, *Asimina*
Peach, *Prunus*
Peacock plant, *Calathea*
Pear, *Pyrus*
Pearlbush, *Exochorda*
Pearlwort, *Sagina*
Peashrub, *Caragana*
Peony, *Paeonia*
Pepperidge, *Nyssa*
Periwinkle, *Vinca*
Persian shield, *Strobilanthes*
Persian violet, *Exacum*
Peruvian lily, *Alstroemeria*
Pheasant's eye, *Adonis*
Photinia, *Photinia*
Pickerel weed, *Pontederia*
Pieris, *Pieris*
Piggyback plant, *Tolmiea*
Pimpernel, *Anagallis*
Pincushion flower, *Scabiosa*
Pine, *Pinus*
Pineapple, *Ananas*
Pineapple lily, *Eucomis*
Pink, *Dianthus*
Pink quill, *Tillandsia*
Pinkroot, *Spigelia*
Pitcher plant, *Nepenthes,*
    Sarracenia
Pittosporum, *Pittosporum*
Plane tree, *Platanus*
Plantain lily, *Hosta*
Plum, *Prunus*
Plum yew, *Cephalotaxus*
Pocketbook plant, *Calceolaria*
Polka-dot plant, *Hypoestes*
Polypody, *Polypodium*
Pomegranate, *Punica*
Poplar, *Populus*
Poppy, *Papaver*
Poppy mallow, *Callirhoe*
Potato vine, *Solanum*
Pot marigold, *Calendula*
Prairie coneflower, *Ratibida*
Prairie dock, *Silphium*
Prickly pear, *Opuntia*
Prickly poppy, *Argemone*
Primrose, *Primula*
Privet, *Ligustrum*
Purple bell vine, *Rhodochiton*

Q
Quaking grass, *Briza*
Quamash, *Camassia*
Queen-of-the-prairie, *Filipendula*
Quince, *Cydonia*

R
Rabbit's-foot fern, *Davallia*
Radiator plant, *Peperomia*
Ragwort, *Senecio*
Raspberry, *Rubus*

Rattlesnake master, *Eryngium*
Rattlesnake plantain, *Goodyera*
Redbud, *Cercis*
Red cedar, *Juniperus*
Red-hot poker, *Kniphofia*
Redroot, *Ceanothus*
Red valerian, *Centranthus*
Redwood, *Sequoia*
Rest harrow, *Ononis*
Resurrection flower, *Lycoris*
Rhubarb, *Rheum*
Rock cress, *Arabis, Aubretia*
Rock rose, *Cistus*
Rodgersia, *Rodgersia*
Rosary vine, *Ceropegia*
Rose, *Rosa*
Rosemary, *Rosmarinus*
Rose-of-Sharon, *Hibiscus*
Rosinweed, *Silphium*
Royal fern, *Osmunda*
Rue, *Ruta*
Rue anemone, *Anemonella*
Rush, *Juncus*
Russian arborvitae, *Microbiota*
Russian sage, *Perovskia*

S
Saffron, *Crocus*
Sage, *Salvia*
Sago palm, *Cycas*
St. John's wort, *Hypericum*
Sandwort, *Arenaria*
Sapphire flower, *Browallia*
Sassafras, *Sassafras*
Saucer plant, *Aeonium*
Saxifrage, *Saxifraga*
Scholar tree, *Sophora*
Scotch thistle, *Onopordum*
Sea holly, *Eryngium*
Sea kale, *Crambe*
Sedge, *Carex*
Senna, *Cassia*
Sensitive fern, *Onoclea*
Serbian queen, *Ramonda*
Serviceberry, *Amelanchier*
Shadbush, *Amelanchier*
Shamrock, *Oxalis*
Shasta daisy, *Chrysanthemum*
Sheep laurel, *Kalmia*
Shield fern, *Polystichum*
Shieldleaf rodgersia, *Astilboides*
Shooting star, *Dodecatheon*
Shrimp plant, *Justicia*
Shrub althaea, *Hibiscus*
Shrub verbena, *Lantana*
Silverbell, *Halesia*
Silver grass, *Miscanthus*
Skimmia, *Skimmia*
Skunk cabbage, *Lysichiton,*
    Symplocarpus
Slipperwort, *Calceolaria*
Smokebush, *Cotinus*
Smoke tree, *Cotinus*
Snake plant, *Sansevieria*
Snakeroot, *Cimicifuga*
Snapdragon, *Antirrhinum*

Sneezeweed, *Helenium*
Snow-in-summer, *Cerastium*
Snow-on-the-mountain,
    Euphorbia
Snowball bush, *Viburnum*
Snowbell, *Styrax*
Snowberry, *Symphoricarpus*
Snowdrop, *Galanthus*
Snowflake, *Leucojum*
Soldenella, *Soldenella*
Solomon's seal, *Polygonatum*
Sorrel, *Oxalis*
Sorrel tree, *Oxydendrum*
Sour gum, *Nyssa*
Sourwood, *Oxydendrum*
Sow bread, *Cyclamen*
Spanish bluebell, *Hyacinthoides*
Spanish dagger, *Yucca*
Spathe flower, *Spathiphyllum*
Spatterdock, *Nuphar*
Speckled wood lily, *Clintonia*
Speedwell, *Veronica*
Spicebush, *Lindera*
Spider flower, *Cleome, Grevillea*
Spider lily, *Lycoris*
Spider plant, *Chlorophytum*
Spiderwort, *Tradescantia*
Spindle tree, *Euonymus*
Spirea, *Spiraea*
Spleenwort, *Asplenium*
Spring beauty, *Claytonia*
Spring meadow saffron,
    Bulbocodium
Spruce, *Picea*
Spurge, *Euphorbia, Pachysandra*
Squill, *Scilla*
Starfish flower, *Stapelia*
Star jasmine, *Trachelospermum*
Star of Bethlehem, *Ornithogalum*
Stewartia, *Stewartia*
Stinking Benjamin, *Trillium*
Stokes' aster, *Stokesia*
Stonecrop, *Sedum*
Strawberry, *Fragaria*
Strawberry bush, *Euonymus*
Strawberry geranium, *Saxifraga*
Strawberry tree, *Arbutus*
String of hearts, *Ceropegia*
Sumac, *Rhus*
Summer hyacinth, *Galtonia*
Summersweet, *Clethra*
Sundrops, *Oenothera*
Sunflower, *Helianthus*
Sun rose, *Helianthemum*
Swamp mallow, *Hibiscus*
Swan River daisy, *Brachychome*
Swedish ivy, *Plectranthus*
Sweet alyssum, *Lobularia*
Sweet bay, *Laurus*
Sweet box, *Sarcococca*
Sweet chervil, *Myrrhis*
Sweet cicely, *Myrrhis*
Sweet fern, *Comptonia*
Sweet flag, *Acorus*
Sweet gum, *Liquidambar*
Sweet pea, *Lathyrus*

Sweet pepperbush, *Clethra*
Sweetspire, *Itea*
Sweet William, *Dianthus*
Sweet woodruff, *Galium*
Swiss cheese plant, *Monstera*
Switch grass, *Panicum*
Sword fern, *Nephrolepis*
Sword lily, *Gladiolus*
Sycamore, *Platanus*

T

Tailflower, *Anthurium*
Tansy, *Tanacetum*
Tea, *Camellia*
Tea olive, *Osmanthus*
Texas pride, *Phlox*
Thoroughwax, *Bupleurum*
Thrift, *Armeria*
Thyme, *Thymus*
Ti, *Cordyline*
Tickseed, *Coreopsis*
Toadflax, *Linaria*
Toad lily, *Tricyrtis*
Tobacco, *Nicotiana*
Tomato tree, *Cyphomandra*

Torch lily, *Kniphofia*
Transvaal daisy, *Gerbera*
Trifoliate orange, *Poncirus*
Trout lily, *Erythronium*
Trumpet vine, *Campsis*
Tulip, *Tulipa*
Tulip poplar, *Liriodendron*
Tulip tree, *Liriodendron*
Tupelo, *Nyssa*
Turtlehead, *Chelone*
Tweedia, *Oxypetalum*

U

Umbrella plant, *Cyperus*
Umbrella tree, *Schefflera*
Urn plant, *Aechmea*

V

Valerian, *Valeriana*
Vancouveria, *Vancouveria*
Vanda, *Vanda*
Veltheimia, *Veltheimia*
Vervain, *Verbena*
Violet, *Viola*
Viper's bugloss, *Echium*

Virginia creeper, *Parthenocissus*
Virgin's bower, *Clematis*

W

Wake robin, *Trillium*
Wallflower, *Erysimum*
 (*Cheiranthus*)
Walnut, *Juglans*
Wandering Jew, *Tradescantia,*
 Zebrina
Wandflower, *Dierama, Sparaxas*
Washington palm, *Washingtonia*
Water lily, *Nymphaea*
Wattle, *Acacia*
Wax flower, *Stephanotis*
Wax plant, *Hoya*
Weigela, *Weigela*
Wickerware cactus, *Rhipsalis*
Wild ginger, *Asarum*
Wild hyacinth, *Camassia*
Wild lilac, *Ceanothus*
Wild oat, *Helictotrichon*
Wild oats, *Chasmanthium*
Wild rye, *Elymus*
Willow, *Salix*

Windflower, *Anemone*
Windowleaf, *Monstera*
Winter aconite, *Eranthis*
Wintergreen, *Gaultheria*
Winter hazel, *Corylopsis*
Wintersweet, *Chimonanthus*
Wisteria, *Wisteria*
Witch alder, *Fothergilla*
Witch hazel, *Hamamelis*
Woodbine, *Parthenocissus*
Wood fern, *Dryopteris*
Wormwood, *Artemisia*

Y

Yarrow, *Achillea*
Yellow jessamine, *Gelsemium*
Yellowroot, *Xanthorhiza*
Yellow waxbells, *Kirengeshoma*
Yellowwood, *Cladrastis*
Yew, *Taxus*

Z

Zebra grass, *Miscanthus*
Zelkova, *Zelkova*
Zenobia, *Zenobia*

RESOURCES

EQUIPMENT

Most of the larger mail-order seed sellers also sell growing supplies. The following companies specialize in tools and materials for gardeners/propagators. Some charge for catalogs; call or write for costs, as these change frequently.

Alternative Garden Supply, Inc.
PO Box 662
Cary, IL 60013
Tel: 800-444-2837
Lights and hydroponics supplies.

A. M. Leonard
241 Fox Dr.
PO Box 816
Piqua, OH 45356
Tel: 800-543-8955
Commercial farm and garden supplies at reasonable prices—many seen elsewhere for more.

Charley's Greenhouse Supply
17979 State Route 536
Mount Vernon, WA 98273-3269
Tel: 800-322-4707
Lots of items for in and around greenhouses, home, and indoor garden. Excellent source.

Early's Farm & Garden Centre
2615 Lorne Ave.
Saskatoon, SK S7J 0S5 Canada
Company sells a wide variety of supplies, along with seeds, to gardeners in that country.

Gardener's Supply Company
128 Intervale Rd.
Burlington, VT 05401
Tel: 800-863-1700
Excellent source for supplies and information. Technical support and some special publications.

Garden Trends
60 Saginaw Dr.
PO Box 22960
Rochester, NY 14692-2960
Tel: 800-514-4441
Supplier of some of the best "floral carts," light stands, propagation supplies, simple greenhouses.

Gothic Arch Greenhouses
PO Box 1564
Mobile, AL 36633
Tel: 334-432-7529
Manufacturer of domestic wooden, metal, fiberglass, or polycarbonate greenhouse kits.

Hydrofarm Gardening Products
1455 East Francisco Blvd.
San Rafael, CA 94901
Tel: 800-634-9999
Hydroponics and high-intensity artificial lighting.

Hydro-Gardens, Inc.
8765 Vollmaer Rd.
Colorado Springs, CO 80908
Tel: 800-634-6362
Complete supplier to the commercial and hobbyist hydroponics grower, with supplies easily adapted for propagation use.

IGS
PO Box 527
Dexter, MI 48130
Tel: 734-426-9080
A wide variety of floral carts—well made and well priced.

Kinsman Company, Inc.
River Rd., PO Box 357
Point Pleasant, PA 18950-0357
Tel: 800-733-4146
A few general propagation supplies, cloches.

Lagenbach
MSC 290
638 Lindero Canyon Rd.
Oak Park, CA 91301-5464
Tel: 800-362-1991
Tools and supplies—distinctive, unusual.

Lee Valley Tools Ltd.
PO Box 1780
Ogdensburg, NY 13669-6780
Tel: 800-871-8158
Some of the best products at the best prices. A must.

The Natural Garden
PO Box 860
Newton, NJ 07860
Propagation supplies, books, and unusual decorative accessories.

Park Seed
1 Parkton Ave.
Greenwood, SC 29647-0001
Tel: 800-845-3369
Seeds, plants, a wide variety of seed-propagation supplies.

Paw Paw Everlast Label Co.
PO Box 93-C
Paw Paw, MI 49079-0093
Many kinds of plant labels.

Peaceful Valley Farm Supply
PO Box 2209
Grass Valley, CA 95945
Tel: 530-272-4769
Tools and supplies for organic farmers and gardeners.

Superior Growers Supply, Inc.
4870 Dawn Ave.
East Lansing, MI 48823
Tel: 517-332-6218
Mostly artificial lights of all types and some growing supplies.

Texas Greenhouse Company, Inc.
2524 White Settlement Rd.
Fort Worth, TX 76107
Tel: 800-227-5447
Many styles of greenhouse structures in a wide range of prices.

Turner Greenhouses
PO Box 1260
Highway 117 South
Goldsboro, NC 27533
Affordable greenhouses, supplies, and accessories.

Walt Nicke Co.
36 McLeod La.
PO Box 433
Topsfield, MA 01983
Tel: 978-887-3388
A wide variety of gardening and propagation supplies.

Worm's Way
7850 North Highway 37
Bloomington, IN 47404
Tel: 800-274-9676
A huge selection of indoor gardening supplies.

MAIL-ORDER SOURCES FOR ORNAMENTALS

The following nurseries sell seed; those selling small plants, tubers, rhizomes, etc., are noted.

The Abundant Life Seed Foundation
PO Box 772
Port Townsend, WA 98368
Tel: 360-385-5660
Heirloom herb and flower seeds.

Aimers Seeds
RR 3
Ilderton, ON N0M 2A0 Canada
Tel: 519-461-0011
Seeds of ornamental plants, woody and herbaceous.

Arrowhead Alpines
PO Box 857
Fowlerville, MI 48836
Tel: 517-223-3581
Seed list available by request.
Mail-order alpine and rare plants.

Aurora Biodynamic Farm
RR1 63-9
Creston, BC V0B 1G0 Canada
Tel: 603-428-4404
Fax: 603-428-4404
Seeds of heirloom vegetables, flowers, and herbs.

Aztekakti
11306 Gateway East
El Paso, TX 79927
Tel: 915-858-1130
Extensive list of seeds for cacti and succulents.

B & T World Seeds
Rue des Marchandes
Paguignan, Olonzac, France 34210
Tel: 33 0 4-68-91-29-63
Fax: 33 0 4-68-91-30-39
Comprehensive seed list.

The Banana Tree, Inc.
715 Northampton St.
Easton, PA 18042
Tel: 610-253-9589
Fax: 610-253-4864
Seeds, tubers, and rhizomes of tropical plants.

Bluestem Prairie Nursery
13197 E. 13th Rd.
Hillsboro, IL 62049
Tel: 217-532-6344
Packets of seed and custom mixes of species native to midwestern prairies and savannas.

Boone's Native Seed Co.
PO Box 10363
Raleigh, NC 27605
Open-pollinated seeds of North American natives, nonnative wildflowers, and vegetable seeds.

Bountiful Gardens
18001 Schaefer Ranch Rd.
Willits, CA 95490
Tel: 707-459-6410
This educational organization dedicated to sustainable agriculture and conservation offers open-pollinated flowers and herbs.

Brudy's Exotics
PO Box 820874
Houston, TX 77282-0874
Tel: 713-946-9557
Fax: 713-960-8887
Tropical plants and seeds.

W. Atlee Burpee & Co.
300 Park Ave.
Warminster, PA 18974
Tel: 800-888-1447
The grandaddy of them all: seeds for ornamental and edible plants, mostly annuals, some heirlooms.

Chiltern Seeds
Bortree Stile
Ulverston, Cumbria
LA12 7PB England
Tel: 44-0 1229 581-137
Fax: 44-0 1229 584-549
Seeds for a wide variety of plants rarely available in the U.S.

Comstock Seed
8520 W. 4th St.
Reno, NV 89523
Tel: 702-746-3681
Fax: 702-746-1701
Shrub, grass, and flower seeds, primarily from the Great Basin, Mojave Desert, Sierra Nevada.

Deep Diversity
PO Box 15189
Sante Fe, NM 87501-5189
Tel: 505-438-8080
Fax: 505-438-7052
Seeds of heirloom flowers and vegetables—many rare and endangered plants.

DiGiorgi Seed Company
6011 N St.
Omaha, NE 68117-1634
Tel: 402-731-3901
Fax: 402-731-8475
Orders: 800-858-2580
Seeds for ornamental grasses, flowers, herbs, vegetables, and North American natives.

Edge of the Rockies
PO Box 1218
Bayfield, CO 81122
Seeds and plants native to the southern Rocky Mountain region.

The English Garden Emporium
Box 222
Manchester, VT 05254
Flower and vegetable seeds from Johnson's Seeds of England.

Far North Gardens
16785 Harrison
Livonia, MI 48154
Tel: 810-486-4203
Rare flower seeds.

Far West Bulb Farm
10289 Candlewood Way
PO Box 515
Oregon House, CA 95962-0515
Tel: 530-692-2565
Fax: 530-692-2565
California native bulbs and their seeds. (Ships Sept.–Oct. only.)

Ferry-Morse Seeds
PO Box 1620
Fulton. KY 42041
Tel: 800-626-3392
Old-time varieties of flowers and vegetables.

Flowery Branch Seed Co.
PO Box 1330
Flowery Branch, GA 30542
Tel: 770-536-8380
Seeds of unusual perennials and annuals from around the world. Culinary and medicinal herbs.

The Fragrant Path
PO Box 328
Fort Calhoun, NE 68023
Seeds for hundreds of flower varieties grown for scent.

Garden City Seeds
778 US Hwy 93N
Hamilton, MT 59840
Tel: 406-961-4837
Seeds for heirloom flowers and herbs, especially hardy varieties.

Gardens North
5984 Third Line Rd. North, RR3
North Gower, ON K0A 2T0
Canada
Tel: 613-489-0065
Fax: 613-489-0065
Seeds of hardy herbaceous perennials for the Far North.

Good Seed Co.
Star Route, Box 73a
Oroville (Chesaw), WA 98844
Herb collection from the 1700s.

Grandma's Garden, Underwood Seeds
4N381 Maple Ave.
Bensenville, IL 60106
Tel: 630-616-0268
Fax: 630-616-0232
Heirloom flowers and information on seed saving and organic growing.

Gurney's Seed and Nursery Co.
110 Capital St.
Yankton, SD 57078
Seeds of familiar flower and vegetable varieties.

Heirloom Garden Seeds
PO Box 138
Guerneville, CA 95446
Tel: 707-887-9129
Seeds of antique and rare herbs and flowers. Interesting and useful catalog.

Heirloom Seed Project
Landis Valley Museum
2451 Kissel Hill Rd.
Lancaster, PA 17601
Tel: 717-569-0401, ext. 202
Seeds of open-pollinated varieties.

Ion Exchange
1878 Old Mission Dr.
Harpers Ferry, IA 52146
Tel: 800-291-2143
Fax: 319-535-7362
Seeds for over 200 species of North American plant.

J. L. Hudson, Seedsman
PO Box 1058
Redwood City, CA 94064
Unusual catalog—decidedly opinionated—with extensive and varied list of seeds.

Thomas Jefferson Center for Historic Plants
Monticello
PO Box 316
Charlottesville, VA 22902
Seeds for antique and heirloom, old-fashioned, rare varieties.

Little Valley Farm
5693 Snead Creek Rd.
Spring Green, WI 53588
Tel: 608-935-3324
Seeds of native plants for the Midwest and Northeast—prairie, woodland, and wetland species.

The Living Desert
Palo Verde Garden Center
47900 Portola Ave.
Palm Desert, CA 92260
Tel: 760-346-5694
Fax: 760-568-9685
Plants and seeds indigenous to the Southwest and Mexico.

Mellinger's Inc.
2310 W. South Range Rd.
North Lima, OH 44452-9731
Tel: 216-549-9861
Typical flower seed varieties and some supplies.

Michigan Wildflower Farm
11770 Cutler Rd.
Portland, MI 48875-9452
Tel: 517-647-6010
Fax: 517-647-6072
Seeds of Michigan wildflowers and grasses.

Midwest Wildflowers
Box 64
Rockton, IL 61072
Seeds of more than 120 species.

Moon Mountain Wildflowers
PO Box 725
Carpinteria, CA 93014
Tel: 805-684-2565
Fax: 805-684-2798
Seeds of North American natives and naturalized aliens.

National Wildflower Research Center
2600 FM 973 North
Austin, TX 78725-4210
Large selection of wildflowers.

Native Seeds Inc.
14590 Triadelphia Mill Rd.
Dayton, MD 21306
Tel: 301-596-9818
Fax: 301-854-3195
Seeds in packets and bulk.

Native Seeds/SEARCH
2509 N. Campbell Ave., #325
526 N. Fourth Ave.(Retail Outlet)
Tucson, AZ 85719
Tel: 520-622-5561
Fax: 520-622-5591
Seeds of heirloom crops from the Southwest and Mexico.

New England Wild Flower Soc.
Garden in the Woods
1180 Hemenway Rd.
Framingham, MA 10701-2699
Tel: 508-877-7630
Mail-order seeds of native plants.

Nichols Garden Nursery
1190 North Pacific Highway
Albany, OR 97321-4580
Tel: 541-928-9280
Fax: 541-967-8406
Seeds of vegetables, culinary herbs, and old-fashioned flowers.

O'Donnell's Fairfax Nursery
1700 Sir Francis Drake Blvd.
Fairfax, CA 94930
Tel: 415-453-0372
Native seeds, bulbs, and plants of rare to familiar species.

Park Seed
1 Parkton Ave.
Greenwood, SC 29647-0001
Tel: 800-845-3369
Fax: 864-941-4502
One of North America's largest suppliers of seeds for flowers.

Prairie Moon Nursery
RR 3, Box 163
Winona, MN 55987
Tel: 507-452-1362
North American natives, including some offered nowhere else.

Prairie Nursery
PO Box 306
Westfield, WI 53964
Tel: 800-476-9453
Seeds and plants for prairie and meadow restoration.

Prairie Oak Seeds
PO Box 382
Maryville, MO 64468
Tel: 660-582-4084
Seeds for annual and perennial flowers, herbs, and grasses.

Prairie Ridge Nursery/CRM Ecosystems
9738 Overland Rd.
Mt. Horeb, WI 53572
Tel: 608-437-5245
North American natives.

Richter's Herbs
357 Highway 47
Goodwood, ON L0C 1A0 Canada
Tel: 905-640-6677
Enormous list of seeds.

SBE Seed Co.
3421 Bream St.
Gautier, MS 39553
Tel: 800-336-2064
Seeds for 6,000 tropical plants.

F. W. Schumacher Co.
36 Spring Hill Rd.
Sandwich, MA 02563
Tel: 508-888-0659
Tree seeds.

Seeds Blum
HC33 Idaho City Stage
Boise, ID 83706
Tel: 800-742-1423
Seeds of open-pollinated flowers.

Seeds of Change
PO Box 15700
Santa Fe, NM 83706
Tel: 888-438-8080
Seeds of organically grown flowers and vegetables.

Seeds Trust—High Altitude Gardens
PO Box 1048
Hailey, ID 83333
Tel: 208-788-4363
Fax: 208-788-3452
Orders: 208-788-4419
Seeds of plants that grow at elevations of 6,000–10,000 feet in the mountains of Idaho.

Select Seeds—Antique Flowers
180 Stickney Rd.
Union, CT 06076
Tel: 860-634-9310
Fax: 860-684-9224
Over 100 varieties of annual and perennial flowers from the 1700s through the 1800s.

Shepherd's Garden Seeds
30 Irene St.
Torrington, CT 06790
Tel: 860-482-3638
Seeds for old-fashioned and European flowers, vegetables, and herbs.

Shooting Star Nursery
444 Bates Rd.
Frankfort, KY 40601
Tel: 502-223-1679
Wildflower and prairie grass seeds. Nursery-propagated native perennials, trees, shrubs, vines, and wetland plants.

Silverhill Seeds
PO Box 53108
Kenilworth, Cape Town 7745
South Africa
Tel: 27-21-762-4245
Seeds of South African plants.

Southern Exposure Seed Exchange
PO Box 170
Earlysville, VA 22901
Tel: 804-973-4703
Fax: 804-973-8717
Open-pollinated seeds of herbs and heirloom flowers. Supplies and information on seed saving.

Stokes Seeds, Inc.
PO Box 548
Buffalo, NY 14240
Tel: 716-695-6980
Hybrid seeds.

Terra Edibles
Box 63
Thomasburg, ON K0K 3H0
Canada
Open-pollinated, heirloom, organically grown vegetable and flower seeds.

Territorial Seed Company
PO Box 157
Cottage Grove, OR 97424
Tel: 541-942-9547
Seeds for ornamentals and edibles geared to the Pacific Northwest.

Theodore Payne Foundation
10459 Tuxford St.
Sun Valley, CA 91352
Tel: 818-768-1802
California wildflower seeds. Information and books.

Thompson & Morgan
Box 1308
Jackson, NJ 08527-0308
Tel: 908-363-2225
Over 2,000 varieties, including seed of rare and unusual plants.

Western Native Seed
PO Box 1463
Salida, CO 81201
Tel: 719-539-1071
Fax: 719-539-6755
Seeds native to Rocky Mountains and western Great Plains.

Weston Gardens
8101 Anglin Dr.
Fort Worth, TX 76140
Tel: 817-572-0549
Fax: 817-572-1628
Plants and seeds of flowering perennials and bulbs.

Wild Flower Seeds
630 Wildlife La.
Anaconda, MT 59711
Tel: 406-563-8048
Seeds native to northern Rocky Mountains, as well as some herbaceous perennials and trees.

Wild Garden Seed
Shoulder to Shoulder Farm
PO Box 1509
Philomath, OR 97320
Tel: 541-929-4068
Seeds, including edible greens and insect-attracting species.

Wildginger Woodlands
PO Box 1091
Webster, NY 14580
Tel: 716-872-4033
Seeds for forest-floor plants and fern spores.

William Dam Seeds Ltd.
Box 8400
Dundas, ON L9H 6M1
Canada
Tel: 905-628-6641
Seeds of European plants.

Scion and understock sources

Fedco Trees
PO Box 520
Waterville, ME 04903
Fax: 207-827-8317
Understock of apple, pear, and plum for grafting. Orchard supplies.

Rocky Meadow Orchard & Nursery
360 Rocky Meadow Rd. NW
New Salisbury, IN 47161
Tel: 812-347-2213
Rootstocks and scion wood of fruiting trees. Custom propagates—top to bottom.

Sonoma Antique Apple Nursery
4395 Westside Rd.
Healdsburg, CA 95448
Tel: 707-433-6420
Scion wood of old varieties. Custom grafting.

PLANT SOCIETIES

The following plant societies offer many benefits for specialists, including seed exchanges or propagation services.

African Violet Society of Canada
Mrs. Bonnie Scanlan
1573 Arbourdale Ave.
Victoria, BC V8N 5J1 Canada

Alpine Garden Society
AGS Centre, Avonbank
Pershore, Worchester
WR10 3JP England

American Begonia Society
John Ingles, Jr.
157 Monument Rd.
Rio Dell, CA 95562
Tel: 707-764-5407

American Conifer Society
Maud Henne, Executive Secretary
PO Box 360
Keswick, VA 22947-0360
Tel: 804-984-3660
Fax: 804-984-3660

American Dahlia Society
Alan Fisher, Membership Chair
1 Rock Falls Ct.
Rockville, MD 20854
Tel: 202-326-3516
Fax: 202-326-3516

American Dianthus Society
Rand B. Lee, President
PO Box 22232
Santa Fe, NM 87502-2282
Tel: 505-438-7038

American Fern Society
David B. Lellinger
326 West St. N.W.
Vienna, VA 22180-4151

American Gourd Society
Jean McClintock
7265 State Route 314
Mount Gilead, OH 43338-0274
Tel: 419-362-6446
Fax: 419-362-6446

American Peony Society
Greta Kessenich
250 Interlachen Rd.
Hopkins, MN 55343
Tel: 612-938-4706

American Primrose Society
Addaline W. Robinson
41809 SW Burgansky Rd.
Gaston, OR 97119-9047
Tel: 503-985-9596

Australian Plants Society
Lyn Thompson
PO Box 38
Woodford, NSW 2778 Australia
Tel: 61 (0) 29621 3437
Fax: 61 (0) 29676 7603

Botanical Society of South Africa
Membership Secretary
BSA, Kirstenbosch
Claremont, Cape Town 7735
South Africa

The British Clematis Society
Mrs. Betty Risdon, Membership
Secretary
The Tropical Bird Gardens
Rode Nr. Bath
Somerset BA3 6QW England

The British Pteridological Society
A. R. Busby
16 Kirby Corner Rd., Canley
Coventry, West Midlands
CV4 8GD England

Cactus & Succulent Society of America
Mindy Fusaro, Treasurer
PO Box 35034
Des Moines, IA 50315-0301
Tel: 515-285-7760
Fax: 515-285-1523

California Horticultural Society
Mrs. Elsie Mueller
1847 34th Ave.
San Francisco, CA 94122-5222
Tel: 415-566-5222

California Native Plant Society
Membership Secretary
1722 J St. #17
Sacramento, CA 95814
Tel: 916-447-2677
Fax: 916-447-2727

The Canadian Wildflower Society
Business Secretary
Unit 12A, Box 228
4981 Highway #7 East
Markham, ON L3R 1N1
Canada
Tel: 905-294-9075
Fax: 416-466-6428

Cottage Garden Society
Clive Lane
Hurstfield House
244 Edleston Rd.
Crewe, Cheshire CW2 7EJ
England
Tel: 44 (0) 2702 50776
Fax: 44 (0) 2702 50118

The Cyclamen Society (UK)
Dr. D. V. Bent
Little Pilgrims
2 Pilgrims Way East
Otford, Sevenoaks, Kent
TN14 5QN England
Tel: 44 (0) 1959 522-322

The Flower & Herb Exchange
Membership Secretary
3076 North Winn Rd.
Decorah, IA 52101
Tel: 319-382-5990
Fax: 319-382-5872

Gesneriad Society International
Richard Dunn
11510 124th Terrace N.
Largo, FL 34648-2505
Tel: 813-559-7772

Hardy Fern Society
Membership
PO Box 166
Medina, WA 98039-0166

Hardy Plant Society (UK)
Mrs. Pam Adams
Little Orchard, Great Comberton
Pershore, Worcester
WR10 3DP England
Tel: 44 (0) 1386 710-317
Fax: 44 (0) 1386 710-117

Hardy Plant Society—Mid-Atlantic Group
Pat Horowitz
801 Concord Rd.
Glen Mills, PA 19342
Tel: 610-558-2857

Hardy Plant Society of Oregon
Julie Maudlin, Membership
Secretary
2148 Summit Dr.
Lake Oswego, OR 97034
Tel: 503-635-2159
Fax: 503-224-5734

Herb Society of America, Inc.
Membership Secretary
9019 Kirtland Chardon Rd.
Mentor, OH 44094
Tel: 216-256-0514
Fax: 216-256-0541

Heritage Roses Group
Beverly Dobson
1034 Taylor Ave.
Alameda, CA 94501
Tel: 510-522-3024

Hobby Greenhouse Association
HGA Membership
8 Glen Terrace
Bedford, MA 01730-2048
Tel: 617-275-0377
Fax: 617-275-5693

Indoor Gardening Society of America
Sharon Zentz
944 S. Munroe Rd.
Tallmadge, OH 44278
Tel: 330-733-8414

International Aroid Society
Don Burns, Membership Chair
PO Box 43-1853
South Miami, FL 33143-1853

International Carnivorous Plant Society
Leo Song, Fullerton Arboretum
California State University
Fullerton, CA 92634

International Geranium Society
Membership Secretary
PO Box 92734
Pasadena, CA 91109-2734

International Oak Society
Lisa Wright
1093 Mill Rd.
Pen Argyl, PA 18072-9670
Tel: 610-588-1037
Fax: 610-599-0968

International Plant Propagators' Society
Dr. John A. Wott, Box 358010
Washington Park Arboretum
Seattle, WA 98195
Tel: 206-543-8602
Fax: 206-527-2796

The Magnolia Society, Inc.
Roberta D. Hagen, Secretary
6616 81st St.
Cabin John, MD 20818
Tel: 301-320-4296
Fax: 301-320-4296

National Gardening Association
Susan Lefebure
180 Flynn Ave.
Burlington, VT 05401
Tel: 802-863-1308
Fax: 802-863-5962

National Wildflower Research Center
4801 La Crosse Ave.
Austin, TX 78739
Tel: 512-292-4200
Fax: 512-292-4627

North American Lily Society, Inc.
Executive Secretary
PO Box 272
Owatonna, MN 55060-0272

North American Rock Garden Society
PO Box 67
Millwood, NY 10546-0067
Tel: 914-762-2948

Northwest Horticultural Society
Heidi Shifflette
Box 354115
University of Washington
Seattle, WA 98195-4115
Tel: 206-527-1794

Northwest Perennial Alliance
Membership Secretary
PO Box 45574
University Station
Seattle, WA 98145
Tel: 206-324-0179
Fax: 206-324-8513

Passiflora Society International
Anna Zinno
c/o Butterfly World
3600 W. Sample Rd.
Coconut Creek, FL 33073
Tel: 954-977-4434
Fax: 954-977-4501

Peperomia & Exotic Plant Society
Anita Baudean
100 Neil Ave.
New Orleans, LA 70131-4014
Tel: 504-394-4146

Perennial Plant Association
ATTN: Steven Still
3383 Schirtzinger Rd.
Hilliard, OH 43026
Tel: 614-771-8431
Fax: 614-876-5238

Rare Pit & Plant Council
Deborah Paterson
17 Circuit Ave.
Scituate, MA 02066
Fax: 617-545-8557

Rhododendron Society of Canada
R. S. Dickhout
5200 Timothy Crescent
Niagara Falls, ON L2E 5G3
Canada
Tel: 905-357-5981
Fax: 905-375-0018

The Royal Horticultural Society
Membership Secretary
PO Box 313
80 Vincent Square
London SW1P 2PE England
Tel: 44 (0) 1718 344-333
Fax: 44 (0) 1716 306-060

Scottish Rock Garden Club
Membership Secretary
PO Box 14063
Edinburgh EH10 4YE Scotland
Tel: 44 (0) 1833 650-068
Fax: 44 (0) 1833 650-068

The Sedum Society
Ron Mills
173 Colchester Rd.
West Bergholt
Colchester, Essex
CO6 3JY England

Seed Savers Exchange
3076 North Winn Rd.
Decorah, IA 52101
Tel: 319-382-5990
Fax: 319-382-5872

Seeds of Diversity Canada
PO Box 36, Station Q
Toronto, ON M4T 2L7 Canada
Tel: 905-623-0353

Sino-Himalayan Plant Association
Chris Chadwell
81 Parlaunt Rd.
Slough, Berkshire
SL3 8BE England
Tel: 44 (0) 1753 542-823

Species Iris Group of North America (SIGNA)
Colin Rigby
18341 Paulson St. S.W.
Rochester, WA 98679

Species Lily Preservation Society
Julius Wadekamper
15980 Canby Ave.
Faribault, MN 55021

GLOSSARY

ACHENE: a small, dry, indehiscent fruit with one seed; sometimes used to describe a fruit with an aggregate of seeds, such as strawberry

ACID (ACIDIC): having a pH value below 7.0

ADVENTITIOUS: appearing in unusual places, as in viviparous plantlets on leaf edges

AERIAL ROOT: a root occurring aboveground

AGGREGATE FRUIT: the product of a single flower with many individual pistils and ovules, such as a raspberry

ALKALINE: having a pH value above 7.0

ANGIOSPERM: a plant that produces seeds in an ovary; i.e., a flowering plant

ANNUAL: a monocarpic (one-fruit) plant that grows, blooms, sets seed, and dies in a single year

ANTHER: the pollen-bearing part of the stamen

APEX: the growing point

APICAL: a term used to describe growth at the extreme tip of a plant, its stem or root

APICAL DOMINANCE: the dominance of young cells in the ascending growth to preclude lateral development via hormones they produce

ARBORESCENT: having the characteristics of a tree

ARIL: a fleshy attachment that partially or totally covers a seed; e.g., as found on plants of the genus *Taxus*

ASEXUAL: without sex, as in asexual reproduction; i.e., vegetative propagation

AUTOGAMOUS: self-fertilizing

AUXIN: a natural (or synthesized) chemical found in plants that controls stem growth and root formation

AWN: a narrow fiber occurring commonly on grass flower bracts

AXIL: the place where a branch or leaf grows from a vertical stem

AXILLARY BUD: a bud growing in the axil

BASAL: originating at the base of a plant organ, usually the crown

BASAL CUTTING: a stocky stem of a plant that is removed at the crown for propagation

BASAL ROSETTE: a disk of leaves originating from the crown of a plant and sometimes including secondary rosettes of plantlets

BERRY: an indehiscent fruit originating from a single pistil with one or many seeds

BIENNIAL: a monocarpic (one-fruit) plant that dies in its second year

BINOMIAL: a two-part name of an organism consisting of its genus and specific epithet

BIPINNATE: a term used to describe compound leaves in which the primary and secondary parts are divided

BISEXUAL: having both pistils and stamens in the same flower

BRACT: the outer leaf or sheath, usually of a flower

BREAK: the act of resuming growth; a chance color deviation in a flower

BUD: nascent organ prior to development

BUD SCALES: bud coverings

BULB: a swollen stem modified to serve as a storage organ—either *tunicate*, with solid concentric layers and a papery covering (tulip), or *nontunicate*, with individual scales attached only at the base (lily)

BULBIL: a small bulblike growth forming at a leaf axil or stem bud

BULBLET: an immature bulb usually attached to a mature bulb

BURR: a fruit covered with barbs

CALLUS: thickened tissue forming at the site of a wound

CALYX: the outer whorl of a flower or perianth created by the sepals

CAMBIUM: the inner or secondary layer of meristem below the bark or epidermis of a dicotyledon

CAPSULE: a dry, dehiscent fruit

CARPEL: a pistil or compound pistil that provides an ovule; the female reproductive organ of a flower

CATKIN: a cylindrical inflorescence composed of individual, petal-less flowers

CELL: the principal constituent of living tissue

CHAFF: dry, papery bracts or scales

CHIMERA (CHIMAERA): plant growth consisting of divergent genetic makeup, often the result of a mutation and which may be manifested by variegation

CLASS: the principal division of taxa between Division and Order; e.g., Monocotyledonae

CLEFT: a wedge-shaped incision

CLONE: an asexually produced offspring that is genetically identical to its single parent

COMPLETE: a term used to describe a flower possessing all four whorls: sepals, petals, stamens, and pistils with ovules

COMPOST: decomposed organic matter prepared by the gardener that is an open and friable source of humus and some nutrition

CONE: overlapping bracts forming an egg-shaped structure in gymnosperms, which in the case of female cones mature to bear seeds

CORDATE: heart-shaped

CORK: a spongy outer layer of some plants

CORM: a solid, enlarged, underground stem modified as a storage organ and from which new corms are generated, most often annually

CORMEL (CORMLET): a small, immature corm forming at a point on a mature one

COROLLA: the whorl around the floral perianth made up of petals

CORYMB: a flat or concave inflorescence in which the outer flowers open first

COTYLEDON: the first, or seed, leaf (monocots) or leaves (dicots) or whorl (some conifers). The cotyledon may emerge and turn green (epigeal germination) or remain underground (hypogeal germination).

CROSS: a hybrid

CROWN: the base of a plant, usually herbaceous, where the top growth meets the ground or roots

CRYPTOGAMA: plant that is neither an angiosperm nor a gymnosperm but still reproduces sexually; e.g., fern

CULTIVAR (FROM *CULTIVATED VARIETY*): a version of a species with distinctive characteristics that is selected and perpetuated through sexual or, more often, vegetative propagation. The cultivar is signified by an epithet in roman characters beginning with a capital letter and set off by single quotation marks or preceded by the abbreviation *cv.* Prior to 1959, the plants could be named after places, things, or individuals (e.g., *Stachys byzantina* 'Countess Helen von Stein' [syn. *S.b.* 'Big Ears']) or have botanical or Latinized epithets (e.g., *Iris laevigata* 'Variegata'). Today the use of "fancy" names (as determined by the International Code of Nomenclature for Cultivated Plants) that are descriptive is encouraged (e.g., *Salvia splendens* 'Scarlet Pygmy').

CYME: a flat-topped inflorescence in which the terminal or inner flowers open first

DAMPING-OFF: the collective name for fungal diseases that attack seedlings

DEADHEAD: to remove spent flowers before they form seed

DECIDUOUS: a plant that sheds its leaves when dormant

DEHISCENT: a term used to describe a seed capsule that splits along determined lines when ripe and spills its contents

DICOTYLEDONOUS: having two cotyledons

DICOTYLEDONS, DICOTS: flowering plants that typically have two seed leaves, cambium, and floral parts in sets of four or five

DIOECIOUS: a term used to describe a species of plant that has male and female flowers or sporophylls on separate individuals

DIVIDED: a term colloquially used to describe deeply lobed or compound leaves

DIVISION: the first rank of members of the plant kingdom, distinguished by the suffix *phyta*, meaning "plant"—Thallophyta (algae, bacteria, fungi, lichens, and slime mold); Bryophyta (mosses and liverworts); Pteridophyta (ferns and fernlike plants); Spermatophyta (seed-bearing plants)

DORMANCY: the resting period a plant undergoes during which growth is stopped or slowed in response to undesirable conditions

DORMANT BUD: an undeveloped leaf, root, or shoot in its inactive state

DOUBLE: having more than the usual number of parts, typically referring to the petals of a flower

DRUPE: an indehiscent fruit in which the seed or seeds are contained in a fibrous cover (endocarp), which is in turn encased in pulp (pericarp); e.g., stone fruits such as peaches

ELAIOSOME: an expendable, oil-rich appendage on some seeds that encourages ants to bring them underground, where the unharmed seeds germinate under appropriate conditions

EMBRYO: the undeveloped plant within a seed

ENDOCARP: the innermost layer of the pericarp, encasing the seed

EPHEMERAL: a plant with a very short season of sexual or vegetative activity; e.g., early spring-blooming plants of the woodland

EPIPHYTE: a nonparasitic plant that grows on another plant, such as in tree-branch crotches

EPIPHYTIC: growing on plants

EPITHET: any name below the rank of genus that qualifies an individual; e.g., *Acer tataricum* ssp. *ginnala,* where *Acer* is the genus, *tataricum* the specific epithet, and *ginnala* the subspecific epithet

ETIOLATION: a condition due to lack of light wherein plant growth is elongated (leggy) and pale

EVERGREEN: a plant that has leaves at all times of the year, because new leaves are produced while older leaves are still evident; having foliage through more than one growing season

EXFOLIATING: sloughing off the outer covering in thin layers

EXOCARP: the outer layer of a pericarp

EXOTIC: a plant that originated in another land

EYE: an undeveloped bud, as on a tuber; the center of a flower with contrasting color

F1: the first-generation seed or subsequent plant resulting from crossbreeding, F2 being the second generation, and so on

FAMILY: a level of plants between Order and genus; e.g., the rose family, Rosaceae

FATHER PLANT: the source of pollen in a cross

FERTILE: able to produce viable seed

FLORET: a small flower, generally one of an inflorescence

FLORIFEROUS: flowering profusely

FORM, FORMA: the lowest-ranking category of plant taxonomy, coming after genus, species, subspecies, and variety, but still with a distinguishing characteristic such as flower color

GAMETE: a single reproductive cell (male or female)

GENE: the part of a chromosome that conveys inheritable data

GENUS (PL. GENERA): the fundamental category in the botanical hierarchy between Family and species (consisting of one or many species); it is the first word in the binomial system of naming plants

GEOPHYTE: a plant that produces an underground stem modified as an organ to store moisture and food during dormancy, usually in dry seasons; i.e., bulbs, tubers, corms, fleshy rhizomes

GYMNOSPERM: a plant that bears naked seed from a sporophyll rather than within a swollen ovary or pericarp that develops from a fertilized flower

HABIT: the manner in which a plant grows and its resulting features

HEAD: a conglomerate of flowers at the end of a floral spike

HEAVING: the action of freezing and thawing soil outdoors, which can push a plant out of the ground

HERB: a soft-tissued, nonwoody plant

HERBACEOUS: a term used to describe an herb or other nonwoody plant that produces new tissue annually and usually lacks evergreen stems or leaves—however, some plants with overwintering foliage, such as *Helleborus,* are considered herbaceous perennials

HIP: the swollen floral cup (calyx) of a fertilized rose blossom containing achenes

HUMU: decayed vegetable matter

HUSK: the outer covering of certain fruits (such as the coconut) formed by a developed perianth or involucre

HYBRID: a plant produced by crossbreeding a genetically dissimilar pair, arising spontaneously (occurring in nature) or induced artificially. The parents may be of the same species (*intraspecific hybrid*); of two species in the same genus (*interspecific hybrid*); or of two distinct genera (*intergeneric hybrid*). Some hybrids are the result of numerous crosses and varied ancestry (*multigeneric hybrids*).

HYPOCOTYL: the point beneath the cotyledons of an embryo that swells to become the radicle during germination

INCOMPLETE: a term used to describe a flower lacking one or more of the four floral whorls

INDEHISCENT: a term used to describe a fruit or fruiting body that does not split open to spill its seeds or spores, usually referring to achenes, berries, drupes, or pomes

INFLORESCENCE: the flowering structure of a plant, usually including the axis and the arrangement of one or more flowers and their parts

IN SITU: a Latin term for sowing seeds in a place where the plant is intended to grow

INTERNODAL CUTTING: a section of stem cut between two leaf nodes

INTRODUCTION: a nonnative plant that may or may not have been intentionally presented to horticulture; a new selection or hybrid produced for commercial cultivation

INVOLUCRE: showy bracts or leaves surrounding flowers

LATEX: a milky juice that appears when certain plants, such as *Asclepias* or *Euphorbia,* are cut or cuttings are taken, which may be irritating to those people with skin sensitive to the liquid

LEGUME: usually, the seed of the pod or plants in the family Leguminosae, which typically bear pods that split open along seams or sutures on either side of a flat vessel, revealing individual valves (as in the fruit of a pea)

LIGNEOUS, LIGNOSE: having cellulose fibers or a woody texture

MARGINAL PLANT: a plant that inhabits the water's edge

MERISTEM: the new tissue of the terminal growth in which the dividing cells are capable of assuming the structure of specific tissues or organs—such as leaves, stems, or roots—and in their early stage may be used in micropropagation

MESOCARP: the middle layer of a pericarp, often fleshy

MONOCOTYLEDONOUS: having one-bladed cotyledon

MONOCOTYLEDONS, MONOCOTS: plants typified by one seed leaf, a lack of cambium and woody tissue, in most cases parallel veins in leaves and stems, and flowers with parts in multiples of threes

MONOECIOUS: having flowers of both sexes on one plant or in each flower on one plant

MONOPODIAL: a stem or rhizome that grows indefinitely in one direction, such as the rhizome of a bearded iris

MONOTYPIC: a term used to describe a genus of only one species

MORPHOLOGY: the science of the physical form and structure of plants

MOTHER PLANT: the parent plant that provides the propagule for reproduction—be it sexual or vegetative (seed or offset)

MULTIPLE FRUIT: a fruit that forms from an entire inflorescence and multiple ovaries that sometimes fuse, as in the pineapple

MUTATION: a chance variation in the cellular makeup of a plant resulting in altered characteristics

MYCORRHIZAL: a term used to describe the symbiotic relationship formed when certain plant roots adapt to derive a nutritional or functional benefit from an association with a fungal mycelium

NECTAR: the sweet liquid offered by flowers to attract pollinators

NECTARY: the glands in which nectar is produced and held

NEUTRAL: having a pH level of 7.0, neither acid nor alkaline

NODE: the place where a leaf or leaves, branches, or flowers are attached to a stem

NODAL CUTTING: a section of stem cut just below a node

NUT: an indehiscent, one-seeded fruit with a hard shell, or more generally referring to the shell's contents

NUTLET: a small nut

OFFSET: a plantlet or bulbous offspring formed next to a mother plant or along the length of a runner or sucker

OVULE: the component in the ovary that becomes a seed after fertilization

OVERWINTER: to care for or carry a plant through dormancy, or seed for conditioning, during cold months of inactivity

PANICLE: a branched inflorescence

PEDUNCLE: the stalk of an inflorescence

PEPO: a multicarpellate fruit with fleshy pulp but a hard outer skin, such as a pumpkin

PERIANTH: a term for the corolla and calyx together, especially when they are fused

PERICARP: a fruit; more precisely, the wall of a ripened ovary

PETAL: a "leaf" of a flower's corolla, usually brightly colored

PETIOLE: the leaf stem

PH: a measure of the acidity or alkalinity in a soil or growing medium, expressed in logarithmic increments. The pH scale ranges from 0 to 14, with pH 7.0 being neutral, values below 7 indicating acidity, and values above 7 indicating alkalinity.

PHLOEM: the tissue within a stem through which nutrients are transported up and down the plant

PHOTOSYNTHESIS: the chemical process in green plants in which the energy in sunlight is absorbed by chlorophyll, which acts as an enzyme to convert carbon dioxide and water to sugars, releasing oxygen in the process

PINCHING: removing the terminal growth of a plant to encourage branching; removing the flower bud to stimulate vegetative growth

PISTIL: the part of the female reproductive organs of a flower usually containing a stigma, a style, and an ovary with one or many ovules

PITH: the spongy tissue in the center of a stem

PLANTLET: a small plant developing on a larger one

POD: a general term for a dry fruit

POLLEN: grains or microspores containing the male gametes

POLLINATION: the delivery and attachment of pollen grains from the anther of a flowering plant to the stigma

POME: a multiloculate fruit that results from the swelling of the calyx cup or perianth tube after fertilization rather than from an ovary alone, e.g., apple, pear

PRICKING OUT: removing seedlings individually from their communal pots

PROTHALLUS (PL. PROTHALLIA): the gametophyte that grows from a spore of a fern or other cryptogam, beneath which male and female gametes unite

PROTOGYNOUS: a term used to describe a flower in which the stigma becomes receptive before the anthers ripen

PSEUDOBULB: a swollen, water-storing organ at the base of the leaves of plants such as epiphytic orchids

PTERIDOPHYTE: a fern or fernlike plant

PULP: the moist flesh of a fruit

RACEME: an elongated, unbranched inflorescence bearing flowers, as produced by *Wisteria*

RADICLE: the embryonic root in a seed

RAY FLOWER: a flower head consisting of fertile flowers in a central disk and a radiating fringe of ray florets, as in a daisy

RHIZOMATOUS: producing rhizomes

RHIZOME: a modified stem that grows horizontally on or below the surface of the soil (or higher in epiphytes) and may be swollen and store moisture, starch, and sugars, and from which eyes will grow into stems, roots, and ultimately inflorescences

ROOTLET: a small root or root branch

ROOTSTOCK: a section of perennial crown and roots; the fleshy rhizome of deciduous herbs; see also *understock*

ROSETTE: a cluster of leaves or stems radiating from a central point

RUNNER: a horizontal stem at or below ground level from which plantlets and roots grow at the nodes or the apex

SAMARA: a one-seeded, indehiscent fruit, as borne by maples

SCALES, SCALE LEAVES: the fleshy concentric layers or radiating succulent leaves of bulbs; the hard, brittle covering of dormant buds

SCAPE: a leafless stalk with terminal flowers, as produced by daylilies

SCHIZOCARP: a dry, dehiscent, syncarpous ovary that splits into two 1-seeded halves, as found in maples

SCION: a piece of a desired plant that is grafted onto an understock or rootstock

SEED: an embryonic plant in a ripe ovule produced through sexual propagation

SEED LEAF: a cotyledon

SELECTION: a unique version of a plant produced through sexual or asexual propagation that is given a cultivar name

SELF-SOW: to grow in situ from seeds that fell to the ground out of ripened fruits

SEPAL: one of the floral whorls occurring outside the petals

SESSILE: without a stalk, as when a flower or leaves spring directly from a stem without, respectively, a flower stalk or leaf petioles

SHRUB: a woody plant with multiple stems originating at or close to ground level

SILIQUA: a slender, dehiscent, two-carpeled fruit, as found in mustard-family members

SORUS (PL. SORI): a cluster of sporangia, usually located on the underside of fern fronds

SPATHE: a showy bract surrounding a spadix, such as the hooded spathe of jack-in-the-pulpits

SPECIES: the first categorization of a genus denoted in the binomial system as the second word, or specific epithet. A species is distinguished by being able to freely interbreed with other individuals of the same species. The naming of the species can be further analyzed into smaller divisions such as subspecies (ssp.), variety (var.), form or forma (f.), and cultivar (cv.).

SPERMATOPHYTE: a seed-bearing plant

SPIKE: an inflorescence with sessile flowers on an unbranched stem

SPORANGIUM (PL. SPORANGIA): the pouch where spores are produced or contained in cryptogams

SPORE: a reproductive cell capable of becoming a gametophyte and ultimately a new organism

SPOROPHYLL: a modified leaf capable of producing spores or pollen

SPORT: a naturally occurring genetic deviation (mutation)

STALK: any stemlike structure

STAMEN: the male floral organ, bearing filaments topped by anthers where pollen is produced

STIGMA: the sticky terminal end of the pistil that accepts pollen

STOLON: a horizontal stem from which plantlets or suckers and roots appear at the terminus or from nodes along its length

STOLONIFEROUS: stolon-producing

STOMA (PL. STOMATA): a pore in a leaf or stem from which gases are exchanged and moisture transpires

STONE FRUIT: a drupe

STRAIN: a version of a plant that comes true from seed and is perpetuated through cultivation in isolation, as in heirloom varieties, but will most likely not persist if allowed to hybridize with other members of its species

STYLE: the slender tube of a pistil supporting the stigma

SUBGENUS (PL. SUBGENERA): a category of plant between genus and Order

SUBSHRUB: a small woody or partially woody plant; e.g., *Lavandula*

SUBSPECIES: a category of plant between species and form

SUCCULENT: a plant with fleshy, moisture-storing leaves, stems, roots

SUCKER: a plantlet growing from the base of a plant or a stolon

SYMPODIAL: a term used to describe growth in which the terminal bud forms an inflorescence and subsequent new tissue is created by lateral shoots

SYNCARP: an aggregate or multiple fruit from one or more flowers

TAPROOT: the main root of a plant, often the extension of the original seed radicle

TAXON (PL. TAXA): a taxonomic group of plants that have common characteristics

TEPAL: a bractlike extension of the perianth that is neither a petal nor a sepal, as in the showy parts of a tulip flower

TERMINAL: at the end or apex of growing tissue, usually of a stem

TESTA: the seed coat

TRANSPIRATION: loss of water through the stomata (pores) in leaves and stems

TREE: a woody perennial plant with a single stem or trunk and branches beginning well above the ground

TRIBE: the category of plant between Subfamily and genus

TUBER: a mostly subterranean stem or root modified to swell and become a storage organ with eyes from which stems and roots grow

TUBERCLE: a small tuberlike outgrowth, not always subterranean

TUBEROUS: having tubers; resembling a tuber

TUNICATE: enclosed by a tunic; having layers of tunics, the outermost being papery

TURGID: of a plant, firm and filled to capacity with water

UMBEL: a flat-topped inflorescence in which all the florets emanate from the same point (like the spokes of an umbrella)

UNDERSTOCK: a section of a plant to be used in grafting that will act as the host for the scion and develop a trunk and/or roots

VALVE: one of the two parts a dehiscent fruit or capsule splits into

VARIEGATED: having markings of different color

VARIETY: a chance variant or form of a species recognized in horticulture that may become a cultivar

VIABLE: of seed, capable of germination

VIVIPAROUS: having seeds, bulbs, or buds that become plantlets while still attached to the parent plant

WHORL: an arrangement of similar parts (such as leaves) in a circle around the same axis

WINTER-OVER: see *overwinter*

WOODY PLANT: a nonherbaceous plant with hard, ligneous tissue

XYLEM: the woody tissue in a stem that transports water and supports the plant

BIBLIOGRAPHY

Bir, Richard E. *Growing and Propagating Showy Native Woody Plants.* Chapel Hill, N.C.: University of North Carolina Press, 1992.

Barton, Barbara. *Gardening by Mail: A Source Book,* 5th ed. Boston: Houghton Mifflin Company, 1997.

Bubel, Nancy. *The New Seed-Starters Handbook.* Emmaus, Pa.: Rodale Press, 1988.

Capon, Brian. *Botany for Gardeners: An Introduction and Guide.* Portland, Oreg.: Timber Press, 1994.

Case, Frederick W., and Roberta B. Case. *Trilliums.* Portland, Oreg.: Timber Press, 1997.

Clarke, Graham, and Alan Toogood. *The Complete Book of Plant Propagation.* London: Ward Lock Ltd., 1992.

Curtis, Will C. *Propagation of Wildflowers.* Revised by William E. Brumback. Framingham, Mass.: New England Wild Flower Society, 1986.

Deno, Norman C. *First Supplement to the Second Half of Seed Germination and Theory and Practice.* State College, Pa.: Self-published*, 1996.

———. *Second Supplement to the Second Half of Seed Germination and Theory and Practice.* State College, Pa.: Self-published*, 1996.

———. *Seed Germination and Theory and Practice,* 2nd ed. State College, Pa.: Self-published*, 1993.

Dirr, Michael A. *Manual of Woody Landscape Plants: Their Identification, Ornamental Characteristics, Culture, Propagation and Uses,* 5th ed.. Champaign, Ill.: Stipes Publishing, 1998.

Dirr, Michael A., and Charles W. Heuser, Jr. *The Reference Manual of Woody Plant Propagation: From Seed to Tissue Culture.* Athens, Ga.: Varsity Press, 1987.

Druse, Ken. *The Collector's Garden.* New York: Clarkson Potter, 1996.

Garner, Robert John. *The Grafter's Handbook.* London: Cassell, 1988.

Hartman, Hudson T., Dale E. Kester, and Fred T. Davies, Jr. *Plant Propagation Principles and Practices,* 5th ed.. Englewood Cliffs, N.J.: Prentice Hall,1990.

Hill, Lewis. *Secrets of Plant Propagation.* Pownal, Vt.: Storey Communications,1985.

Jefferson-Brown, Michael, and Harris Howland, *The Gardener's Guide to Growing Lilies.* Portland, Oreg.: Timber Press, 1995.

Kyte, Lydiane, and John Kleyn. *Plants from Test Tubes: An Introduction to Micropropagation,* 3rd ed.. Portland, Oreg.: Timber Press, 1996.

Lloyd, Christopher, and Graham Rice. *Garden Flowers from Seed.* Portland, Oreg.: Timber Press, 1994.

Macdonald, Bruce. *Practical Woody Plant Propagation for Nursery Growers,* Vol. I. Portland, Oreg.: Timber Press, 1993.

Mickel, John. *Ferns for American Gardens.* New York: Macmillan Publishing Company, 1994.

Phillips, Harry R. *Growing and Propagating Wild Flowers.* Chapel Hill, N.C.: University of North Carolina Press, 1985.

Reilly, Ann. *Park's Success with Seeds.* Greenwood, S.C.: George W. Park Seed Co., 1978.

Still, Steven M. *Manual of Herbaceous Plants,* 5th ed.. Champaign, Ill.: Stipes Publishing, 1994.

Thompson, Peter. *Creative Propagation: A Grower's Guide.* Portland, Oreg.: Timber Press, 1992.

Toogood, Alan. *Plant Propagation Made Easy.* Portland, Oreg.: Timber Press, 1993.

———. *Royal Horticultural Society Plant Propagation.* London: DK Publishing, 1999.

Young, James A., and Cheryl G. Young. *Collecting, Processing and Germinating Seeds of Wildland Plants.* Portland, Oreg.: Timber Press, 1986.

* Books by Norman C. Deno are published and distributed by the author. Address inquiries to Norman C. Deno, 139 Lenor Dr., State College, PA 16801.

INDEX